HRBIO

APR 2007

AFTER JACKIE

PRIDE, PREJUDICE, AND
BASEBALL'S FORGOTTEN HEROES:
AN ORAL HISTORY

Cal Fussman

AFTER JACKIE

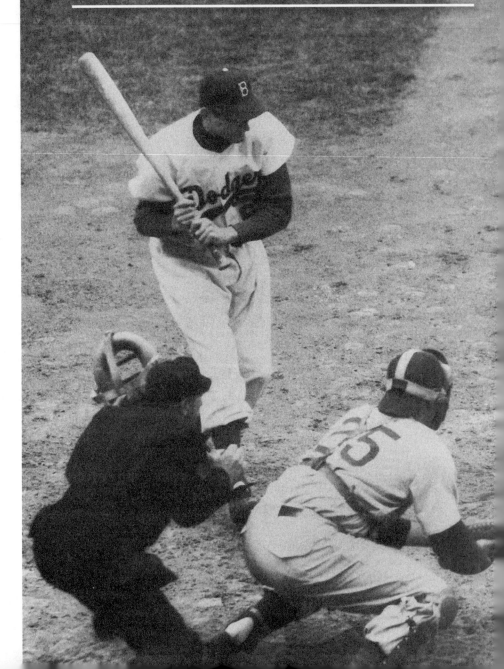

PRIDE, PREJUDICE, AND BASEBALL'S FORGOTTEN HEROES: AN ORAL HISTORY

Cal Fussman

ISBN-13: 978-1-933060-18-7
ISBN-10: 1-933060-18-2

ESPN books are available for special promotions and premiums. For details contact Michael Rentas, Assistant Director, Inventory Operations, Hyperion, 77 West 66th Street, 11th floor, New York, New York 10023, or call 212-456-0133.

FIRST EDITION

10 9 8 7 6 5 4 3 2 1

**TO MY MOTHER,
AND THE PURPLE HAT**

Table of Contents

TIME
THE WEEKLY NEWSMAGAZINE

JACKIE ROBINSON
He and the boss took a chance.
(Sport)

PERMISSION TO DREAM

◆◆

I CAN REMEMBER being a kid back in Mobile sitting on the back porch when an airplane flew over. I told my father when I grew up I was going to be a pilot. You know what he said? He said, "Ain't no colored pilots."

So I told him I'd be a ballplayer. And he said, "Ain't no colored ballplayers."

There were a lot of things blacks couldn't be back then. There weren't any colored pilots. There weren't any colored ballplayers in the major leagues. So it was hard to have those dreams.

Then Jackie came with the Brooklyn Dodgers to Mobile for an exhibition game in 1948. I went to hear him talk to a crowd in front of a drugstore. I skipped school to meet Jackie Robinson. If it were on videotape, you'd probably see me standing there with my mouth wide open.

I don't remember what he said. It didn't matter what he said. *He was standing there.*

My father took me to see Jackie play in that exhibition game. After that day, he never told me ever again that I couldn't be a ballplayer.

I was allowed to dream after that.

—HENRY AARON

THE MEANING OF JACKIE ROBINSON

IT WAS MADE clear to me, not long ago, how careful a man must be in writing a book such as this. I was telling a teenager and his father about my subject and mentioned that toward the end of Jackie Robinson's life, there were African-Americans who called him an Uncle Tom.

"Do you know who Uncle Tom is?" the teenager's father asked him.

"Yeah," the boy responded with assurance. "He's the guy with the beard and the tall hat who says, 'We Want You!'"

"No, no!" his father and I chorused. "That's Uncle *Sam*!"

Then we both chuckled at the irony of a mythical black man who cozied up to whites to gain their favor being confused with a mythical white man who recruited young men, some of them black, to fight in wars.

Crazy as it sounds, surveys show that 40% of America's recent high school graduates believe the United States fought on the side of the Germans in World War II.

But do you know what's even crazier? Sometimes I find myself wondering if a lack of education might be *helpful* when it comes to race in America. If ignorance is part of the problem, maybe it's also part of the solution.

What if you had no idea? What if you couldn't tell the difference between Uncle Tom and Uncle Sam by their skin color? What if you hadn't grown up absorbing all the stereotypes and fears of your family, friends, and culture?

What if the young were left, unguided, to figure out race on their own?

Well, we all know the world's turned way too many times for that. Every step of progress made since the day Jackie Robinson integrated Major League Baseball has come from education, learning, knowledge.

The distance covered by so many footsteps since 1947 is hard to fathom. We've come so far so fast in some areas that it's impossible for the young—or the old—to get a grip on race in America.

We no longer have laws forcing people with black skin to the back of the bus. The police don't unleash attack dogs on people marching for the right to eat a sandwich at a lunch counter. Hotels are now open to anyone with a credit card.

No, attitudes on race these days are much more complicated because they're usually concealed and virtually impossible to put a finger on.

Listening to the ballplayers who came after Jackie helps us see our past. Their voices help us understand what's in front of our eyes right now, what's coloring and shaping so much of our world . . . but often can't be seen.

The more I spoke with the men who came after Jackie, the more certain I became of one thing: The only way to unlearn is to learn. The surest way for us to move forward is to know where the old have been.

—CAL FUSSMAN

CHAPTER ONE

A DEFINITION OF PRESSURE

IT'S HARD TO imagine the past. So let's start by trying to imagine the present.

Imagine a star in the world of sports we all know, Shaquille O'Neal, standing on the free throw line in the seventh game of the NBA Finals. One second remains. His team trails by a point. Thousands of people are shouting and waving their arms to distract him, and millions more are watching at home. He's one of the best players—and worst free throw shooters—in basketball history.

Now, *that's* pressure, you'd probably say.

Funny, I always thought that was pressure too. See, I grew up watching the great black ballplayers who followed in Jackie Robinson's footsteps, but I didn't have a clue about what I was seeing because I had no idea what was going on inside their heads or their hearts, in their personal lives, or even on the field.

I had no idea what real pressure was.

So let's go back in time and reconsider that word. Let's say you're standing, like Jackie Robinson, in a major league batter's box in April 1947.

You're a little tired because you're living in a hotel room with a wife and a 5-month-old baby. That's because you didn't know you'd be playing for the Brooklyn Dodgers until a few weeks before the season opener and haven't had time to find an apartment.

There's no place to escape to at night when the baby cries. And there's no place to escape to in the afternoon when you're the only black man on the ball field and the bigots in the box seats are screaming insults at you that everyone can hear.

Are they the ones, you wonder, who've been writing those letters that you've received, threatening to kill you, to harm your wife, and to kidnap your son?

You're staring at a pitcher who's holding a hard ball that, any second now, might be whistling 90 miles an hour at your skull. What makes you think so? The manager of the opposing team, the Philadelphia Phillies, has ordered his players to scream racial filth at you. Some of those players, having learned of the death threats, are holding their bats like machine guns, aiming them at you and imitating the sound of rapid fire. They're screaming at you to "Go back to the cotton fields, nigger!" They're asking which one of your teammates' wives you'll be with after the game.

You'd like to think that your teammates, at least, are on your side—but how can you? During spring training some of them passed around a petition to boycott the team if you were on it. Some of them, raised in the segregated South, are likely afraid they'll be sneered at or spit on when they return home once it's known that they've shared a shower with a black man. Some, perhaps, are afraid that if you succeed, more blacks will follow you and take their jobs.

So you don't let off steam with the guys on your side about what the guys on the other side are yelling at you. You wait until your teammates have showered before you do. And you sit alone during the long train rides between big league cities.

And then one time, on one of those train rides, when they invite you to come over and play cards with them, one says, "You know what I used to do down in Georgia when I ran into bad luck? I used to go out and find me the biggest, blackest nigger woman I could find and rub her tits to change my luck."

At least you can count on all the people of your color, right? Well, sure . . . but not so fast. You've been chosen to be the first black major league ballplayer because you're college educated and have competed against whites on a football field at UCLA, not because you're the best black baseball player of your time. Plenty of Negro League players, jealous that you're the chosen one, are waiting for you to prove yourself to them.

If you fail . . .

"It might have been 50 *more* years before they'd let a black play," said 94-year-old Buck O'Neil, a superb black ballplayer who never became one of the chosen ones, before he died last October. "They would have said, 'You picked the best, and he couldn't make it. So there's nobody else out there. They just can't think well enough to play major league baseball.' "

And if a black man isn't considered smart enough to play baseball, what chance is there that he'll be considered smart enough to be a doctor, a business executive, a professor, or a politician? So there are 15 million black Americans counting on you.

All of that's coiled inside of you, and has to stay there, because you've promised the white man who hired you that you won't raise a finger against anyone: not the heckling fans, the opponents or your teammates. All of that's boiling inside of you because, far from being the passive man you must appear to be, you're the ex-Army officer who was nearly court-martialed for refusing to back down when ordered to get to the back of a bus. You're the man who, as an 8-year-old, got in a rock-throwing fight with the father of a white girl from across the street in Pasadena, California, who called you a nigger.

Isn't that what a man does when he's being abused like this?

All of that's swirling through and around you in the 0:00:48 that you have to decide whether to swing at that white missile leaving the pitcher's hand—or to duck.

Now we begin to know that word: *pressure*.

Now we begin to understand what the 28-year-old man named Jackie Robinson faced in 1947.

The man who brought Jackie into the Dodgers organization in August 1945 did his best to ease that pressure. Branch Rickey had sent Jackie as far from the flames of American racism as possible to prove himself in baseball's minor leagues: to Montreal. Rickey had scheduled spring training in 1947 in Cuba, far away from colored and white drinking fountains, so that Jackie could get his footing. He'd housed Jackie in quarters separate from those of white teammates to avoid racial conflict. He'd met with black ministers in Brooklyn and persuaded them to encourage their congregations to cheer for all the Dodgers, not just Jackie, to prevent provocations or fights in the stands. He'd met with the team's radio announcer, Red Barber, to make sure the Mississippian didn't sabotage Jackie with unfair comments. And he'd faced down the players on his team who'd planned the boycott.

But Branch Rickey couldn't fathom what it felt like to be Jackie.

"To hell with the image of the patient black freak I was supposed to create," Jackie would later write in his autobiography about that 1947 game against the Phillies. "I could throw down my bat, stride over to the Phillies' dugout, grab one of those white sons of bitches, and smash in his teeth with my despised black fist. Then I could walk away from it all. I'd never become a sports star. But my son could tell his son someday what his daddy could have been if he hadn't been too much of a man."

By the end of that first season, Jackie had swallowed centuries of condensed pressure and performed above it. He'd bounced back from an injury sustained when—while he was playing first base—St. Louis Cardinals outfielder Enos "Country" Slaughter ran straight toward him instead of the base, leaped, and dug his spikes into Jackie's leg. He'd gotten the Dodgers to recognize his dignity and rally to his defense. As racial abuse poured down upon Jackie in Cincinnati, the team captain, a white man from Kentucky named Pee Wee Reese, simply walked over and put a hand on Jackie's shoulder.

By the end of that first season, Jackie had helped lift the Dodgers into the World Series. He'd been voted Rookie of the Year. And four other black men had entered the major leagues.

More were on the way, and teams began to seek out the best young black prospects. One of them, Henry Aaron, would break Babe Ruth's home run record three decades later. Another, Willie Mays, would be hailed as perhaps the greatest baseball player who ever lived.

A door had been opened. A wrong had been righted. A Jackie

Robinson postage stamp would be commissioned. Sport was able to guide society toward a better place. And that's how the Jackie Robinson story is usually told to America.

But that still leaves you, like me, back when I was a kid, watching Henry and Willie, eyes wide open—and missing so much.

◆ ◆ ◆

CHAPTER TWO

DAYS OF THE ZULU CANNIBAL GIANTS

BASEBALL
IN PERSON
ZULU CANNIBAL GIANTS

PLAYING AGAINST AN ALL-STAR LOCAL TEAM

WILSON PARK
SATURDAY
JUNE 12 2 P.M.

Y OU CAN'T HOPE to understand what came After Jackie unless you understand how it was Before Jackie. That's complicated, of course, but there's a simple way to begin.

Take a look at a $20 bill.

Go ahead: Open your wallet, pull out a $20 bill, and take a long, close look at it.

We can disagree on many things about race, but a $20 bill is something everyone can agree upon, right? Nobody will dispute that it's just over six inches long and two and a half inches wide, that it's green, and that the man pictured in the center has bushy eyebrows and a fancy hairdo. Nor will anyone argue that there is a name at the bottom of the picture identifying the man: Jackson.

He's certainly not as famous as the man pictured on the one-dollar bill, George Washington, or the five, Abraham Lincoln. So now that you're staring at that $20 bill, it's only natural to wonder how his face got on it.

Andrew Jackson was born in 1767 in the backwoods of South Carolina but headed west as a young man after the Revolutionary War. Jackson became a national hero in the War of 1812 when he defeated the British at the Battle of New Orleans. His success as a lawyer and land speculator created the wealth to build a grand mansion near Nashville called the Hermitage. But his gruff frontier style never left him, even as he served as a congressman and then senator from Tennessee. That's why folks called him Old Hickory. A co-founder of the Democratic Party, he was elected the seventh president of the United States in 1828.

But a deeper look into his life suggests a different way to view his picture. Jackson climbed from his humble beginnings to become one of the largest slave owners in the state of Tennessee. As president, he presided over the removal of nearly 50,000 Native Americans from their land in the South in order to free up about 100 million acres for plantations to be worked by slaves. To this day, there are members of the Cherokee tribe who carry two ten-dollar bills rather than a single twenty. You look a little deeper. Then, in 1836, Jackson's nominee for Chief Justice of the United States was confirmed, a man named Roger Taney.

This is important, because when a president leaves office his influence lives on through the rulings made by the justices he's placed on our highest court. So now you've got to look into the life of Chief Justice Taney. And the most famous thing Justice Taney ever did was write the majority opinion in a single case.

The case was *Dred Scott v. Sanford*, in 1857. In this case, the court ruled that people of African ancestry—slaves as well as free men—could never become citizens of the United States.

Taney wrote that Negroes "had for more than a century before been regarded as beings of an inferior order, and altogether unfit to associate with the white race."

As far as "all men being created equal" in the Declaration of Independence? Well, Taney reasoned that "the enslaved African race were not intended to be included, and formed no part of the people who framed and adopted this declaration . . . "

And the framers of the Consitution, Taney went on, certainly believed that blacks "had no rights which the white man was bound to respect; and that the negro might justly and lawfully be reduced to slavery for his benefit."

Sounds like Old Hickory would have been proud.

Maybe that $20 bill feels a little different if your fingers are black.

Maybe, if they're white, you didn't realize what you were carrying around in your wallet.

But let's take a positive approach. Let's say that so much has been overcome in 170 years that every time you go to the music store to buy a CD made by a black musician with a $20 bill, you're triumphing over what the man in the middle of that bill stood for.

Only when you hand the $20 to the cashier for the $16.99 CD, he doesn't give you your change.

"I think there's been a mistake," you say.

"No mistake," says the cashier. "You don't know how to do math. That's what it costs. Now, get out of here."

That's pretty much what happened year after year back in the 1920s in a general store in Haleburg, Alabama, to the father of a terrific ballplayer named Monte Irvin.

Wait, you say, why not just call the police?

Well, would you make that call if the policeman was the cashier's buddy, or if the cop would take the cashier's side simply because they shared skin color and the two of them would start accusing *you* of something? No, Monte Irvin's father wasn't going to call the police in rural Alabama in the 1920s just to get correct change from a $20 bill.

But that's Alabama, you say. Okay, let's say your music store's in Los Angeles, and the cashier *does* hand over your change, and you take it to a restaurant to get some lunch. You're feeling pretty good, because—unlike the Irvins—you at least are allowed to enter the same restaurant as a person of another color. A waitress hands you a menu, and you notice that it's different from the menu at the next table where diners of a different skin shade sit. You crane your neck and see that the prices on your menu are higher than the ones on theirs.

That's what happened to the father of Rachel Robinson before Rachel married Jackie.

So you see, in the days before Jackie, $20 bills weren't all the same, nor were they all that simple. In fact, you might find out that you weren't even wanted inside that music store or restaurant, and then your $20 is worth nothing.

Keep your eyes on the money. That's the one thing that'll help you see what's really going on, even when things get as murky as they did for legendary Negro Leagues player Buck O'Neil back in the days of the Zulu Cannibal Giants.

BUCK O'NEIL

Buck O'Neil was one of the great stars of the Negro Leagues. He died on October 6, 2006. For biographical information about O'Neil and others whose testimony appears in this book, see Voices, pages 236–240.

◆◆

ONE OF THE saddest moments in my life might have been at a pageant in Sarasota when I was young. Every year, this pageant would have a parade. On this one day, they rounded up four of us black boys, had us pull off our shirts, and painted our bodies.

The idea was for a white boy and a white girl to be carried through the streets like on a chariot. There were two long poles at the bottom of the chariot, and the four of us boys were at the ends of the poles carrying the white kids in the parade. We're walking down Main Street, and everybody in Sarasota is lined up watching. I look over and see that my friends are lookin' at me. I said to myself, Oh, *maaannnn*!

When it was over, I got back to school and cried. Mrs. Booker comforted me, told me she knew just how I felt. But ohhhhhhh, it took me a long time to get over that.

Many years later, I was playing in the Negro Leagues with the Memphis Red Sox when I ran into Charlie Henry, who at the time was promotin' the Zulu Cannibal Giants. I knew about the Zulu Cannibal Giants because we had played against them. The Zulu Cannibal Giants painted their faces, put rings through their noses, and took the field in straw skirts. They dressed like they were out of a Tarzan movie to attract a crowd—and they sure brought folks in. How they looked didn't really hit me when we played against them. It was a show.

Anyway, Charlie Henry says to me, "How much you makin'?"

I say, "About $90 a month."

He says, "I can get you that in about two or three days if you join up with the Zulu Cannibal Giants. We're going up north to Canada."

In those days, jumping around from team to team was how it was. We never had any written contracts. The money Charlie Henry was offering was too good to pass up, so I decided to go.

Well, we get up in Canada, and I put on that damn straw dress, and I go out on the field. And at first I'm thinking, I'm not in America, and none of my people can see me. But I look around at all these white Canadian people, and

I'm wonderin' if they even know it's a show. They're lookin' at me like I just come right out of the bush.

At that moment a feeling came rushin' back to me, the same feeling I had as a boy when my friends saw me carryin' the white kids through the street.

And I say, "*Sheeee*-it! I'm gettin' outta here! And this is *never* gonna happen again!"

Now, I never got a chance to play major league baseball. A lot of people think that hurt me. But I'll tell you what hurt me more. See, when I played for the Kansas City Monarchs in the Negro Leagues, I thought I *was* playing the best baseball in America. What really hurt me was not being able to attend Sarasota High School. What really hurt me was not being able to attend the University of Florida, even though my father was paying taxes to support those institutions, just like the white man.

What the white man was thinking was this: If I keep him dumb, I can work him for a dollar an hour.

You understand?

The white man didn't want us to realize that we had a lot to do with makin' this country. *I* picked that cotton. I sure did. *I* cut that timber in the woods for the sawmill. I did that, too.

But I didn't see it that way when I was young. I was a shoe-shine boy. The man who owned the shoe-shine shop was white. He was the boss. So it was a natural thing to think that white men were above me.

This is a capitalistic country. I'm looking at this country right now, and I see people coming up from Mexico. I see companies sending their jobs overseas. Cheap labor. There you go. *There you go.* Everything is geared up on the side of the rich man.

Now, Jackie understood it was about the money.

Here's how I know. I left the Monarchs for the service in World War II, but Hilton Smith, a pitcher on the team, told me a story after I got back. The Monarchs were traveling through the South on the team bus, and this bus stopped for gas. It was a big bus, with two 50-gallon tanks. Jackie got out and started to go to the restroom, but the white attendant stopped him.

"Where you going?"

"To the restroom," Jackie said.

All the other players on the bus were used to segregation. They accepted that they couldn't use the restroom at a white gas station. But not Jackie. He'd come to the Monarchs from college in California. So Jackie, he said, "Take the pump out. If I can't go to the bathroom, then you can't sell me any gas."

Now, this white man's thinking: That's a big bus there. It's gonna take more gas than I'm gonna sell to any other customer today. If I pull the pump out, I'm gonna lose all that money. So he said to Jackie, "Okay, go on to the restroom, but don't stay long."

Jackie showed the whole team that things didn't have to be that way. Oh yeah, Jackie understood it was about the money.

Why do you think it took so long for the Yankees to have a black player? The Yankees were winning and drawing big crowds in every ballpark they played in. They didn't need a black guy to put fans in the seats.

But the Dodgers were in competition with the Yankees and the Giants in New York, and there were 10,000 empty seats at their games in Brooklyn.

Branch Rickey saw the handwriting on the wall when the Negro Leagues played in Yankee Stadium before 40,000 people. You don't need a calculator to figure it out. Forty thousand payin' fans, 99.9% of 'em black. They could fill those 10,000 empty seats in Ebbets Field at your average Dodgers game. Now, that's a brand-new clientele.

It's *all* about the money . . .

BRANCH RICKEY III

BRANCH RICKEY, the man who signed Jackie Robinson to a contract with the Brooklyn Dodgers in 1945, is often described as baseball's ABRAHAM LINCOLN. Many who negotiated with RICKEY called him something else: El Cheapo. But The Mahatma—another nickname—was a lot more complicated than that. Here he's seen through the eyes of his grandson.

◆◆

WHEN MY GRANDFATHER was young and wanted to go off and play baseball, his father probably thought, Well, at least he won't have to follow around behind the tail of a mule.

My grandfather's people were rural farmers in southern Ohio. One-room schoolhouse. Church every Sunday. Simple life. Probably the only thing they had to pass down to the children was the family Bible.

But his mother objected to the idea of him playing baseball because baseball players, back at the turn of the century, often rode to the games on the back of a wagon drinking, and just as often, they came home with women in the back of the same wagon. They were a loose crowd. There wasn't much morality around a baseball team back then.

Well, my grandfather had to figure out a way to win the support of both his parents, so he asked them, "What if I would agree never to play on Sunday?"

I don't think he understood what the power of that offer was going to be. This wasn't a religious thing with him. This was a negotiating tactic to win the argument. And he did win.

Now, can you imagine the catcher of a team going to his manager after a game on Saturday and saying, "See ya Monday!"

My grandfather was a catcher and an outfielder who played 120 games in the majors over four seasons, but never on a Sunday. He managed almost a decade in the major leagues, but never on a Sunday. After his parents died, my grandfather was in the front office for another 15 to 20 years. Never went to the ballpark on Sunday. Now, he'd call in to find out what the attendance was. But that wasn't a violation of the original agreement.

Now, there *was* an accusation once that, during a very important Sunday game, my grandfather was on the roof of a YMCA two blocks away from Ebbets Field, watching through a pair of binoculars . . .

◆ ◆ ◆

PLEASE UNDERSTAND THAT the Robinson signing was not a quirk. It was not a spontaneous aberration. It followed the thread that ran through the course of my grandfather's life.

My grandfather coached the Ohio Wesleyan baseball team that had a black player way back in 1904. One day, they went over to Indiana for a game, but when they checked in to the hotel, the black player was refused lodging. My grandfather went after the clerk, who simply said, "No, we don't allow them in here."

While the argument continued, my grandfather got permission for this player—Charles Thomas—to wait in his room. Not Thomas' room. He didn't have one. My grandfather's room.

Finally, my grandfather went up to his room and found Thomas at the foot of the bed with tears streaming down his face. One hand was pulling on the fingers of the other, as if he were trying to wipe them clean. Thomas looked up and said to my grandfather, "If only I could rub away this color, I'd be just as good as any other man."

I saw my grandfather reenact that scene around the supper table when I was young, and it just reached inside to your heart and pulled it right out of you.

Now, when was Robinson signed? End of 1945. This happened in 1904. There's a 41-year gap here.

So you need to understand the thread that started in 1904 and ran through my grandfather's entire life, because it never really could be seen in the time when he was working in the front office in St. Louis.

In those days, there were 16 teams in the major leagues, and the southernmost was St. Louis. It had a deep Southern tradition. Very conservative, very racist. Well, my grandfather took over the front office there near the end of World War I and was responsible for a couple of decades of innovation.

Permanent spring training camp. An organized system of scouts. The farm system. Stop watches to measure speed. Sliding pits. Batting helmets . . .

I can name probably 20 other innovations that he brought forth.

But it was *impossible* for him to integrate the game in such a conservative city.

Things were different in Brooklyn. Within a year of landing there, in 1943, he had a meeting with the Dodgers owners, and he got them to sign on to the idea of bringing in a player from black baseball, from the Negro Leagues.

Now, put yourself in my grandfather's shoes. He was going up against the commissioner and the owners of the other teams, who were all adamantly opposed to this. Why would a man in his 60s risk his reputation on a 25-year-old black man who'd nearly been court-martialed by the U.S. Army for refusing to back down? Why would he risk his own reputation for some vague financial advantage that might come from attracting more black fans?

When Jackie Robinson and my grandfather met in Granddad's office in August 1945, it was the first time they ever saw each other. After reading a passage from Giovanni Papini's *Life of Christ*, a devotional book that had been hugely popular in the 1920s, my grandfather asked Jackie if he would agree to turn the other cheek no matter what he faced for the first three years.

What was it about my grandfather that Jackie trusted enough to agree to do that—if not the invisible thread that went back to 1904?

◆ ◆ ◆

OVER THE YEARS, I heard the old Pirates slugger Ralph Kiner, who went on to a long career as a broadcaster, denigrate my grandfather at every opportunity. Kiner loved to tell about the time he led the National League in home runs and went in to see my grandfather about a new contract. My grandfather offered him a minimal raise—or maybe no raise at all. "Ralph," he said, "we could have finished last without you."

So I grew up with a conflict. I have an image of this warm grandfather who was so full of spirit, mirth, stimulation, and innovation. But I also have an image of him through the eyes of the players who feared him as a negotiator who could be completely overwhelming. In their accounts, he came off as almost subjugating the ballplayers.

Ultimately, I think my grandfather was trying to sell the idea not only that integrating baseball was right, socially just, and morally necessary—the 1904 thread—but that it enhanced the team, the ownership, baseball, Brooklyn, and society in general.

When money and morality come together, you realize the ideal of free enterprise.

BILL VEECK

Eleven weeks after JACKIE ROBINSON broke the Major League color barrier with the Dodgers, Cleveland Indians owner BILL VEECK signed LARRY DOBY, the first African-American to play in the American League. Here MIKE VEECK, Bill's son, reflects on his father's role in the integration of baseball.

◆◆◆

ONE DAY, WHEN my father was a boy, his father, who ran the Chicago Cubs at the time, took him down to the box office at Wrigley Field and dumped all the money in the till on the table. And my grandfather said to my father, "What color is the money?"

My father looked up at him and said, "It's green."

And my grandfather said, "What color is the man who put that money in the till?"

My father looked at him in silence.

And my grandfather said, "Always remember that, son."

I love that story. From the number of times my father told it, I know he did too. I believe it marked the beginning of his interest in people.

The beauty of my dad was that he was so simple in so many ways. As you get older, you realize how valuable—and how hard—it is to maintain that simplicity.

When he tried to buy the Philadelphia Phillies before the 1943 season, his idea was to stock the team with great black players. I think he looked at the labor supply during the war years and thought to himself, Wow! Here's a tremendous opportunity.

The fact that they happened to be Negroes or blacks or whatever the term was back then had little bearing. My father was as color-blind as any man I've ever met. I've met a lot of people who are fake color-blind. It looks good because the cameras are rolling, and it looks good because it's liberal. But my father didn't really have that. It was pure economics.

And I think it was upsetting to him that the other owners figured out a way to stop him from getting the Phillies, especially since he offered twice the amount that the guy who bought them had. Later in life, he came to call major league owners "the most elite men's club in the hemisphere." But back in 1943, he hadn't really seen the full arsenal of their duplicitous ways. He was 28 at the time. These days we worship youth, but back then, he was an upstart. He was almost virginal in the tough world of business. And I think he was really surprised and disappointed.

I never once heard my dad utter the idea that he would have brought in a black ballplayer if he'd have gotten the Philadelphia ball club. It would have been an interesting thing. But he never said he would have paved the way.

My father brought Larry Doby to the Indians 11 weeks after Jackie went to Brooklyn. Bringing Larry Doby into the Rust Belt was a lot tougher than bringing a handpicked guy like Jackie Robinson into New York. My dad got 15,000 letters. I usually don't talk about this, but the one that really got to him was the excrement in a box. I know if I received a box of excrement in the mail that it would really, really offend me. But my father was intrigued by the moron who sent it.

All the letters were racist and hateful. He answered every one of them—except those that weren't signed. But the one he always talked about was the box of excrement: "You think the guy did it out on the lawn and picked it up and put it in the box?"

He was almost childlike that way. Understand, he was very similar to Bob Dylan. I think Bob Dylan wrote "Blowin' in the Wind" because that song *was* blowin' in the wind, and he was picking up on it. But I don't think he stepped out and wanted to be the leader of the band.

If you asked my father what the proudest moment of his life was, he'd tell you that he marched with Dr. King. But he didn't sign Larry Doby so that he could march with Dr. King.

In 1948, the Indians drew a major-league record 2.6 million. And that doesn't count the other 800,000 or so women and children who got in free or on discount tickets and weren't counted through the turnstiles. So that's really 3.5 million people in a season—30 years before any other major league team drew over three million.

◆ ◆ ◆

CHAPTER THREE

GUESS WHO?

THE NEXT THING we must do is a lot harder than staring at a $20 bill. We must look at people who are different from us without making assumptions.

Perhaps you don't think you're guilty of stereotyping, but I'll bet I know what runs through your mind when you find yourself sitting on an airplane next to a man speaking Arabic. Double or nothing, you know how many Poles it takes to change a lightbulb.

We can't help it, none of us. Not long ago, I found myself smiling while watching a movie titled *Guess Who*, a remake of a classic comedy about interracial marriage that reverses the plot so that a black woman brings home a white guy to meet her parents. When her sister comes through the front door and gets a glimpse of the preppy white fellow in the hallway, her first thought is, Are we being audited?

All of the black players who came in after Jackie had to play past the stereotypes. They were seen as lethargic, not leaders. And when they did do well it was because they were natural athletes, not gamers.

Listen carefully to sportscasters today, and you'll still hear traces of that stereotyping. "He's a very articulate young man" is a comment made far more often about a black athlete than a white one, as if it is surprising to discover in a person of color the ability to express himself in correct English.

If you had sat down to dinner with Jackie and his successors, you wouldn't have needed to get all the way to dessert to find out that not one of them came from a cookie cutter.

Larry Doby, the first black man to follow Jackie into the majors, was an introvert who tucked his wounds inside. He struggled to find ways to keep his bitterness from spreading to his children.

Monte Irvin, who joined the Giants in 1949, was an extrovert and a peacemaker. After his Hall of Fame career, he worked at the baseball commissioner's right hand—and tried to build bridges over racial waters.

Dan Bankhead, a pitcher who followed Jackie to the Dodgers, saw his career suffer because he had a powerful fear of hitting a white batter. Bankhead could never throw the brushback pitch that every pitcher must employ from time to time in order to claim the outside corner of the plate from hitters.

Bankhead's catcher, Roy Campanella, had an Italian father and an African-American mother. He was as comfortable around spaghetti as around collard greens. Whereas Jackie played baseball to bring about social change, Campy played baseball in disbelief that people would actually pay him to do it.

Each man's temperament and experiences would send him down a different path—not a stereotypical one. For instance, everyone knows that all African-Americans are Democrats, right? Well, Jackie Robinson, by the end of his life, campaigned for Republican Richard Nixon against Democrat John F. Kennedy in the 1960 election.

Just as surprising and singular were the paths that the first black ballplayers' children took. Who would've dreamed that Jackie Robinson's son would grow up to be a coffee farmer in Africa, or that Roy Campanella's son would become a documentary filmmaker with a degree in anthropology from Harvard?

See where I'm going here? The fact that their careers surprise me shows that I too haven't taken a broom to all the old stereotypes.

❖ ❖ ❖

MONTE IRVIN

◆◆

MY FATHER TOLD me many times that you've got to play the hand that's dealt you. Learn how to get along with people. Always make things better than they were. Rise above the bitterness. That served me well. It wasn't always easy, though.

Tell you a story from my days in the Negro Leagues. We were traveling from Montgomery to Birmingham one afternoon. Hot as hell, and we came upon this café that was built on a terrace. We pulled the bus off the road, and a few of us got out. A white lady was serving people, and when she saw us, she started shakin' her head.

I said, "Why you shakin' your head, ma'am? You don't even know what we want."

"I don't give a damn," she said. "Whatever you want, I don't have any. The answer is no."

"Well," I said, "that's too bad, because we only wanted to buy a hamburger or a hot dog. But mainly what we wanted was a cool glass of water."

"I'm not going to sell you anything," she said. "But if you want some water, there's a well in the back."

So we went back to the well and hoisted up a bucket of water. There was a gourd nearby. We drank from this gourd, then walked back to the bus to head on down the road.

When I looked back, I saw this woman breaking the gourd that we'd drunk out of, smashing it into little pieces.

Not everyone was that way. There were people who wanted to help but felt trapped by the laws. On that same trip, we stopped in a gas station late at night. It was really dark, and the colored bathroom was way, way in the back. The white bathroom in the front was lit. So we asked the attendant if we could use it.

"The place is empty," we said. "Who's gonna know the difference?" We were filling up the bus, meaning we were buying plenty of gas. And we bought some peanuts and sodas, too.

The attendant said, "Yeah, okay, go ahead."

So we go to the white bathroom, and just then, some white guys pull up in a truck and get out to use the restroom. Right then this attendant hollers, "Hey, what are you niggers doing? Goddamn it, I told you the colored restroom is in the back. Get your asses back there!"

So we went back to the colored restroom. When we returned to the front, the attendant was alone again. We patted him on the back and said, "It's okay. You tried, and we appreciate it."

The real problem was that anything and everything could be done to you, and you had no recourse.

The Newark Eagles trained every spring in Daytona Beach, Florida, near Bethune-Cookman College. We didn't have a black hotel, so we stayed in the private homes of black families. One night, I went to the movies with a pitcher named Max Manning. It was about nine o'clock when the picture was over, and we were walking home.

"Hey, boy, where you goin'?"

It was a white cop.

I said to him, "Officer, we were just at the movies, and now we're on our way home."

At that time in Daytona Beach, blacks weren't supposed to be on the other side of the railroad tracks. When blacks worked on the white side of the tracks, for upscale people, they needed notes to go back and forth.

So I said, "Officer, we're baseball players down here to get in shape so we can entertain you folks. That's all we want to do. We don't want any trouble here."

The policeman said, "I notice you're doing all the talkin'. Can't that boy talk for himself?"

I said, "Yes, sir. Sure, he can."

"Hey, boy," the officer said to Max, "don't you know how to talk?"

"Yeah," Max said. "I can talk."

"Yeah? Don't you know how to say 'Yes, sir'?"

The policeman's holster was already unbuttoned.

And I was whispering, "Max, Max, say 'Yes, sir.'" At that time, they could do anything they wanted to you. They could rape your mother, your sister, your wife. They could trump up any charge and say you did it. And whatever they said you did, well, that was the way it was gonna be. Understand?

Anyway, when that's the hand you're dealt, you have to think fast. So I was thinking, if the cop goes for that pistol, I'll hit him with a right, knock him out, and we'll get us the hell out of there.

But Max said, "Yes, sir," and the policeman goes, "All right, you're out here too late. Now you boys get your asses out of here and inside."

◆ ◆ ◆

EVERY ONCE IN a while, we'd play exhibition games against local white teams. Strictly black vs. white. The teams were never integrated.

Sometimes, a few of the white guys had been in the majors before, and we figured there was a chance that they might get called back up. So we'd say, "Hey, if you go back, talk it up. Bring us up to the majors, and we'll help you guys win a pennant."

They'd say, "We don't think the owners would let you."

"Why not?" we'd say. "We play the same rules. Use the same bats, same balls. We just played black against white. There were no problems. Why not?"

"Sure, we'll talk it up," they'd say. "Won't do any good, but we'll talk it up."

A lot of the guys from the Negro Leagues went to play in Mexico, including me, in 1942. There, you were just like anybody else. You could go to the movies, restaurants, whatever. Nobody stopped you. At the time, the economy down there was booming—they called it the Mexican Mira—and it was beautiful. It was a wonderful, wonderful place to play ball. Six or seven players got married there. When it got time to return home to the ol' segregated USA, they said, I'm not going back.

I was a popular man in Mexico. In 1942, I hit .397 for Veracruz and led the league in home runs. I played for Jorge Pasquel, the George Steinbrenner of Mexico. He was very rich, very impulsive, and very, very demanding. I mean, he once ordered me to hit a home run.

We were playing the team from Monterrey that had a great Cuban pitcher, Lazaro Salazar. He had us shut out, 1-0, and we were down to our last out in the ninth inning. Ray Dandridge went to the plate, and I was on deck.

Now, Ray was a truly great fielder. Played third base like nobody you'd ever seen. Bowlegged. They said a train might go through his legs, but not a baseball. Well, Ray singled, and I started walking up to the plate.

As I was going up to hit, Jorge waved for me to come to his box right behind the plate: "¡Monte, ven aquí! Come here!"

"Jorge, I'm getting ready to hit."

"Never mind that," he said. "Come over here!"

So I went over to his box. He put his arm around me and said, "Hit a home run and win the ball game for me."

I said to him, "Jorge, do you know how hard it is to hit a home run?"

"Never mind about that," he said. "You just hit a home run for me."

All this time, the game was being held up. Finally, I got to the batter's box. Roy Campanella was catching, and he asked me, "What did Jorge want?"

"He wants me to hit a home run."

"Are you crazy?" Campy said. "Is *he* crazy?"

The first pitch I took for a strike.

The second pitch was a sharp breaking curve that I fouled over the grandstand. But something inside me said, Campy isn't going to waste one backing you off the plate. He's going to want to strike you out on three pitches. Be ready.

The third pitch was a low fastball. I guessed right and hit it 410 feet over the centerfield fence. The crowd was going crazy as I rounded the bases. We'd won the game, and Jorge was waiting for me at home plate with 500 pesos in his hand.

"Man," Campy said to me afterward, "you are the luckiest son of a gun I ever saw!"

"Calm down, Campy," I said. "Jorge just gave me 500 pesos, and he told me to give you 250 for calling the right pitch."

True story, true story . . .

It was a beautiful time, and I was at the top of my game. No question about it, I was a much better ballplayer than Jackie Robinson at the time. Matter of fact, we didn't even see Jackie as a baseball player back then. We knew him as a college football star.

Anyway, the following winter I was at home in New Jersey, preparing to go back to Mexico, when I got news that I'd been inducted into the Army.

Now, there's a conflict, right there. First, you say to yourself, Why the hell should I go over and fight to preserve a system that we detest, for Christ's sake? But then another side of you says, I wish they'd let us fight because we want to prove that we can fight as well as anybody else.

See, that was the thing about being in the Negro Leagues. You could never really know how you measured up to the best white players, because you weren't allowed to compete with them.

I had a brother-in-law in World War I. He said it was terrible the way the blacks were treated. They were treated like dogs. And on top of that, they weren't even allowed to fight. If they won't let us fight, he wanted to know, why are we here?

Pretty soon, I was on this troop ship with 10,000 soldiers going over to Liverpool, England. We were on that ship for 19 days. When we got off the boat, it was hard to stand up.

D-Day was June 6, 1944. We didn't get to Omaha Beach until two months later. When we got there, the beach had been cleaned up. There was a long banner on the way to camp. It said, "Through these portals, America's finest soldiers have trod."

Lot of things happened while I was in France. At one point, a French girl was raped. All us black soldiers had to line up so that this little French girl could identify who raped her. Pretty French girl. Then it came to light that it was white soldiers who'd done it. They'd gotten some shoe polish and painted their faces.

I came home with the war jitters. But see, I got the war jitters from my own side. When I got home, I just wasn't the same man. On top of that, I hadn't played any for a long spell, and I'd lost my timing.

The Dodgers sent one of their top scouts to see me and asked me to sign with them. This was 1945. Maybe I would have been the first instead of Jackie. But I had to tell Branch Rickey that I just wasn't ready. It took me a while to get back to where I was before I went into the service. But by the time I was ready—I hit .401 in 1946—Rickey had settled on Jackie. Plus, he didn't want to spend the money to buy out my contract with the Eagles.

◆　◆　◆

IF I'D BEEN Branch Rickey, I'd have picked Roy Campanella to go first. Roy had proven himself for almost ten years in the Negro Leagues. Not only could he hit, he also had a rifle for an arm, and he had more baseball knowledge than any other catcher I ever saw. Plus, his father was Italian, so it was easier for him to blend in. And in the field, he'd be behind the plate, his back'd be to the fans, and he'd have a mask on. Almost nobody would know.

The only thing I can come up with is that Rickey wanted to pick a full-blooded black man. Jackie was out there on first base that first year, visible to everyone. Rickey took that chance and won.

◆　◆　◆

A FEW MONTHS later, Larry Doby joined the Indians. He was told he was going to play first base in the second game of a doubleheader. Now, Larry didn't ordinarily play first base, so he asked the regular first baseman, Eddie Robinson, if he could use his mitt. But Robinson wouldn't loan him his glove. Nobody would loan him a first baseman's mitt.

Larry never did play first base for the Indians. Fact is, he didn't play much of anything after he was called up. They used him mostly as a pinch hitter.

That first season he was with the Indians, Larry sat way over at the end of the dugout by himself. See, with me, I would have made sure to sit in the middle. But he stayed off by himself.

Joe Gordon saw what the situation was. He went over and put his arm around Larry and said, "Some of these guys are just stupid. You're a helluva ballplayer. I wish you well."

The following year, they moved Larry to the outfield. He'd never played there before, and the next year he made the All-Star team. Shows you how much raw talent he had.

See, Larry was a better ballplayer than Jackie. He could outrun Jackie, and he had more power—Larry hit a whole lot more home runs. But he was withdrawn. He wasn't outgoing. He didn't know how to handle difficult social situations like Jackie did. Larry would get mad and go back to the hotel and sulk.

Somebody once said it was too bad that Doby didn't have Luke Easter's personality. Big Ol' Luke! Now, he could laugh at anything. He didn't let anything anybody said get under his skin. But Doby would keep things within him. He had what they call a persecution complex. I guess it took him a while to get over that.

BOB FELLER

◆◆

LARRY CAME UP as a second baseman, but he wasn't going to play second base for us. Joe Gordon was our second baseman. So Larry was told to borrow a first baseman's glove so he could play first. And Eddie Robinson wouldn't loan his to him.

But you know what? I wouldn't loan my glove to Bob Lemon or Early Wynn or anybody else. That's because you mold the glove to the shape of your hand. I've got a thumb that comes way back very deep. It would fit in the glove very differently from anybody else's. That's the reason you don't loan out your glove or your shoes or anything else.

In my opinion, it wasn't fair to blast Eddie Robinson for not loaning his glove. I'm not saying that because he's a deep friend of mine. He's not a deep friend of mine. I know him. But I think it was about the fit of the glove, not about racism.

Hell, a lot of people thought I was a racist because I said once that Jackie Robinson couldn't hit a high fastball.

Can anybody tell me exactly what that has to do with race? I know a lot of white guys who couldn't hit a high fastball. I couldn't hit a curveball whether the guy who threw it was black or green or yellow or pink.

What does that have to do with race? Nothing. It's just a matter of strong points and weaknesses.

MONTE IRVIN
◆◆

THE GIANTS BOUGHT my contract from the Newark Eagles for $5,000 in January 1949. Sent me to Jersey City in the International League that spring. I was hitting close to .400 when they called me up. Hank Thompson was also playing very well. We reported at the same time. The manager, Leo Durocher, introduced himself.

When the regulars came in to the clubhouse, Durocher said, "Fellas, listen up. We're gonna have a short meeting. This is all I'm going to say about race. I don't give a damn what color you are. As long as you can play good baseball, you can play on this team. We got Monte and Hank here. They got good credentials. I'm sure they'll help us get out of fifth place. We're all one team. Let's go out and play hard, and that's all I'm going to ask of any of you."

And that was it.

Once you put on that uniform, it wasn't between black and white. It was the Giants against the Dodgers. That was a big change. When Bobby Thomson won the pennant in 1951 with his ninth-inning home run, there weren't any thoughts of race. I had made the only out that inning, so I was grateful that Bobby got me off the hook. And Willie Mays was a rookie in the batting circle, so he was happy he didn't have to come up to the plate and hit in that situation.

The name of the team on the front of your uniform mattered more than the color of your skin. Give you another example of that: the fight in 1953 between Carl Furillo and Durocher.

Carl was leading the league in hitting. He'd been killing us all summer. Every time he got up against us, it seemed like he got a base hit. So we were playing them at the Polo Grounds near the end of the season, and Leo told our pitcher, Ruben Gomez, to go out there and knock Furillo on his ass. You know, don't let him take the bread out of your mouth.

So Gomez brushed Furillo back a couple of times and finally hit him. Carl went on down to first base. Didn't say anything to Gomez.

But he looked over at our dugout and yelled, "I don't blame him, Leo. I blame you, you no-good son of a bitch."

And Leo yelled right back, "You're goddamn right, dago!"

As soon as Leo said it, Carl left first base and came charging for him. Carl would have killed Leo. I mean, Leo was an old man. So my first thought was to break it up. I got between them, but in the melee, somebody stepped on Carl's finger and broke it. He didn't play the last month of the season because of the injury, and that's how he hung on to win the batting title—by not playing.

That didn't make him any happier. Much later, Campy told me, "Furillo's mad as hell at you."

"Why?" I asked.

"Because you kept him from breaking Leo's head, that's why."

"Hey," I said, "all I wanted to do was keep those guys from killing each other."

◆ ◆ ◆

AFTER I RETIRED, I got a job in the commissioner's office, and I tried to bring people together.

I can't imagine how somebody can hate you and not even know you. How can you hate me when you don't even know what I think, what my values are, what kind of contribution I can make?

Ever see the countenance of a person who likes to help somebody as opposed to the face of a bigot? Ever see that look? The look of a bigot?

Oh man . . .

Slaughter. Enos Slaughter. Enos "Country" Slaughter. I didn't know him personally, but back when he was with the Cardinals, he had a reputation for being one of the biggest racists in baseball. Really outspoken. No two ways about where he stood.

Well, about a year before he died, we happened to be in the dining room at Cooperstown. I was sitting there with my two granddaughters. He was sitting by himself.

So I walked over and said to him, "Enos, would you like to join my granddaughters and me?"

He said, "No, I'll stay here."

JERRY IZENBERG

A longtime columnist for the *Newark Star-Ledger,* JERRY IZENBERG became close friends and neighbors with LARRY DOBY after Doby retired from baseball following the 1959 season and returned home to New Jersey.

◆◆◆

LARRY DOBY CAME up to the major leagues 11 weeks after Jackie Robinson did. In a way, those 11 weeks were like a curse, because who remembers No. 2?

It's like a football player once told me: "You know what's so unfair about getting to the Super Bowl and losing? Everybody remembers you as the loser. Nobody remembers all the other teams that didn't get there."

That's a good analogy. When you're No. 2, you were there—that's all.

Jackie went through hell. All that's well documented because Jackie was outspoken and played in a media center. But Larry was quiet, and he played in Cleveland. Not many people knew what Larry went through, because he kept it all bottled up inside.

Let me tell you a story that sets up everything Larry went through.

Larry played football for Eastside High School in Paterson. He was the only black on the team. He was also the best running back in the state of New Jersey. In those days, high schools played bowl games in Florida. And Paterson Eastside was invited to come down there for a postseason game. But when Florida officials found out that the Jersey team's star running back was black, they told the Paterson Eastside coaches that they couldn't bring Larry Doby.

What happened? The Paterson team voted unanimously not to go. That's the kind of respect Larry drew from people. That was the world he came from.

The Dodgers gave Jackie a year in the minors. They were ready for him. But for Larry, the change happened in a single day in 1947 when he was playing for the Newark Eagles in the Negro National League.

In the first game of a doubleheader against the Homestead Grays, he hit a home run. Then, between games, he was given a shaving kit and was sent to meet Bill Veeck and join the Cleveland Indians. Just like that. No fanfare. No preparation.

You know, I think a lot of Branch Rickey was a charade. But Bill Veeck was genuine. If it weren't for Bill Veeck, Larry would have gone mad. Every time things would start going wrong, Veeck would be there.

"Tough, isn't it, Lawrence?" Bill would say.

"It ain't good, Bill."

"Come on, we'll knock down some beers and go hear some jazz."

And it would be a message from Veeck to Larry: I care.

Anyway, on that first day, Veeck told Indians manager Lou Boudreau to treat Doby like everybody else. So Boudreau took him into the clubhouse to introduce him to the other players, and most of the guys just turned their backs. Larry would stick out his hand to shake, and they'd turn away. A few guys told him they were glad he was there—Bill McKechnie, the coach, was one—but only a few.

Larry was still a kid—only 23 years old—and he got a little rattled. He put on a uniform, went to the bathroom, and looked at himself in the mirror. Well, he thought, I'm here, so I might as well go out. He walked up the tunnel and out onto the field, stood near the dugout where everybody was warming up—and nobody would throw him a ball.

Finally, Joe Gordon, the Indians second baseman, turned to him and said, "You gonna stand there and wait for your picture to be taken? Or do you want to warm up?"

From that day on, Doby and Gordon always played catch before games.

BOB FELLER

◆◆◆

I NEVER UNDERSTOOD where that story came from about nobody shaking Larry Doby's hand when he came to the Indians. That's not so. I was there.

I think Larry was very insecure and apprehensive about what might happen. And nothing did happen that I know of.

JERRY IZENBERG

❖❖❖

IT WAS SO bad in Washington, which back then was essentially a Deep South town, that Larry wasn't allowed to use the visitors' clubhouse—he had to change in a black boardinghouse. No cab would pick him up, and there he was, walking down the street with his uniform on and his cleats over his shoulder, going to the tradesman's entrance at the ballpark so he could play against the Senators.

Unless you've lived it, you don't know. Walk a mile in my shoes.

In St. Louis, the fans were pretty close to the field. Sportsman's Park was a bandbox of a place. Once Larry was in the batter's box, and some guy in the boxes was yelling, Nigger this! Nigger that! Go pick cotton!—that sort of thing. Larry just looked straight ahead and didn't let on that he heard anything. Then the guy started telling the crowd all the things he was gonna do with Larry's wife.

At that, Larry turned and sprinted for the railing. He got one leg over the railing, and the next thing he knew, he was on his back and there were guys on top of him. His arms were pinned down, and someone was saying to him, "Don't make a single move. If you make one more move, we won't have a black player in this league for another 20 years."

It was Bill McKechnie, the Indians coach. McKechnie saved Larry Doby's career—and saved integration in the American League.

You see, the powers that be in the American League didn't want black ball-players. They really didn't. The American League believed it was the elite league. The Yankees were winning the World Series every year, and they figured that proved their argument. At least until the National League began to bring in the elite black players and started to win every All-Star Game.

Once the National League began to be integrated, Jackie became the feisty guy that we always knew he was, a you-spike-me-and-I'll-spike-you-back type of guy. Doby didn't have that luxury. If you check the numbers, you'll see that Larry was in the American League virtually alone for a number of years. The Yankees, for instance, didn't bring in a black player—Elston Howard—until 1955. For a long time, Doby was out there being thrown at simply because he was black. And he had to restrain himself.

❖ ❖ ❖

LARRY DID STRIKE back in little ways. Throughout the 1950s, there was segregation in spring training. The team would stop and get something to eat on the way back from games, and of course, the restaurants wouldn't serve Larry.

Joe Gordon would say, "Hey, Doby, you want me to get you something to eat? I'll get it." And Larry would say, "Don't give them one quarter. I'd rather starve."

Gordon would apologize for the racists, and Larry would say, "Forget it, Joe. Just have your meal."

That was how Larry won. They didn't know Larry had won. Only Larry did.

◆ ◆ ◆

IT WASN'T LIKE you could see any of this on television. I know these stories because Larry became one of my best friends. We lived in the same town, and one day, after he retired, there was a knock on my door. Larry wanted to know what I was doing that night. He wanted to talk. Don't ask me why he chose me. I have no idea. But it all started to come out in bits and pieces until, finally, I had the whole story as he saw it.

I remember saying to him, "You know, you're the bitterest ex-athlete I've ever known."

He said to me, "You think so?"

I did think so. And I still do.

◆ ◆ ◆

LOOK UP THE year. Was it 1957? Ten years after he came in? I think that's the year Larry finally felt like he had teammates. He was with the White Sox then, and they were playing the Yankees, and Art Ditmar threw behind him.

You understand what that means? It's very simple. If a pitcher wants to hit a guy, he throws behind him. The batter's natural reflex, once he sees the ball coming toward him out of the strike zone, is to pull back. If you throw behind a guy's head, he'll pull back, and there's a much better chance you'll hit him.

Doby went down and said to himself, That's it, I'm not taking this shit anymore, and he charged the mound. Larry was a big guy, and he could fight.

He didn't take the bat with him. He just went after Ditmar, and the Yankees ran out and piled on.

"There I was, in this pile," Larry told me, "and people were clawing at me, and I was clawing at them. I looked toward my dugout, and suddenly I saw my teammates coming. The first face I saw was big Walt Dropo. Then I saw four more guys, all of them white. And I thought to myself, I finally have teammates."

That was one of the two most important moments—in racial terms—in Larry Doby's major league career.

The other moment was one he talked about at the end of his Hall of Fame speech, in 1998. It had to do with a wire photo taken in 1948 after Larry had hit a home run to help win a game in the World Series. After the game, the winning pitcher, Steve Gromek, and Larry hugged each other, and the wire photo of them was subsequently plastered on the front page of the sports section of most of America's newspapers. It was the first time a photograph of a white athlete and a black athlete hugging each other had ever appeared on a national level.

Larry said in his speech, "America really needed that picture, and I'm proud I was able to give it to them."

LARRY DOBY, JR.

◆◆◆

THAT PICTURE OF my dad and Steve Gromek has been in my house since I can remember. I walked by it every day as a kid without any idea what it meant. It was just two people happy that they had won a game. That's all I thought. And I think that's what my father wanted me to think.

"What's that, Dad?"

"Oh, I hit a home run, and we won a World Series game."

My father was one of those people who didn't talk about the past. There were no kitchen table conversations about "when I did this" and "when I did that."

When I was little and asked to hear his baseball stories, he would say, "What I did is in the history books. If you want to read it, fine. But I'm here to take care of today and to think about the future."

But sometimes I'd come into the house, and my mother would ask me to be quiet because my dad was doing a phone interview. And I'd hear the name

Gromek mentioned. Then I'd have a reason to ask. As I got older, he began to talk a little.

So it took me a while to realize how close that picture was to his heart.

Gromek was from Hamtramck, Michigan—a very Polish area—and from what I understand, he took some flak for hugging my dad. One of my biggest disappointments is I never got to meet Steve Gromek and tell him how much that moment meant to my father.

As I grew older, my father talked about the people who did something nice for him. Ask him about Joe Gordon's playing catch with him before every game, and he'd go on and on and on.

But he wouldn't talk about the people who didn't treat him well. I think he got over the fact that he was always second and that he never got all the accolades. But he never forgot what he'd been through. That stayed inside.

A little of it would come out 50 years later, when players would show up on TV and say things like, "I never signed any petition to keep Jackie out of the major leagues." My father would just shake his head and say, "I was there."

Sometimes it was hard for me to understand how he felt. I didn't have to go through what my father went through. They didn't spit on me. They didn't call me nigger. They didn't refuse to shake my hand. So it's not to be forgotten, not to be minimized, but it just wasn't me. Because of his taking that stuff, some white people were nicer to me, I'm sure.

Maybe this will help explain him. When I was deciding whether to play college baseball at Duke, the coach there was Enos Slaughter. Supposedly, Slaughter had been one of those players who'd signed a petition saying they didn't want Jackie Robinson playing in the majors. My father said to me, "Don't take anything that you've heard from me or anyone else about past experiences. You treat him the way he treats you."

And that was what I did.

I became the first black baseball player at Duke. And let me tell you something, Enos Slaughter never treated me anything but good.

ROY CAMPANELLA II

◆◆

PEOPLE MAKE A big deal about the differences between Jackie and my dad, but I think it all really came down to a simple difference in personality.

My dad was just as much in favor of improved race relations and progress and integration as Jackie. But he wasn't interested in pressing the argument at every turn. So if they wanted a ride to a black hotel in the South and a white cabbie stopped and said, "I'm not taking any black folks," then Jackie would argue with him. My dad would simply say, "The heck with him. He's a racist. Let me get a black cab company to pick us up."

Meals—the same way. Certain restaurants wouldn't let blacks sit inside, so meals would be prepared for them to eat on the bus. Well, Jackie might refuse: "Why should I have to eat here when I'm an equal to the guys sitting in the restaurant?" My dad would say, "I'm not gonna let this stop me from getting a meal I like and enjoying it."

It's not that one way is any better than the other—they're just different approaches to life. A lot of people who are nonconfrontational don't want to admit the disparities and inequalities. They're living in denial.

But my father wasn't living in denial. When I was a little kid, I came home from school one day and started talking about George Washington with the kind of pride any young American boy would after hearing about the father of his nation. My dad was proud of me and my enthusiasm, but he did say to me, "Remember, this is also somebody who sold the black man for a barrel of molasses."

Now, that was a very insightful counterpoint to the normal interpretation of George Washington that a 6-year-old would get.

Let me give you another example. I was a big reader of Ernest Hemingway's work when I was growing up. I read all of his short stories and novels all the way into my late teens. My dad knew what a big fan I was, but he didn't tell me until I was in my early 30s that he and Jackie had been excluded from a meeting with Hemingway at his home during spring training in Cuba. Hemingway had invited the white ballplayers but asked that Jackie and my dad not be included.

I said, "Pop, why didn't you tell me about that? You know how much I loved his books."

He said, "You were doing so well in school, I didn't want to take that away from you. You might have said, 'The heck with these novels. I don't need to read any of these white guys.'"

◆ ◆ ◆

WHAT JACKIE BROUGHT to baseball and America was a unifying ethos. If I were to give you a visual metaphor, it would be of Jackie as a vessel that traveled on very troubled waters and cut a wake deep and wide enough so that others coming behind him would encounter less turbulence. That protected a lot of people coming behind him.

Doesn't mean that these guys didn't go through horrible situations. But they were fortunate that Jackie went first.

The ethos was that the African-Americans who followed Jackie owed their community and the nation their best effort. Jackie established a tradition for a couple of waves of ballplayers. They became disciples. Only each spread the message in his own way.

◆ ◆ ◆

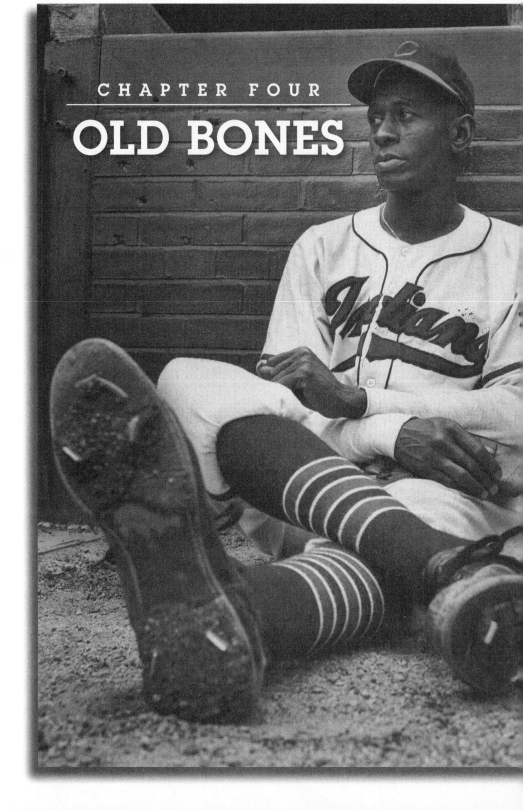

CHAPTER FOUR

OLD BONES

HERE'S A TOUGH one for you: Imagine an all-Caucasian NBA. Now, I know that's a bit of a stretch—especially if you're in high school—because I read about a kid who not long ago wondered when the NBA had been integrated with *white* players.

But let's say the NBA *was* all white and nobody black was allowed to play in it . . . while Michael Jordan was in his prime.

What would Michael do? Well, he'd probably play against Magic Johnson and Charles Barkley in a league of black players. But let's say there wasn't all that much money in a league that had few white fans.

It's no secret that Michael has a keen instinct for making a buck. So imagine that on his days off from the African-American League, he travels from town to town with his black All-Star buddies and plays against teams made up of guys working in the local auto plant or fire department. The people who play against him don't care that he's black and they're white—they just want to see Michael fly. Years later, the guys at the auto plant will still be talking about the day that Michael Jordan dunked on them.

In fact, Michael is such an attraction that he doesn't even need a team. He buys himself a plane and hires himself out to *three different teams* in a single day, playing a quarter of a game, getting his check, then traveling to the next town and the next game . . .

The biggest star of the Caucasian NBA knows how good Michael Jordan is. Larry Bird thinks it's a shame that he and Michael can't play on the same court, so he organizes an off-season tour. Larry and his white All-Stars will play against Michael and his black All-Stars with a whole lot of $20 bills in it for everybody.

The tour sells out all over America, and everybody who sees Michael knows he could dominate the NBA if only given a chance. But his skin color has doomed him to a gypsy's life.

Then, one day, when Michael is 42 and long past his prime, a monumental decision is announced: The NBA will finally allow black players. But the first one won't be Michael. He's too old. Instead it will be a relatively untested college football star.

That's what it was like to be Satchel Paige.

Because he'd been marginalized by his sport, and because there was no slick sporting goods company like Nike to build an ad campaign around him, Satch had to do all that marketing by himself. He gave his pitches nicknames like the Bee Ball, the Long Tom, and the Hesitation Pitch. Occasionally he'd motion for the seven fielders behind him to sit down, or he'd tell the batters which pitch he was gonna throw—and then strike out the side. And if anything seemed like too tall a tale, so much the better: More people would pay down the road to see for themselves.

Paige always refused to divulge his age. He told writers who pressed him on it that his mother had put his birth certificate in a Bible whose pages were eaten by a goat. And when asked if his Hesitation Pitch was legal, he once responded, "I ain't never throwed an illegal pitch. Just once in awhile I used to toss one that ain't never been seen by this generation."

The owner of the Cleveland Indians, Bill Veeck, knew what made the cash register jingle. In 1948, a year after he brought in Larry Doby as the first black American Leaguer, he signed Leroy Robert "Satchel" Paige.

Think about that: a baseball legend's walking out of the shadows and into the sunshine as a 42-year-old rookie, and everyone's still expecting him to be the maestro he was at 29. How would he do?

Oh, and let's not forget another thing, which almost always *is* forgotten: What about all those black All-Stars who were out traveling like vagabonds and playing with Satch? They might have dominated major league baseball too. Now that they were past their prime, what would become of them?

◆ ◆ ◆

MONTE IRVIN

◆◆◆

THERE'LL NEVER BE another Satchel Paige.

One day I was 0-for-4 against Satchel. Afterward, he came over to me and said, "Big'un"—he always called me Big'un—"you'll never hit me. Let's go to the bar and have a beer."

We sat down at the bar and started talking, and Satch said, "You got your bat too high. It's way up there," and he demonstrates. "By the time you get it down, I'm by you and gone."

What he was saying is that he was gonna pitch me inside, and I'd never have time to get the bat around and hit the ball. "Man," he said, "you better drop that damn bat."

I said to him, "You're gonna tell me how to hit you?"

And he said, "Just 'cause I tell you doesn't mean you're gonna do it."

BOB FELLER

◆◆◆

I PITCHED AGAINST Satchel in Des Moines way back in 1935, when I was 16 years old. A bunch of local semipros against the Kansas City Monarchs. Years later, I got to know him well, and we got to be friends. Not drinking-buddy kind of friends. We didn't go out to nightclubs. It was probably a friendship based on respect.

We never talked about the fact that he couldn't play in the major leagues. It was all under the surface. That's just the way it was. Nothing you could do about it.

What could you do? Then, I thought: Why not capitalize on the separation? The racial rivalry tour came to me when I was aboard the battleship *Alabama* during World War II: the best blacks against the best whites across the country. When the war ended, in the summer of 1945, there was no time to organize anything. But there was plenty of time to figure something out for the winter of 1946.

I leased two DC-3's from the Flying Tiger Line, one for the white players, and one for the blacks. Booked 'em for a dollar a mile. Booked a schedule. Rented all the ballparks. Started in Pittsburgh, then went to Yankee Stadium. Played in New Haven in a racetrack. On to Columbus, Des Moines. Council

Bluffs. We got snowed out in Minneapolis. Then we went on to the West Coast and played from San Diego all the way up to Vancouver.

Couldn't play anywhere south of the Mason-Dixon Line, of course. Wouldn't even waste a phone call trying to set anything up.

I paid all expenses and divided up 35% of the gross equally among all the players, white and black. Buck O'Neil said his wife thought he was out robbing banks because he was sending home so much money. It was good business to be friendly.

The two teams didn't associate much—only at the ballpark, really. We were too tired for any folderol. We played 35 games in 30 days. Who won the most? Buck O'Neil used to say that they did, but I've got the scorecards. We won more, but not many more, and anyway, it wasn't important.

After it was over, I remember the black players coming over to shake my hand. Later on, some people said it really opened a door.

LARRY LESTER
A leading historian of the Negro Leagues.
◆◆

SATCHEL PAIGE COULD not have been the first African-American to go to the major leagues. He had age working against him. His best years were behind him. He was overused. Look at 1942: He pitched every game in the Negro League World Series. Maybe he didn't start every game, but he was in them. People were paying to see him.

Paige had a reputation for being undependable. Like a rock star today, he would show up late for the concert. It was all about making the people beg for your appearance. Sometimes he'd show up five minutes before the game, throw a few warmups, and he was ready. He didn't go through all that bullpen stuff. He had to find ways to keep his arm fresh.

◆ ◆ ◆

YOGI BERRA

◆◆

ONCE WE WERE in an All-Star game together—it was 1952 or 1953—and we hit the showers at the same time. Satch turned on the hot water as hot as it could go, and he stood right under it and let it hit his right arm. Scalding water. Didn't bother him a damn bit. I mean, the water in that shower was so hot that smoke was coming off his arm.

I said to him, "What the hell are you doing?"

He said, "Makin' money."

MIKE VEECK

◆◆

THE ONLY STORY I know from when Satchel Paige joined the Indians is the stick-of-gum story.

Our manager, Lou Boudreau, wasn't really certain that bringing Paige up was a good move because of his age. Nobody really knew how old Satchel was. They say there were seven different birth certificates. So I'm sure my father set this up, because this was vintage Bill Veeck.

Dad said, "Let's give him a simple test. We'll put a stick of gum on home plate. And if he throws nine pitches out of 10 over the stick of gum, we'll sign him."

So they did, and Satchel came in and threw nine straight pitches over the stick of gum, and Boudreau said, "I think this is a good idea."

I don't think that one's a myth.

BOB FELLER

◆◆

SATCH WAS THE oldest rookie in history, but he was not the type of guy to be nervous. He would've been recognized as one of the top five pitchers in the history of the game if he'd played in the majors his entire career. He was that good. Great motion, threw from different angles, perfect control. He helped us win the pennant and the World Series in 1948. That's the last time they won it in Cleveland.

You could always have a good time around Satch. I remember one time in Detroit, the soap in the clubhouse looked exactly like the ice cream in the middle of a Nabisco ice cream sandwich. So we took out the ice cream and put the bar of soap between the wafers, and I handed it to Satch between games of a doubleheader. Of course, everybody in the clubhouse knew what was gonna happen. He took a bite, and his false teeth stayed in the soap. It was funny, and Satch went along with the gag.

He was known to play a few of his own, too.

LARRY LESTER

◆◆

PAIGE WAS A very intelligent man, and he played to the hype. He did a little step-n-fetch-it for the white folks. He did the Bojangles tap dance to entertain them.

Jackie never would do that. He would never showboat or do a minstrel show. But Satchel was raking in the money, and he was a lot more sophisticated than people give him credit for. He was an antiques collector, you know.

ROBERT PAIGE

◆◆

I'VE NEVER MET anybody who was at that first game my father pitched in the majors in 1948. I've had family members of players mention it—maybe their grandfather played in it or something. But I never met anyone who paid to get in.

I think of my father making that walk from the warmup cage out to the mound. There must have been a tremendous amount of weight on his shoulders. Can you imagine them bringing somebody up to the major leagues at the age of 42? But it's more than that. They were expecting him to perform as if he were 22.

He was being judged by millions, and it wasn't like he was close to being in his prime. That's a phenomenal amount of pressure to place on anybody. And of course you had the racial undertones. Members of his own team didn't want to sit next to him, eat with him, or get dressed in the same dressing room.

Sometimes I try to imagine myself at that age trying to play in the NBA. Can you picture that? All my basketball skills diminished, going out and trying to run with Dwyane Wade?

MONTE IRVIN

◆◆

SATCH INVENTED WHAT he called the Hesitation Pitch. After throwin' all that fire, Satch would get two strikes on a batter and then wind up, put that left foot down, and . . . throw. It wasn't a full stop, exactly. It was just a little, well, hesitation at the top of his windup. Nobody could hit it. So they outlawed the Hesitation Pitch. They said there had to be a continuous motion, no hesitation. Satchel had this individual talent that nobody else had and the creativity to invent this pitch. But the major leagues banned it.

◆ ◆ ◆

AUTHOR'S NOTE

PAIGE'S FIRST MAJOR league start, on August 3, 1948, attracted 72,434 people to Municipal Stadium in Cleveland. His second start, against the White Sox in Chicago, ignited a virtual riot. The official attendance was announced as 51,103, Comiskey Park's first sellout since 1945. Thousands more were turned away, and one of the turnstiles was uprooted by the surging crowd.

Paige finished the year with a 6–1 record and a 2.48 ERA as the Indians won the American League pennant and went on to defeat the Boston Braves in the World Series.

He pitched two seasons for the Indians (1948-49), left the majors for a year after a contract dispute, and then pitched three more seasons for the St. Louis Browns (1951-53).

Twelve years later, he came out of retirement to pitch in the major leagues one more time.

Here, Satchel's son describes his father's extraordinary "comeback" on September 25, 1965, at the age of 59.

ROBERT PAIGE

◆◆

I WAS LUCKY enough to see Dad pitch in the major leagues. But it took 20 years before I realized what a historical event it was. At the time, I just didn't think it was all that significant. We didn't even take a camera to the game. This is the way it happened.

My dad knew he was going to be put on the Kansas City Athletics roster in order to qualify for his major league pension. He thought he'd spend the time coaching the pitchers and giving advice. Dad had no idea that he would be put in the game. I mean, he was *59 years old.*

But it turned out he needed to appear in an actual game to get his pension. Or that's what he was told. I don't know exactly how it all came together. I do know that Charlie Finley, the owner of the Athletics, was quite a showman, so it may have been his scheme to have Dad pitch. I also know this turned out to be quite a show.

I was 14 years old at the time. I'd been used to hearing about what my dad had done when he was young. I grew up seeing him get stopped for autographs and photographs. So to me, this was just him doing what he did.

Anyway, he didn't have much notice that he was going to pitch, and he decided to check out his control in our backyard. I was his "official catcher." Playing catch was something we'd done from time to time, like what other fathers and sons did on an average weekend throughout America. Only this time I was helping get my 59-year-old father ready to pitch against the Boston Red Sox.

I didn't really play much baseball as a kid. My mother didn't want me to be an athlete. She had a critical view of the professional sports world because of what she went through with my father. It wasn't only the constant travel. It was also the constant adversity that blacks faced in that era. She wanted me to get a college degree and pursue life from that direction.

The thing you have to understand is that I had no idea of the intricacies involved in being a catcher for a major league pitcher, even one who was 59 years old.

So he got me all suited up in catcher's gear. The mask, the chest protector, the shin guards—everything. Then he pulled out this laundry basket full of balls from the garage. There must've been about three dozen balls in that basket. We needed 'em because we didn't chase balls—the ones that got away just got away.

My mother was out there with us watching, more than a little nervous for me. She knew my father was going to have to bear down to see what kind of control he had. She was afraid I might get hurt.

Dad would tell me what he was going to throw—"This is gonna be a curveball, it's gonna break this way" . . . "This is gonna be a sinker" . . . "This one's gonna have a little speed on it"—just so I'd have an idea what was coming.

He wasn't throwing as hard as he could. He was taking a lot off of it. But when he did put on some heat, the balls were getting by me. My reaction time just wasn't good enough. Looking back now, I can only imagine how hard he must've been able to throw at 20 or 25. It's mind-blowing.

We went through that basket of balls, and he was quite pleased with his control. We called it quits, and the next day he went out to pitch against the Boston Red Sox.

Everybody was wondering how a 59-year-old man could possibly play in the major leagues. But I didn't expect anything less than a good performance because of all the stories I'd heard about him. And from my experience trying to catch him.

The crowd that day in Kansas City was plenty excited. A few of the Red Sox made some pretty good contact, but they were mostly flyouts. In three innings, Dad gave up no runs and only one a hit—a double by Carl Yastrzemski.

In the locker room afterward, everyone came over to hug him.

The Red Sox, too.

All the while, I'm thinking to myself, Hey, this is just what my father does.

MONTE IRVIN

JACKIE DREW GREAT crowds wherever he played, at home and on the road. Don't think the other owners in the majors didn't take notice.

A few months after Jackie joined the Dodgers, the people running the St. Louis Browns brought in Willard Brown and Hank Thompson from the Negro Leagues, hoping they would be instant successes too. The Browns were a terrible team, and the ownership figured these guys might be able to attract the same kind of huge crowds as Jackie.

And make no mistake, you would have paid to see Willard in his prime. The man could flat-out hit home runs. Don't throw him anything high. They loved Willard in Puerto Rico. He was the greatest player in the Puerto Rican League. Down there, they called him *Ese Hombre.*

The other players on the Browns didn't want Willard and Hank around: "Why are they here? They're taking jobs away from us." That was the attitude.

It was a shock for the guys coming out of the Negro Leagues. More like a real cultural collision. Willard Brown and Hank Thompson didn't go to college and didn't have the education or experiences that Jackie did. The teams made a big mistake by not sending them to the minor leagues, if only for a month, just like the Dodgers sent Jackie to Montreal for a year.

In the minors, you got used to playing baseball in a major league way. Understand? You could learn from the ground floor up. When Willard and Hank got to St. Louis, they had to learn by lookin'. You know, see how the other guys do it.

BUCK O'NEIL

◆◆

PROBLEM WAS, WHERE could you send a black ballplayer for some minor league seasoning back then? If your farm team was in South Carolina or Georgia or Louisiana, there was no way you could send him there. They didn't want a black man there.

So where you gonna send him?

MONTE IRVIN

◆◆

GUYS LIKE WILLARD Brown never had a period of acclimation to doing things the major league way.

See, Willard was the kind of guy who wasn't takin' orders from anybody. I don't give a damn who it was. He was gonna do things his own way.

Without a period of acclimation, he never could have played in the major leagues. He wouldn't have made it, in my estimation. *Who are you to tell me how to play? I know how to play.* Once in St. Louis, Willard came up with a runner on. The sign was for him to bunt down the third baseline to move the runners over. First pitch, he didn't advance the runners. Second pitch, a high fastball. Now, Willard was a high fastball hitter, and he knocked it off the wall for a two-run, inside-the-park homer—the first home run ever by a black man in the American League.

But when Willard got to the dugout, the manager, Muddy Ruel, was all over him for ignoring the sign. And you know what Willard said? He said he knew he wouldn't be able to play for the Browns because anytime you get chewed out for hitting a home run, you know you're in the wrong place.

QUINCY TROUPE

An acclaimed poet and biographer of Miles Davis, Quincy Troupe—he dropped the "Jr." following his name when he reached young adulthood—talks about his father, Quincy Trouppe, a fabled catcher in the Negro League who didn't get his shot in the majors until he was well past his prime. (Quincy Sr. added a "p" to his last name while playing in Latin America.)

◆◆◆

My FATHER WAS 39 when he finally got his chance with the Indians, in 1952. But he played only six games in two and a half months, and one day near the end of the season, he got a message to go see the GM, Hank Greenberg, in his office. When Dad got there, Greenberg told him to take a seat. Let me read what happened next from Dad's autobiography, *20 Years Too Soon*:

> "I don't know how to say this," Hank said, "but I'm afraid I have bad news for you. We've decided to send you down to Indianapolis."
>
> This hit me with such force that I was speechless for a few minutes. Greenberg saw how it affected me, and he spoke up again:
>
> "Quincy, I want you to know that I feel that you should be our second catcher. I even talked to Al Lopez, but he won't go along with the idea. Well, you understand. He's the manager, and there are certain things that we can't do over his head." The terrible disappointment nearly choked me. I finally said, "Well, look, Hank. I don't think I'm being treated right."
>
> Hank interrupted before I could say more: "Quincy, one thing you don't have is a record that we can go on."

Didn't have a record?

How could Greenberg say that? Everybody knew who my father was. My dad had been an All-Star 18 times in the Negro Leagues and Latin America. Not only that, but my father was a great manager. He hit .400 and led the Cleveland Buckeyes to the Negro Leagues championship. They beat the Homestead Grays. He was the catcher and the manager. He was behind the plate when Cleveland pitchers held the great Josh Gibson to .123 in the World Series.

Hank Greenberg knew that. Al Lopez knew that. Everybody in the Indians organization knew that.

No record?

So you say, Okay, that was just a poor choice of words. What Greenberg should have said was, "Quincy, you're not the player you once were. And we need somebody who's going to deliver for us. Somebody who's 29, not 39. Somebody who's younger." That would have been a *baseball* answer.

And I know my dad could have accepted that, because we talked about it. He could have accepted it because he'd been a manager, and he'd had to do the same thing. The message should have been, "If we'd gotten you when you were 29 or 30, it would be different. But you're 39, and you're a catcher. You're not like Satchel Paige, who draws those big crowds."

But Greenberg didn't say that. He said, "You don't have a record."

That's the kind of willful, self-serving ignorance that goes into a lot of decisions, not only in baseball but in all areas, when it comes to black folks.

No record?

Man, Roy Campanella went on to win three MVP awards in the National League. And in the Negro Leagues, Campanella was my dad's *backup*!

◆ ◆ ◆

MY FATHER INTIMIDATED people with his power, his size, and his ability.

He was 6′3″ and weighed 215 pounds. He'd been a Golden Gloves champion. They thought he might be the next Joe Louis. All-state in football. All-state in basketball. All-state in baseball. He spoke Spanish and French. Smart as hell. Great dancer. All the women loved him—black, white, Cuban, Chinese, whatever. Now, that's scary to a lot of people. So he had to figure out a way to negotiate through a world that was frightened of him. And to make it palatable for everybody, what he did was hold everything inside.

When I came along, times were different. I came along in the time of Muhammad Ali: I'm out there, and I'm letting you know that nobody's putting a foot on my neck.

Now, I don't know if Muhammad Ali was able to say the things he said because of what Jackie Robinson went through. It's a big question. But I do know that he said them. He had a voice.

And I had a voice. My father looked at me, and he saw there was no submerging going on. I was expressing myself, and he still couldn't. He couldn't express himself, and I think because of that he felt a sense of shame.

The shift in time and voice created tension between us. My father taught me everything about baseball. He taught me how to throw fastballs and curves. I must've been throwing 90 miles an hour. One day he said to me, "You know, you ought to try to make it in baseball. You can be a great pitcher if you apply yourself. I can get you in."

He kept bugging me about it when I was in high school. So one day I said to him, "Dad, do you see any girls at baseball games? No! They're all at the basketball games."

I didn't realize what I was saying. But it hurt him to his heart. What I was really saying to him was, I'm going my own way. Don't talk to me about playing baseball. I want to play *basketball*. You want me to be a baseball player. I want to be a basketball player. This is the way it's gonna be. And he was pissed.

Later, this tension between us came out in ways I couldn't have anticipated.

Once, about 15 of my poems got translated into Spanish in the literary section of a Sunday newspaper in Mexico City. One of the editors wanted to send them to me, and when he looked for my address in the Los Angeles directory, he saw a listing for Quincy Trouppe's Dugout, the restaurant my dad owned. I was living in New York at the time, but the editor didn't know it, so he sent the poems to my dad.

Well, one day the phone rang: "Junior?"

"Hey, Dad, how you doing?"

"Look here, you tell these people from Mexico who are sending these poems not to send them to me no more."

"What?" I asked. I didn't even know what he was talking about. The conversation went back and forth until finally he said to me, "Man, I was a *star* in Mexico. And you ain't nothin' but a poet."

That's how it came out. My dad just didn't have a voice to get out all the stuff that was bottled up deep down inside.

I used to tell him, "Dad, they weren't ever gonna give you shit, so you might as well have told 'em what you thought. Every time someone mentions Roy Campanella's name, you get mad. You're mad because Roy Campanella was your backup, and he's in the Hall of Fame. But it wasn't *his* fault that he played in the major leagues. Campanella got the opportunity, and he took it. He went on and became a great player. He won championships. He won MVP awards."

But that only dug deeper into my dad's heart. Because he was thinking to himself, If Roy could be MVP, what could *I* have been? *He was my backup.*

I'd say to him, "You own a big restaurant in LA. You're independent. You own big houses. You make money. You can say whatever you want. You don't have to keep silent. What are you keeping silent about?"

"You don't understand," he'd always say. "You just don't understand."

"Yeah, but I *do*," I'd tell him. "I *do* understand. You're keeping silent because you think they might put you in the Hall of Fame, and you don't want to hurt your chances. You deserve to be in the Hall of Fame on your merits. You deserve to be in the Hall of Fame on your record. Why get mad at Roy Campanella?"

But he just couldn't get through to the bottom of his anger.

Once I asked him, "Why don't you ever talk about the people who fired you when you were a scout for the St. Louis Cardinals?"

But he couldn't go there because that was a deep wound.

You see, after he left baseball as a player, he joined the Cardinals as a scout. And early on, he recommended Roberto Clemente and Vic Power.

The first thing that the manager, Eddie Stanky, asked my dad when he recommended that the Cardinals sign Vic Power was, "Does he date white girls?"

And my dad told him, "Vic Power is from Puerto Rico. They don't think about it like that. In Puerto Rico, you can date anybody you want."

Only Stanky wasn't thinking first about talent. He wasn't thinking that this guy Power might help him win a championship. He was thinking about whether he dated white women.

So then my dad recommended Roberto Clemente. Well, he was also from Puerto Rico, and that meant he also thought he could date anybody he wanted to. So Vic Power went to the Philadelphia Athletics, and Roberto Clemente went to the Pittsburgh Pirates.

Now, you're gonna tell my dad he can't scout? He'd just found two bona fide major leaguers, one of them a future Hall of Famer, and the team he found 'em for wouldn't sign 'em.

And then they came to him and said, "We're going to have to let you go because you haven't signed anybody."

Dad said, "Hey, look at the people I recommended."

And they said, "It's not enough for you to recommend them. You have to sign them."

But *they* were the ones who wouldn't sign them. I mean, hold on. My dad wasn't an ignorant person. He was a brilliant man. You can't say that to him.

He knew that the people who hired him were racist. But he was going along with it because he wanted to contribute to the Cardinals—in the city where he grew up—by bringing in great players.

But he could never express the rage that this wound brought him. And because he couldn't express it, it came out in other ways. It came out in arguments with me or at the very mention of Roy Campanella.

Once, just once, my father let it out when he went to talk with Cool Papa Bell. It's in his book, which I'm proud he finally wrote. In fact, he published it himself.

Anyway, my father said to Cool Papa, "I know I held my own with the best."

"Most people close to baseball know that about you, Quincy," Cool Papa said. "But remember, he who hollers the loudest will be seen and recognized. I guess you haven't hollered loud enough."

◆ ◆ ◆

AUTHOR'S NOTE

THE GREATEST SLUGGER in Negro League history, JOSH GIBSON (1911-47) once hit 75 homers in a single season (1931). Legend has it that a 500-foot home run he hit as a rookie in a playoff game for the Homestead Grays in 1930 was the longest shot ever in Yankee Stadium. He played 17 seasons for the Grays and the Pittsburgh Crawfords. Gibson died following a stroke in January 1947, just three months before Jackie Robinson made his debut with the Brooklyn Dodgers. He was 35. In 1972, Gibson followed SATCHEL PAIGE into the Hall of Fame. Here MONTE IRVIN, BOB VEALE, BUCK O'NEIL, ORLANDO CEPEDA, and Gibson's great-grandson, SEAN GIBSON, talk about "the Black Babe Ruth."

◆ ◆ ◆

MONTE IRVIN
◆◆◆

EVERY TIME I go up to Cooperstown and start talking baseball, people always ask me, "How good was Josh Gibson?"

And I'll always say, "He was as good as I say he was. And I'm one of the few guys still living who saw him play. I've seen Ruth, Gehrig, DiMaggio, Mays,

Mantle, Aaron, and Bonds. None of 'em could hit like Josh Gibson."

Then they'll say, "Well, describe him."

Josh was about 6′1″, 215. Muscular. Ran like a deer. Rifle for an arm. But more than anything else, he was as strong as two men. And he had a swing unlike any I've ever seen.

BOB VEALE
◆◆

INSANE POWER! JUST insane! He was a behemoth. God gave Josh his strength, like he gave it to Samson. I've seen pitchers throw at Josh's head, and he'd just lean back and knock it over the right field fence.

MONTE IRVIN
◆◆

IN PUERTO RICO, we played in a stadium that had tall, skinny palm trees out past the outfield fence. They made a nice background to hit against, and beyond them was the ocean. Man, Josh would hit 'em over those trees!

The way the ball is souped-up today, I'm sure he'd have hit 'em into the ocean.

You know who I always felt sorry for? I felt sorry for the major league fans back home who never got a chance to see so many great ballplayers. Never got a chance to see Cool Papa Bell run. Never got a chance to see Buck Leonard hit—and he was every bit as good as Lou Gehrig, maybe even better. Smokey Joe Williams, Bullet Joe Rogan—never saw them. Willie Foster, a great left-hander—never saw him.

And man, they never got a chance to see Satchel Paige go up against Josh Gibson . . .

BUCK O'NEIL
◆◆

I'LL TELL YOU what you didn't see. And you're never gonna see it again. Oh no!

I mean, nobody's going to pitch to Barry Bonds in the World Series. You walk him. You don't walk batters to get *to* Barry Bonds. But back then, it was different. It was an era of personal competition. You *lived* to pitch to Josh Gibson. This is how I get my kicks, a pitcher's sayin' to himself, pitchin' to the best.

Let me tell you about the second game of the 1942 Negro League World Series. Kansas City Monarchs and the Homestead Grays in Pittsburgh. We're ahead 2-0 in the seventh inning. Satchel's pitchin'. The batter knocks a triple down the leftfield line. I go over to the mound, and Satchel says to me, "You know what I'm fixin' to do?"

And I say, "You're gonna get this guy out, and we goin' home."

Satchel just shakes his head and says, "No, I'm gonna walk him. And I'm gonna walk the next guy, too. I'm going to pitch to Josh."

Fill the bases to pitch to Josh Gibson?!

I say, "Man, don't be facetious."-

Then I call out our manager, Frank Duncan, and I say to him, "Listen to what this fool is sayin'!"

And Frank says, "All these people in the ballpark came out here today to see Satchel Paige and Josh Gibson. Let the man do what he wants to do."

Now, there was some history here. See, years before, Satchel and Josh played for the same team. They were sitting next to each other on a bus once as they were travelin' through the Blue Ridge Mountains, and Satchel said to Josh, "They say you're the best hitter in the world, and I know I'm the best pitcher. One day we're gonna meet up on different teams and see who the best really is."

So anyway, Satchel walks the first batter, and as he's walking the second, he looks over to Josh in the on-deck circle and says, "Remember that time in the Blue Ridge Mountains?"

As Josh heads up to the plate, the crowd is feeling it, but Satchel isn't through yet. Oh no. He's just setting the stage. He puts his glove down on the mound, and he motions for our trainer, Jewbaby Floyd.

Now it's showtime. Jewbaby goes out to the mound with a glass foaming over with bicarbonate of soda. Understand, Satchel was famous for having stomach problems. So Satchel drinks that glass right down, and he lets out a great belch. Big old belch! And he makes the motion, too, so if you were sitting way up in the stands and couldn't hear it, you could see that belch.

Then he turns back to Josh and hollers down to him, "Okay, you ready?"

Josh just nods that yes, he's ready, and he steps into the batter's box with that great, great body of his, after two guys have walked *just to get to him.* Let me tell you, it was scary. All you could do was hope Josh didn't kill somebody.

You know what I'd have done? I'd have walked Josh, too. That's right. I'd have walked him and gave up one run instead of four.

But Satchel throws a fastball, and Josh doesn't even move his bat.

Strike one!

"Okay, Josh, now I'm gonna throw you another fastball, just about the same place," Satchel calls down to him. "But it's gonna be a little harder than the last one."

Again, Josh doesn't move his bat.

Strike two!

Now Satchel yells out, "I got you 0-and-2, and I'm supposed to knock you down. But I'm not gonna throw no smoke at yo' yolk. I'm gonna throw a pea at yo' knee."

Satchel was about 6′4″, but when he wound up and kicked that leg up, he looked to be upwards of seven feet tall. Josh never even swung.

Strike three!

Let me tell you, when Satchel walked off the mound, he was *10* feet tall.

And he said, "*Nobody* hits Satchel's fastball."

You know, I must have told that story a million times. But I never get tired of it. Why would I? Every time I tell it, I'm 30 years old again and playin' in the World Series.

◆ ◆ ◆

HERE'S THE THING. I tell that story all the time, but there's another part to it that I hardly ever tell.

A couple of seasons after that, Satchel was on the mound again, and up comes Josh Gibson again. This time, Josh hits a line drive right back at Satchel's head. I mean, Satchel ducks and it buzzes his head. But the ball keeps risin' and carries right over the centerfield fence.

Satchel's head comes up all slow, like a turtle peeking out of its shell. He looks over to me, and he says, "You know, a man can get *killed* out here."

◆ ◆ ◆

ORLANDO CEPEDA

◆◆◆

ONCE, WHEN I was a boy, I met Josh Gibson. My father was a big star down in Puerto Rico, and that day, Dad was playing second base and Josh was catching.

What I remember was how much Josh scared me. He was drinking at the time and having mental problems. The day after I met him at the ballpark, he was caught walking naked through his hotel.

They say he was drinking so much because he was angry that he'd been passed over by Branch Rickey and that he wouldn't be the first Negro star in the major leagues.

A few months later, he died of a stroke.

MONTE IRVIN

◆◆◆

I REMEMBER WALKING through Allegheny Cemetery in Pittsburgh back in the 1960s, trying to find Josh Gibson's grave. There was no marker on it. We had to find it by tracking down a grave number provided by the cemetery attendant.

SEAN GIBSON

◆◆◆

PEOPLE ARE ALWAYS asking me questions about my great-grandfather that I can only speculate on.

Do you think Josh Gibson could have done what he did in major league baseball?

Do you think he was bitter because he didn't make it into the major leagues?

Do you think he died of a broken heart?

I can't answer those questions. My great-grandfather died so young—he was only 35—and I came along so much later.

Everything I know about him I learned from family members and friends.

More and more people have become interested in Josh Gibson recently with the major league home run record being challenged. We're now looking at Barry Bonds maybe passing Henry Aaron as the all-time leader. Aaron hit 755. Some say Josh hit more than 800.

CHAPTER FIVE

A LITTLE DISCUSSION

WHENEVER OL' SATCH and Rapid Robert got together, they spoke only about what they had in common: throwing a baseball.

Satchel Paige and Bob Feller never spoke about the invisible wall between them. The two pitching greats formed a bond based on mutual respect in 1946, when they went barnstorming together. Probably they didn't want to jeopardize that bond. Or maybe a black Alabama railroad porter and a white Iowa farm boy simply didn't know where to start.

Neither ever learned how the other truly felt about the invisible wall, because neither ever asked.

Now let's take a step forward.

The Dodgers integrate baseball. They have Jackie Robinson and Roy Campanella and a fireballing pitcher named Don Newcombe. They're a crowd magnet at home and on the road. Yet when the team arrives at Union Station in St. Louis, the white players walk straight to their bus to head for the plush Chase Hotel, while Jackie, Roy, and Don grab their luggage and find a cab to take them to a crummy hotel on the black side of town, one without air-conditioning.

As the trio waits for a taxi in the St. Louis heat, a burn begins to spread through Newcombe that still smolders more than half a century later.

At that very moment, a white pitcher for the Dodgers named Carl Erskine, who grew up in Indiana with a black childhood friend, sees the same scene through very different eyes. Oisk, as fans back in Brooklyn called him, doesn't dwell on the unfairness in lodging. He sees the Dodgers as at the cutting edge of racial relations and himself as part of something huge and wonderful, a team helping to change America.

Neither Newk nor Oisk could know how the other truly felt, because neither ever asked.

What's changed since then? Much—and nothing. After all this

time, we still don't talk about race, as if afraid that old problems could spark new ones.

"It's more than the elephant in the room," says Bryant Gumbel. "It's the *zoo* in the room."

The first black man to host a national sports show and then a network morning show, Gumbel believes that the issue of race is "right in front of us, and everyone wants to walk around it and talk around it. Anytime you mention something black-white, people go into conniptions. It's unfortunate, because there are a lot of serious discussions that need to be had."

Perhaps the most unfortunate part is how race emerges from our TV screens, typically popping up before us only when something dramatic happens that we can't possibly turn away from. Black superstar O.J. Simpson goes on trial for allegedly murdering his white wife. A black erotic dancer accuses white players on the Duke lacrosse team of rape.

How do we discuss race then? We point fingers and shout at each other on talk shows, mostly because of all the conversations that never took place.

But what if you could sit down and listen to Don Newcombe? He's 80 now, the last black man alive to have played with Jackie. He'd make you very comfortable in his home. Get you an iced tea. Make sure your seat was to your liking. And then he'd make you a little *un*comfortable—remember, this is a man who once tried to pitch a doubleheader all by himself, and he's still coming at you full force. There's no warm and fuzzy blurring of memories for Don Newcombe. Those memories are still raw and sharp at age 80, and when he gets down deep enough, a tear appears in the corner of his eye.

Afterward, you go to Erskine, and you tell him some of the things that Newcombe said. You register his reaction. And as you think about the views of the two men, you can only wonder about all the conversations that never happened.

DON NEWCOMBE

◆◆

WHY? WHY? WHY?

What is it about us that we had to be treated as subhuman beings?

What did we do to be treated like we were treated?

Were they afraid of us?

Maybe so, because the Robinsons and the Dobys and the Campanellas and the Newcombes and then the great players who came after us—the Mayses and the Gibsons and the Aarons—we set all kinds of records.

I'm the only player in baseball history to have won the Rookie of the Year award, the Most Valuable Player award, and the Cy Young Award. Nobody else in baseball history—black, white, brown, tan, yellow, or whatever—has won those three awards in his career.

Was the white man afraid of that, afraid of what we would do to baseball?

Baseball had a famous commissioner named Kenesaw Mountain Landis back when I was growing up. And Kenesaw Mountain Landis once said, "As long as I'm the commissioner of baseball . . ."—and here Landis used the n-word—"will never play in the major leagues."

Thank God, he died in 1944. I didn't know who he was, didn't know where he came from, didn't know a thing about him. But I was glad when I read the bastard had died. If Kenesaw Mountain Landis had lived another 20 years, you never would have seen me or Jackie in baseball.

I could go to the Army, go to war, fight and die for my country like some of my friends did. This country would take my taxes. But I couldn't play the all-American pastime.

Bitter? Oh yeah, we were bitter.

But Jackie always said that one day we were going to change the spelling and the meaning of the word "bitter." We were going to replace the "i" with an "e" and make it "better."

That's why we had to go through all that stuff that we did: to make things better.

Do you know what Jackie's impact was? Well, let Martin Luther King tell you. In 1968, Martin had dinner in my house with my family. This was 28 days before he was assassinated. He said to me, "Don, I don't know what I would've done without you guys setting up the minds of people for change. You, Jackie, and Roy will never know how easy you made it for me to do my job."

Can you imagine that? How easy *we* made it for Martin Luther King!

◆ ◆ ◆

SOMETIMES THE WHITE guys wondered why we were so bitter. Black guys experienced it. White guys tried to interpret it. But how can somebody else interpret what I feel inside my skin?

Can you know how I feel just because *you think* it's the way I'm supposed to feel?

One day, I got on the team bus to go over to the ballpark for a game, and sitting there were six white men in suits who weren't part of our usual party. Jackie handed me a letter and said, "Read this."

"If you so-and-sos show up at the ballpark today," the letter said, "we're gonna kill all of you."

"Who are these guys on the bus, anyway?" I asked.

"FBI," Jackie said. "It's a really serious threat today."

Me, Jackie, and Roy went to the ballpark and into the clubhouse and then into the dugout with one of these guys on each side of us. I was looking around, and I saw a guy walking on top of a building just beyond the outfield wall with a rifle. I turned to Jackie and said, "Hey, look over there."

"It's okay," Jackie said. "He's with us. FBI."

I said, "What are we gonna do?"

Jackie said, "We're gonna play ball."

All that tension and pressure just because we had the audacity to want to play baseball in the major leagues?

Jackie had his fears. He'd probably have had a nervous breakdown or something after he took the Dodgers to the World Series in his rookie year if it weren't for his wife, Rachel.

Jackie faced a real threat every time he stepped up to the plate. Opposing pitchers threw at him all the time. That was a given. It was hard to hit Jackie because his reflexes were good and he could get out of the way. But how many times did I see Roy Campanella lying on the ground after being hit? He was a big guy and a bad ducker. He was one of the first in baseball to use the hard plastic insert in his cap. That's right, Roy Campanella. They threw at him because he had black skin, and they couldn't hit the other guy with black skin often enough to satisfy them.

They can deny it all they want. They can talk all they want about how much they cared about Jackie and how much they loved Jackie and Roy and what great guys they were. But they didn't care about Jackie and Roy when we first joined that club. And that includes some of our own teammates.

Every time we'd arrive in St. Louis on the train, me and Jackie and Roy would have to get our suitcases and carry them through Union Station and stand on the curb trying to find a cab. Sometimes we had to wait 30 to 45 minutes, because white drivers wouldn't pick up black guys. They'd just drive by us in that St. Louis heat—and only God knows how hot it gets in St. Louis. (And maybe even God doesn't know.)

We'd finally get a cab that would take us to a substandard hotel with no air-conditioning, while the white players went on their air-conditioned bus from Union Station to the Chase Hotel and didn't have to even so much as touch their shaving kits until they got to their rooms. Not one of them—not *one* of the white guys on the Brooklyn Dodgers—ever got off that bus and said, "I'm going to go with Jackie, Don, and Roy just to see how they have to live, just to find out."

The first St. Louis hotel Jackie had to stay in back in 1947, then Roy in 1948, and me in 1949, was called the Princess. It was a slum. We moved to the Adams Hotel after a friend of ours bought it, but he couldn't afford air-conditioning. Many nights, we had to soak our sheets in ice water and put them on the bed just to get a little relief from the heat and humidity. Try that sometime. We kept our windows open even with the trolleys running up and down the street below, because in that heat, you needed to get some air.

There we were, members of the great Brooklyn Dodgers.

We later heard that one of our teammates, who will remain nameless, was sitting on the bus in St. Louis and said to nobody in particular, "Fuck them black sonsabitches. Let them go for themselves. We didn't ask them to be here. They asked to be here."

Our teammate.

◆ ◆ ◆

NOT ONLY DID we have to worry about opposing players, we also had to be very careful about the guys in our own dugout. Jackie, Roy, and me had to find out which guys were on our side and which weren't. We didn't socialize with the white guys. We never went out to dinner with white teammates. We never had breakfast in the hotel with them.

In Cincinnati, where we did get rooms in the team hotel, word came down from a Dodgers executive that the Negro players had to eat in their rooms, because he didn't want us to cause a problem so close to Kentucky.

One day, we decided to smoke out the guy in the organization responsible for this. So Jackie, Roy, and me ordered everything on the menu and signed our names. Our little banquet went onto the Dodgers' tab, and when the bill got back to Brooklyn, word of it got to Mr. Rickey, and he called us in.

We had our answer ready: "Well, Mr. Rickey, we were told it would be a good idea to eat in our rooms so that we wouldn't cause any problems in the dining room . . ."

Rickey fired that executive's ass.

Some of us became very confrontational. The Phillies had a coach who'd sit over in the corner of the dugout and call us all kinds of names.

One day he was really at it at Ebbets Field, and Jackie came over to the mound. "Newk," he said, "do you hear what he's saying to us?"

I said, "Yeah, Jackie. I'm closer to him than you are."

"What are you going to do about it?"

I thought for a moment. Del Ennis was their best hitter, and I said, "When Ennis comes up, I'm going to undress his ass."

Jackie said, "If he comes out to the mound, give him to me. Don't you get into it. Give him to me. I want him."

When Ennis came up, I did what I said I was going to do: I undressed him. Didn't hit him, just put him flat on the ground.

Del got up, brushed his uniform off, and put his bat down.

By this time, Jackie had already come over to the mound. "You think he's coming out?" he asked.

"I don't know."

Well, Ennis turned toward the dugout, took a few steps, and said something to that dude sitting in the corner. We didn't know what he said, but then he came back up to the plate. I struck him out, and that was that.

Years later, when I was with the Reds, I played with Del, and I asked him, "What did you say to that guy that day in the dugout in Ebbets Field?"

Del said, "I told that son of a bitch to shut his mouth and leave you alone or I was gonna pull his tongue out. *He* didn't have to go out there and hit against you."

◆ ◆ ◆

THAT GUY SITTING in the corner of the dugout calling us all kinds of stuff back then? He denies saying all that stuff. He denies it to this day. But me, Roy, and Jackie heard him. And I'm still here to tell you about it.

What was he thinking? Did he think he could change my pitching approach? He just made me mad. He made Jackie mad. Made Roy mad.

He made us perform better.

Same thing in that other game I mentioned, the one we went to on the bus with the FBI guards in Cincinnati. In that one I pitched a shutout, Jackie hit a home run, and the next day Roy hit three home runs.

In the end, all that crap they heaped on us only made us better players and better people.

❖ ❖ ❖

IN ST. LOUIS one day, there was some noise outside the park, and Jackie got up on a stool to see what was going on. Turns out there were all these black people lined up on the street trying to get a ticket, but they couldn't get in. There was a 3,000-seat bleacher area for black people in Sportsman's Park in 1949, and it was sold out. The rest of the place was open only to white people, even though the ballpark had been "officially" desegregated five years earlier.

Jackie told me and Roy, "We're not going to play." Our manager, old Burt Shotton, heard about what Jackie'd said, and he asked, "What's the matter?"

"Get up on the stool," Jackie said. "Look out the window, and you'll see what I'm talking about."

Shotton got on the stool and saw maybe 10,000 people on the street who couldn't get in because the bigots who ran the Cardinals wouldn't open the stadium up to them. He sent our traveling secretary to tell the Cardinals management what was going on with Robinson, Newcombe, and Campanella.

Do you know what? They opened the gates to everybody.

Tell me, did we hurt a single person by doing this? Who does a change like that hurt?

You say some of the white players were scared of losing their jobs to blacks. Listen, this is a game of competition. What difference is it where the competition comes from? What difference does it make if it comes from a black man?

A team is always trying to get the best possible talent so it can win championships. Look what the Brooklyn Dodgers accomplished between 1947 and 1957. We won six National League championships. We almost won two others in

1950 and 1951. Did the Dodgers do that before?

And here's another thing: During that time, me and Jackie and Roy, between us, we won the Most Valuable Player award five times.

Five times!

So you've got to attribute a huge piece of the Dodgers' success to black players. They didn't bring us up because we were black. They brought us up because they thought we were better than the white guy at that position. And they thought we could help the team win.

And we did.

There was a social aspect to Branch Rickey's signing Jackie Robinson, and there was a competition aspect and a business aspect to it, as well. Branch Rickey brought in black players at the right time, and he won a lot of games and made a lot of money doin' it.

What he did also gave a 12th-grade dropout like myself a chance to earn a good living, to meet a lot of important people, and to buy a nice car. But let me tell you what happened with that car, because it shows you how a black man could go only so far. We had to "know our place" is the way they put it. What it meant was, we had to be subjugated.

I was inducted into the military in 1952, during the Korean War. The age limit was 26, and I was 25 years and 8 months old. But I went like any other red-blooded American to serve my country when called.

I went to Camp Pickett in Virginia to do my basic training, and I was held over as part of a cadre to train new recruits. I stayed there for a year. I asked for and received permission to drive my car on the post, the same Cadillac I'd bought with my own money that I'd made pitching for the Dodgers.

Well, one day I got called in to see a bird colonel who'd just gotten back from Korea. He made me stand at attention while he read me the riot act about driving my Cadillac around "his" post.

I said to him, "Colonel, I'm sorry you feel that way. But I just happen to be a baseball player with the Brooklyn Dodgers. I just happen to be on this post. I just happen to have asked for and received permission to drive it before you showed up here. Frankly, I can't figure out why a full colonel like yourself would be so concerned about a buck private like me. There's got to be a reason."

"Whatever that reason is," he said, "you're not going to drive that Cadillac on this post. I'm going to send you to Korea. And you won't get a chance to drive it there."

Turns out he was wrong about that. He didn't know who I knew through baseball. I went to the public telephone, called a friend of mine who was in charge of Army personnel in the Pentagon, and told him what this colonel was trying to do to me. My friend said, "You're not going to Korea. You're going to Fort Sam Houston in San Antonio. If you have any more problems with him, you call me."

When I got discharged, I drove that Cadillac from San Antonio to Vero Beach, where I got ready for training camp in 1954. During that drive, I thought about a white soldier from Georgia who came under my jurisdiction and told me straight to my face, "My mom and dad told me not to take no orders from no . . ." (You know the word he said. I don't use that word. Just won't say it.)

Well, I grabbed that soldier by his ears and took him over to the commanding officer. And once this little fellow found out that unless he changed his attitude he was going to spend the rest of his time in that camp in the stockade, he went on to become my best soldier.

During that drive to Vero Beach, I also thought about all the things that Jackie and Roy and Larry Doby had gone through because of the makeup of this country. This same country had just taken two years of my life, and I decided I wasn't going to be treated as a subhuman anymore.

I was going to find out, on the first trip we made to St. Louis that season, why me and Jackie and Roy and now Jim Gilliam couldn't stay at the Chase Hotel like the other Dodgers. Damned if I wasn't.

Well, we pulled into the St. Louis train station, and we went on over to our hotel, and then I headed back out.

"Where you going, Newk?" Jackie said.

"I'm going over to the Chase."

"Why?"

"I'm going to find out why we can't stay there. Look, Jackie, you came to the Dodgers in 1947. Here we are in 1954. It's been *seven* years now."

"Wait up," Jackie said, "I'm going with you."

When we got there, he said, "And we're not going through the back door."

We walked right through the front door, and everyone was looking at us as we waited for the manager. He took us into the dining room and offered us a cup of coffee. He seemed to be a generous guy, but I turned him down because I didn't drink coffee.

Jackie said, "Do you know why we're here?"

The manager said, "I think I have an idea. Why don't you tell me."

Jackie said, "Me and Don want to know why after all these years we haven't been able to stay at your hotel. Don just got back from two years of service to his country. He's mad, and he wants to know. So do I."

The manager said, "The only thing I can think of, gentlemen, is we don't want you in the swimming pool."

Did that make me want to smack my forehead? No, it made me want to smack him in the mouth.

But Jackie said, "I don't even know how to swim."

And I said, "I never swim in baseball season. Afraid to hurt my arm."

And just like that, the manager said, "All right, you can stay here."

"You mean to tell me," Jackie said, "that all the years we've been coming to St. Louis, we didn't get to stay here just because you didn't want us in the swimming pool?"

The manager said, "That's the only reason I can think of."

Jackie and I went back to the other hotel to get our bags. We told Roy and Jim, but they wouldn't come with us. "They didn't want us before," Roy said, "and I'm not goin' there now."

So me and Jackie moved into the Chase. The thing is, then, and in all the years we stayed there after that, they never gave us a room on the side of the hotel where the pool was located.

We had our ideas why. They didn't want us looking at those pretty white women walking around in their bathing suits. Maybe they didn't want the black ink in our bodies to muddy their pool. Hell, I don't know what they thought. You never can tell what goes through a bigot's mind.

Now, if I wanted to look at pretty women, I could walk all over St. Louis. If I wanted to see pretty women in bathing suits, I could walk around the corner and look through the fence. All I wanted was to be given the same accommodations as the rest of the Dodgers.

We got us an air-conditioned room. But every time we'd open our venetian blinds in the Chase Hotel, the view would be the side of a big, red apartment building.

That's how it worked, you see, in steps. And what did that first step do? I'll tell you what it did. It opened the hotels to all black people coming into St. Louis to see the Dodgers play. Or to see any other major league team with black players on it. The fans would come in on the train—the Fried Chicken

Expresses, they called them—and they wouldn't have a good place to stay, just like we didn't have a good place to stay. But when the Chase Hotel tore down its barriers, black people could come in from that terrible heat and have some relative comfort. And not just in the Chase, but in other "white" hotels, as well.

Tell me we weren't doing something to change society.

We were part of a major historical change in this country—in the world, for that matter. You can see my career that way.

Or you can look at my career the way it was described by the press. Look what the press did to me. Look what they did to my career.

I won 27 games in 1956. But the press vilified me after the Yankees beat my ass in the World Series. The writers said I couldn't win the big one. They called me gutless. Yeah, I got kicked around by the Yankees, but I was one of the big reasons we were in the damned World Series in the first place.

Pee Wee Reese—God bless him!—used to tell reporters all the time, "What are you guys talking about? Didn't he win 27 games in a season? Didn't he get us to the World Series in his rookie year? What big games are you talking about? Because he didn't beat the Yankees? Bob Feller got knocked around by the Yankees, but you never called him a choke-up. You never said he had no guts and no backbone."

But I used to wonder—in fact, sometimes I still wonder—whether some of my other teammates thought that I didn't have any guts and couldn't win the big ones. I'll never forget what the press said about me. It remains etched in my mind as if it'd been cut there in acid.

I'd go to schools after that 1956 season to speak to kids, and I'd hear, "Why can't you win the big ones? What do they mean when they say you're gutless?" So I stopped speaking to kids. I just went out to drink.

I'm not saying that all that unfair criticism made me drink. But it made me feel like drinking. The people who wrote that stuff made me a very venomous person for years. Tell the truth, I still have some of that venom in me.

I put most of my baseball savings into a liquor business in Newark. It was a cocktail lounge and liquor store, and after I retired, I drank it into bankruptcy. My weight ballooned up to 320 pounds. I was going to racetracks and losing money I couldn't afford to lose. I was an animal when I was drinking. I was getting ready to lose my mind, really. My wife didn't drink, and she saw it all. We decided to move out to California—that's where she was from—to make a new start.

The guys who were buying the liquor business from me knew I needed the money, and they made me sit in their office for eight hours, and every hour they came out with an offer that was lower than the last one. That's how they treated Don Newcombe. In the end, they gave me $2,500. When we moved to California, that was all I had. And $2,300 went to the van for moving furniture. So I started all over again with $200.

At one point, my wife was going to divorce me. She had her bags packed. I asked her why she was leaving, and she said, "Because of what you do and say when you drink, Don. I can't live with it anymore, not with three babies."

I said to her, "I can stop drinking anytime I want to."

She said, "You're a goddamn liar."

I said, "Okay. You think I'm lying? Watch."

I turned to my son, Don Jr., and I said, "Don, c'mere." He was 3 years old. I got on my knees, and I put my hand on his head, and I swore to God I'd never drink another drop for as long as I lived.

And for 40 years, I have never had another drop.

◆ ◆ ◆

WHAT MAKES ME happy? What makes *me* happy is that I was able to pull my life together and turn it around and make my son proud of me. That, more than anything else, is what a dad looks forward to—that, and being able to be proud of his son.

I thank God I've been able to live as long as I have, and I hope to live longer. As long as I'm around, I'm going to try to do things that help people a little less fortunate than myself. I've worked with a community relations program for the Dodgers since 1970. I'm Director of Community Relations. I have a charity program that's linked to diabetes, blindness, cancer, autism, and the school system.

We auction off a Night With Don Newcombe at Dodgers Stadium. People get to come on the field, meet the players, get autographs, go to dinner, and see the game with me. The money goes to 13 charities.

◆ ◆ ◆

RESPECT! I THINK that's what everybody wants. I think that's what black people have been asking for, fighting for, and dying for ever since America was born. They're still fighting and dying for it in some way. Maybe it's not in a literal way, but they're doing whatever they need to do to get that respect.

We've made strides. But we're still in a mixed-up society. I won't live long enough—and neither will you—to see us get as far as we need to go. So much of it is subtle now. But with racism, let me tell you, dealing with covert is worse than dealing with overt.

There are a lot of good white people. There were back then, and there are now. But will we ever be able to walk down the street side by side and not be recognized as someone different because of skin color?

On the 50th anniversary of Jackie's coming up to the Dodgers, Lou Johnson and myself and quite a few other athletes were asked questions about race by a writer for the *Los Angeles Daily News*. They were honest questions, and I gave honest answers.

Peter O'Malley owned the Dodgers at the time, and I had arguments with him about what I said, seeing as I was a Dodgers employee.

He said, "Why did you talk to the paper about race?"

"Peter," I said, "was what I said the truth?"

He said, "Yeah, it was the truth, but you're embarrassing the Dodgers."

"If it's the truth," I said, "then get on me for telling the truth. But don't get on me for embarrassing the Dodgers."

Seems to me that a lot of people don't want to hear the truth or face the truth.

Do I love baseball? Hell, no. I don't love baseball. Never did. And never will. I do love the Dodgers. But I'll be damned if I love baseball, because of what baseball did to us, because of all the things we had to endure just to play the damned game.

Look how long it took them to put Larry Doby in the Hall. And he got in only because he came through AL president Gene Budig's office. What stopped them from putting him in earlier, when he could have enjoyed and benefited from it, when he could have made some money, like all the other Hall of Famers do?

And let me tell you something else as far as the Hall of Fame is concerned: If I'm selected, I may be the first one to turn them down. I don't know if anyone's turned them down before, but I've told my son, if they try to put me in after I die, tell 'em to take it and ram it somewhere. It's even in my will.

They didn't give it to Doby when he had a chance to benefit from it. And they didn't give it to me when other people with lesser records benefited from it. Dizzy Dean didn't do any more than I did. Hell, he didn't do *as much* as I did.

The newspaper guys didn't vote me in because they didn't like me. The most votes I ever got was 59, back in 1980. So somebody's going to come up with some idea *now* that it's time to put Don Newcombe in the Hall of Fame?

No.

This is the greatest country on earth, and I love it. But I'll be damned if I'm not gonna speak my mind. I'm the last black man alive who played on the Brooklyn Dodgers with Jackie Robinson, and I'm gonna speak my mind until the day I die.

CARL ERSKINE

◆◆

THERE WERE A couple of guys on the Dodgers from the Deep South that you probably heard about—Dixie Walker and Bobby Bragan—who had a more or less predictable response when Jackie came up. The way they figured it, they had to go back home and answer to their buddies: *Do you shower with this guy? Do you eat with this guy? Do you share a hotel room with this guy?*

Back then, all that was taboo where they came from. So the fact that they resisted up front, even to the point of asking to be traded, was just a natural response. But they were about the only ones who felt that way, or at least who said it out loud.

The way I saw it, there was a pretty quick acceptance from the Dodgers. Jackie was with us, he was fighting his battle, and we were on his side.

Looking back, maybe I should have taken the lead in talking to the Chase Hotel in St. Louis. I was the player representative of the Dodgers for eight years or so, and I could've gone to the Chase management and said, "Hey, why are you the only hotel in the league that won't allow our black players to stay?"

But you have to understand the psychology of the times. Back then, the Chase had a top entertainer in its nightclub: Lena Horne. She was a black woman. She was the headliner at the Chase, but she couldn't enter the hotel through the front door. She entered through the kitchen and went straight to her dressing room.

All the small steps toward breaking down these barriers of discrimination we saw as a big plus. We didn't go around with the sense of what's still wrong. Being around Jackie, *because* of Jackie, we had the sense of, look how much is becoming right.

◆ ◆ ◆

I DON'T THINK we saw the civil rights picture quite the way people looking back today see it. Plus, we all had our own pressures at the time, and we all reacted in our own individual ways.

Most of us were young guys totally consumed with our performance, focused entirely on making the team, on playing baseball at the highest level for as long as we could.

Let me tell you about an exhibition game in 1949 in Atlanta. The game was probably going to determine who was going to stay on the club and who was going to be sent down to the minors. We all had one-year contracts back then. All of us were battling to try to make the team and stay there. So we each had our own pressures.

When we got to Atlanta, the Ku Klux Klan was picketing the ballpark, and there were death threats. I remember Jackie's sister being very scared. Burt Shotton, our manager, read one letter in the clubhouse that said, "Take the field, and you're going to be shot!"

That was a very tense moment. We couldn't believe that anybody would actually think of shooting someone because of his race and because he wanted to play baseball. Then Gene Hermanski came out with a line that broke us all up. Gene said, "Hey, Skipper, I got an idea. If we all wear No. 42, the guy won't know who to shoot at."

Pee Wee always had a pretty good needle. When we got out on the field, he asked Jackie not to stand too close to him because the guy might be a bad shot.

Thank God there was no shot that day—or any other day, for that matter. I'm not trying to defend baseball, but the way I saw it, there was a minimum amount of racial things with the other teams when Jackie played.

You have to realize that baseball is a game in which the guys on the other bench will say almost anything to upset you. They yell about your mother. They yell about your wife. They call you names. If it gets to you, then it makes you less effective.

So a lot of what happened with Jackie in those early years—throwing the black cat on the field, the racial barbs, that kind of stuff—was a part of baseball designed to upset him. Ben Chapman, the Phillies manager, was an open opponent of blacks in baseball, and he ordered his pitchers—according to Robin Roberts and other guys on that team—to throw at Jackie. But after a few games, they realized that the more they tried to get to Jackie, the more stuff they heaped on him, the harder he hit them, so Chapman killed the strategy.

This is only my perspective. I'm not speaking for anybody else here. This is what I saw, what I heard, and what I felt. You've got to realize that other people are going to see it and feel it in different ways. Also, I wasn't with the club the first year Jackie came up, in 1947, when all the really nasty racial barbs came at him in Cincinnati and Pee Wee went over and put his arm around Jackie's shoulder.

Now, I knew Pee Wee as intimately as I knew Jackie. Pee Wee always took the position that Jackie was a Dodgers teammate: *You belong here . . . You're a full major-leaguer . . . I'll defend you to the hilt.* But Pee Wee wasn't some Great White Father. He wouldn't go to marches and carry the banner of civil rights. I think that's an honest, open expression of where Pee Wee stood. And it explains the bowling alley in Louisville that Pee Wee bought a piece of after he retired. Pee Wee accepted Jackie fully, and yet he went on to own a bowling alley that was segregated.

◆ ◆ ◆

JACKIE NEVER QUIT challenging anything he sniffed out as being racist or discriminatory. The birthday party the Dodgers threw for Pee Wee at Ebbets Field is a pretty good example of that.

It seemed like a perfect night. We won the game. Pee Wee got a car. In the middle of the fifth inning, the lights were turned out, and everyone lit a match. A huge cake was rolled out, and the crowd sang "Happy Birthday" to Pee Wee. While the lights were out, the grounds crew paid their own special tribute: They replaced the eight pennants representing the eight teams in the National League with eight Confederate flags.

It had no racial overtones of any kind. It was just that Pee Wee was from Kentucky, and the grounds crew was honoring someone they respected.

But Jackie didn't read it that way. To him, it was like opening the gate of the ballpark that Jim Crow had been thrown out of and inviting Jim Crow back inside.

To tell you the truth, I didn't even notice the Confederate flags. But later, in the privacy of the clubhouse, Jackie went to war, denouncing the idea that somebody would have the audacity to raise those flags.

You have never read—at least I've never read—where Jackie went public with his feelings about the inappropriateness of what happened on Pee Wee's birthday. Part of that is because of what we did. Duke Snider's locker was right by Jackie's. Duke and a bunch of us told Jackie to settle down, that it was Pee Wee's night. The message: "You're going to make more enemies than friends going to war about the flags."

And Jackie let it go. He never said anything more about it. At least not publicly.

❖ ❖ ❖

IT WAS REALLY complicated for Jackie. It was complicated for him in so many ways.

It was complicated between Jackie and Roy Campanella because they disagreed on their status in the major leagues, and they were both right—if you can believe that.

Jackie wanted to shake up the system. He wanted to show that America was not doing it right, that the Constitution says one thing and that society had adopted a social behavior and culture that said something else.

Jackie wanted to use baseball as a platform from which to challenge all of the things that were hypocritical in society. Making the team was incidental to Jackie. His mission was getting black people in America to be respected as citizens like anybody else.

Campanella didn't want to make any noise. He'd say, "Man, we're in the big leagues. Holy Columbus! This is wonderful. We've waited so long to get here. Don't mess it up." Campanella's only goal was to become the best catcher in baseball, and that's where he went with it.

Now, those are two opposite positions, and I think they were right for each person. But it gives you an idea of how complicated it could be for Jackie even in his own clubhouse.

I remember a doubleheader in Cincinnati in 1954. Before we took the field for the second game, a boisterous African-American fan came down the stands just to get close to Jackie. "Where's my Jackie?" he called out. But his voice was slurred, and he wasn't walking straight. He was unmistakably intoxicated, and though he was dressed to the hilt, his clothes were in a shambles.

"Get out of my face, you slob!" Jackie said. "I bet your front yard looks as bad as you do. Go home and clean up."

The guy stopped dead in his tracks, turned around, and walked away.

When I asked why the guy had bothered him so much, Jackie said the guy was just as damaging to what he was trying to do as were the white people who tried to put him down.

You have to understand. The one quality about Jackie that stood out over all others was self-control. "He's not ready for the day," Jackie said about that fan. "We need to be prepared, Carl, not drunk."

A lot of people don't realize that many members of the black community thought Jackie was too bright and too brash. Some thought Jackie was doing more harm than good with his controversial, outspoken behavior. He had a radio show at one time, and also a syndicated printed column. He used both of those platforms to battle for civil rights.

Jackie took exception to anything and everything that remotely resembled racism. He would challenge anybody—it didn't matter how high up. He challenged the president of the United States. He once said that "Eisenhower says all the right words on civil rights but doesn't do a thing."

As time went on, I think Jackie saw himself as a martyr. He became more and more selfless. He spoke less about baseball and more about what needed to be done. He became more dedicated to the course that Mr. Rickey had set for him.

You know, you've got to give credit to Mr. Rickey. Yes, Mr. Rickey wanted a good ballplayer, and yes, he wanted a winner in Brooklyn, and yes, he wanted to bring people into the ballpark. But the underlying reason he brought Jackie into baseball was to break a tradition in America that Mr. Rickey thought was just plain wrong. He had to buck society to do that. He had to go up against a tradition that was solidly in place.

And it seems unreal to me now that one man's idea and one man's performance actually changed social behavior in America.

Take a leap in time from that exhibition game in Atlanta back in 1949 when Jackie was threatened. Go to Atlanta today, and right there in front of the stadium, you'll see a statue of the man who holds the major league home run record.

That statue is of Henry Aaron—a black man.

CHAPTER SIX

NEW OBSTACLES

LET'S SAY YOU'RE going off to college. Chances are, one or both of your parents will help you pack, travel with you, then help you set up your new room and new life. They'll make sure you're linked to them by a cell phone, connected to friends by the Internet, and provided with a meal plan and some spending money. When they leave, resident assistants will be there to smooth your way.

Sound like what you expect? Or what happened to you already?

Now imagine that you're a black teenage ballplayer leaving home for the first time to join your minor league team in the Deep South—half a century ago. You kiss your mother, take the bag of sandwiches she made for you, and get on a bus alone because she can't possibly afford to accompany you.

You look around at the passengers. Crouching in the back of your mind is the story of a black teenager named Emmett Till, who'd recently left Chicago to visit family in Mississippi only to be found in a river with an eye gouged out and his head partially crushed. Some white folks said he'd whistled at a white woman. His mother said he had a lisp.

Or imagine going to the registration desk of the hotel housing your team and asking for your room key only to be told there was no key for you or anybody else of your skin color. That's what happened to Curt Flood during his first spring training in the Cincinnati Reds minor league system in 1956.

Or imagine that one day in your new minor league home, you're getting on a public bus with your new white teammates. You're a team, so it only seems natural to sit among them. But then you're ordered by the driver to get to the back of the bus. That's what happened to Maury Wills when he joined the Fort Worth Cats to play Double-A ball in the Texas League in 1955.

Maybe you're too cautious to make Maury's mistake. You know you're supposed to sit in the back when you catch the trolley to go across town to the ballpark. What you don't know, and what you learn the hard way, is that you have to enter the front door to pay the driver, then get out of the trolley and reenter by the back door so you won't accidentally brush against white people on the way through. The trouble is, plenty of times the driver takes your money and pulls away before you make it to the back door, leaving you stranded on the street. That means you've got to leave real early to get to the ballpark on time. That's what Bill Greason learned when he left Atlanta to play for the Birmingham Black Barons in the Negro Leagues in 1948.

Or maybe you take your position in the outfield during a game in Greensboro and hear a fan yell that if you catch one fly ball he's going to shoot you. You turn, and there's a man hidden in a cluster of fans in the leftfield stands pointing a shotgun at you. So you purposely drop an easy fly ball. That's what happened to Leon Wagner while playing for Danville in the Carolina League in 1956.

Or maybe you miss the bus altogether while heading back to your team's camp after getting a haircut in Waycross, Georgia, and you take a shortcut through the woods only to be shot at by a security guard. That's what happened to Henry Aaron in 1953.

Let's say you've been assigned to a team that's not in the Deep South, and you're thanking your lucky stars. You're playing for a minor league team in Trenton, New Jersey, but your first game's in Hagerstown, Maryland, and you're stunned when you take the field and racial taunts are dumped on you like garbage. That's what happened to Willie Mays in 1950.

◆ ◆ ◆

IN MANY WAYS, the young black ballplayers of the late 1940s, 1950s, and 1960s had it worse than Jackie Robinson.

They didn't have Branch Rickey carefully managing all the details and easing their transition into what had until then been a white man's game.

They didn't have reporters providing a different sort of protection by following their every move and chronicling the insults and abuses.

They weren't 28 years old, college educated, already mature, and well traveled, the way Jackie was.

And they usually didn't have a wife at their side like Rachel Robinson, who used to sit up as tall as she could in the stands and imagine her shoulder blades as a shield that could block the racial filth directed at her husband.

More than a half century later, Hagerstown formally apologized to Willie Mays. But "We're sorry" didn't come up much back then, back when it might have meant something. Imagine what it took for teenagers like Mays and Wills and Aaron and Frank Robinson and Dick Allen. Imagine what it took to walk into a ballpark and gather the focus just to stand out on the field . . . when it could be that hard, that complicated, that risky, just to sit down.

◆ ◆ ◆

MAURY WILLS

◆◆

WORD OF THE Washington Senators never even got to the DC projects where I grew up. We didn't even know there was a major league baseball team in town.

Our baseball heroes were these old guys who played on Sundays in mismatched uniforms, argyle socks under the stirrups, and a half-pint of whiskey in the back pocket. A half-pint, because that fit right in. If these guys didn't get too drunk on Saturday nights, they were out there playing on Sundays. And all us kids wanted to do was grow up and be just like them—including the half-pint.

But one day when I was about 11 years old, a baseball player from the Senators came to our playground to conduct a clinic—and he was white. It was the very first time I had ever looked a white guy in the eyes. Honest. People just didn't interact as we do today. This guy was wearing an official Washington Senators home uniform, crisp and white with piping around the sleeves and *Senators* embroidered across his chest. Everything matched. His shoes were all clean and polished. And his eyes weren't all red.

The player's name was Gerry Priddy, and he was the second baseman for the Senators. Maybe Priddy had lost a coin toss or something and had to be the one to go over to our part of town and do a little clinic for the organization. But he came over, and he didn't stay for just 15 minutes or half an hour. The man talked to us for at least two hours, and I just couldn't believe it.

Priddy even singled me out. He told the other kids to move back and said, "Watch this kid." He bounced a grounder to me, and I got my little feet in place, grabbed the ball, and I took a little hop—just like the guys I'd seen playing on Sundays. I threw it overhand to him, and the ball made a loud pop in his mitt. I still remember what he said: *"Wow!"*

Priddy looked down at my feet and said, "Hey, kid, you've got a chance to be a good baseball player one day. Where's your shoes?"

I was barefoot.

◆ ◆ ◆

I WAS THE first black player to play for the Dodgers in Fort Worth. Texas League, Double-A ball. It was my only bad year in 23 years of playing professional baseball. I hit .202. Man, I couldn't buy a hit all season.

I remember getting on a bus in Fort Worth to go to the ballpark one day. Right behind the driver they had benches that faced each other. Two of my teammates were already sitting there. I said, "Hey, guys, how ya doin'?" and sat down with them. The bus didn't move. Three or four minutes later, the bus still hadn't moved an inch.

Finally, the driver turned and looked at me. "Move to the back," he said. "Colored in the back."

The black people in the back were looking at me like, *Fool, are you crazy!* As if I were trying to start some stuff or something. I felt like goin' under the floorboards. But I went to the back, and when the bus got to the ballpark, all my teammates up front hopped off and ran into the clubhouse. By the time I got there, everybody was laughing at me and making wiseass jokes.

And that was playing *at home.*

Once we got on a bus and drove nine hours to Beaumont. We got there after dark, and I walked into the lobby of the hotel with the team and waited in line for my key, but when I got to the desk, there wasn't one for me.

I went to the traveling secretary—a teammate. (Back then, that's how they did it in the minors.) I won't say his name—I mentioned it once before, and it hurt his feelings so bad—and I asked him, "Where am I going to stay?"

"I don't know," he said. "Didn't they tell you?"

So there I was, walking through the streets of Beaumont in the wee hours of the morning with a black trainer, knocking on doors in the black neighborhood, trying to find a place to sleep. I ended up staying outside on a porch. Fortunately, it was screened in and kept out the mosquitoes. I slept on a little Army cot that folded up. In the morning, the people at the house said, "We didn't say we were gonna feed you."

There weren't any restaurants around, so I ended up at a drugstore down on the corner, where I had some Oreo cookies and hot chocolate. I called for a cab, with plenty of time left to get to the ballpark. But there was only one black cab in the whole town. By the time the cab picked me up and drove me to the park, I was about 15 minutes late and I ended up getting chewed out by the manager.

It was just tough to play after that, seeing as that was only the beginning of one damned thing after another. All year long I was uneasy, lonely, and anxious.

Oh, man, I know exactly what Jackie went through—except I failed utterly. What I don't know is how he succeeded.

CURT FLOOD

In the words of his widow, JUDY PACE.

◆◆

CURT WAS THE second black ballplayer on the minor league team in High Point-Thomasville in North Carolina. The player before him could take it for only three weeks—then he left. Got out of town.

When Curt arrived, his teammates at the time wouldn't even speak to him. It was against the law for a colored man and a white man to dress and shower in the same space. The fans really let him have it. The message behind the treatment came through loud and clear: *You will leave in a few weeks, just like the last guy.*

You have to understand what the young black ballplayers after Jackie were walking into. This was racist turmoil far and above anything that had existed since slavery. Think about it. The patterns had been set. My water fountain, your water fountain. You don't go to school with me, I don't go to school with you.

A mind-set had been established. But after Jackie, you had the *Brown v. Board of Education* case, in Topeka, Kansas. You now had Negroes thinking they could go to school with whites. Curt arrived in North Carolina to play within three months of Rosa Parks' refusal to give up her seat on the bus in Alabama. You now had the bus boycott. The pattern had been broken. You now had Negroes thinking about sitting in the front of the bus.

That uprising brought an opposing swell of venomous energy. Again, the message was loud and clear: *We will put them back in their place.* That's what these young black men, who only wanted to play baseball, were confronted with when they crossed the Mason-Dixon Line.

Many of them, like Curt, came from California and had absolutely no exposure to this. I find it a miracle that one of those young men didn't come up missing like Emmett Till.

It was the same era.

◆ ◆ ◆

FRANK ROBINSON

◆◆

MY OUTLET WHEN I was young was the movies. I was always a quiet kid. I didn't reach out to people easily. Sometimes I'd go into the theater, watch a movie, stay in the same seat, and watch it all over again.

Here I am, 17 years old, just signed by the Cincinnati Reds, and I join the minor league team in Ogden, Utah. Only the second time I'd ever been away from home. Where I grew up, in Oakland, there just didn't seem to be many restrictions. If you wanted to do something, and you could afford to do it, you just went and did it. I knew about skin color. But restrictions—that was in the Deep South.

First minute I get some free time in Ogden, I go over to a movie theater. I get to the front of the line and put $10 on the counter. The woman behind the counter says, "We don't serve your kind."

I say, "Excuse me?" I mean, I'd heard her say something to me, but I wasn't really focused on what she was saying.

"We don't serve your kind."

"Well, what kind am I?"

She says, "We don't serve blacks. You can't come into this theater."

It's hard to describe the shock. Nobody had ever flat-out rejected me before for being black. I took my $10 off the counter and, as I turned away, my eyes filled up with tears. It was the way the lady said it. It set a tone.

Go back to where you're staying and don't come out. And that's what I did. I just withdrew. I didn't go anywhere. Probably I should have told people at the ball club what happened. Normally, I think I would have. But I was so crushed that I didn't even think about telling them.

My roommate was a Cuban kid named Chico Terry. Spoke no English. None. Zero. Now, we gotta make do and get by, and *I've* got to show *him* the way. Well, Chico didn't ask to go out anyplace, and I didn't invite him anyplace, because I never went anyplace. All we did was play baseball and go back to the hotel. We finished first by something like 10 or 12 games. But if you asked me about Ogden, Utah, I couldn't tell you a thing.

◆ ◆ ◆

NEXT YEAR I was sent to Columbia, South Carolina. I made myself a promise. Gonna go down there. Gonna have a big year. Gonna get the hell out of there.

At least you could go to the movie theater in Columbia. Blacks had to sit upstairs in the balcony, but at least you could go to a movie. I didn't try to go to the movies on the road. Wouldn't venture out. After Ogden, I wasn't going to be rejected again.

Montgomery, Alabama . . . Macon, Georgia . . . Charlotte, North Carolina. The only thing I could tell you about those places is I'd step on the field and get called all kinds of names. I just put up with it and tried to get out of there as fast as I could.

But by the end of the year, my arm was kind of bothering me. Every time I threw, it was like someone was sticking a pin in my shoulder. Our manager, Ernie White, told me to play through it, and I finished the season.

The Reds wanted me to play winter ball, so I went down to Puerto Rico. In a game against Santurce, Willie Mays hit a fly ball to rightfield with a man on third. I caught the ball, the runner tagged up, and I made the throw home. Ever slept on your arm wrong and when you wake up it's tingling? That's what my whole arm felt like—until it went dead limp.

I flew back home. Ten doctors looked at my arm, and each of them said it was something different.

The next season I was back in Columbia, but my arm was so bad they had to put me at first base. I couldn't even throw the ball around the infield for warmups between innings. Couldn't throw the ball back to the pitcher after an out. Through April, May, June, and July, I couldn't hit for shit. Couldn't really swing the bat. No power. Couldn't extend. As you can imagine, there was a lot going on in my head.

Before the start of each series, our manager went over the opposing hitters with the team. One time Ernie White was going over the rival lineup and got to a guy named Al Pinkston. And White said, "This nigger, you can't pitch him in because he'll hit the ball out of the park. The way to get this nigger out is to pitch him away."

I just sat there with my mouth open. *Am I hearing what I think I'm hearing?* My teammates were just kind of frozen. I remember their faces. Blank stares: *I hope Frank didn't hear that.* They didn't look at me. The other black player on the team didn't say anything. I was dumbfounded. We'd gone over teams that had black players before, and nothing like that had ever come out. This was the second year I'd played for Ernie.

Afterward, players were coming over to me and apologizing. I told them, "*You* don't have to apologize to me for anything."

I lost a lot of respect for Ernie at that time, as a manager and as a person. I'd do what he asked me to do on the field, but that was it. I just had to get past that whole situation to get up to the Reds. What made it all worse was that our fans were starting to get on me because I wasn't hitting.

In those small ballparks we played in, they had bleachers down the lines. Blacks couldn't sit on the home side. Only whites, and they were really on me. Being on the road in the South conditioned you to take the verbal abuse from the other side. But this was at home, and it started to get personal. When they got to my family, that became too much.

One home game, I hit a long fly ball to the outfield. I was running it out toward second base when the outfielder made the catch. As I headed back to the dugout, some people in the stands were really giving it to me. When they got on my family, that was too much. I picked up a bat and took off down the line toward the stands after them. Fortunately, my teammates grabbed me. Right behind them, Ernie White was yelling, "Who was it? Who was it? I'll get them for you!"

Can you believe it? Ernie White, taking my back. I really appreciated that.

◆ ◆ ◆

Now LET ME tell you about something that happened after the minor leagues.

This was 1958. I was starting my third season in the majors, and the Reds were playing our way up north near the end of spring training. That's how it was done in those days. We'd play exhibition games on the way north from Florida to Cincinnati.

When we got to Baltimore, it was raining, and I told my roommate, Brooks Lawrence, that I was going to a movie.

"You're going *where?*"

I thought he was puzzled because I was talking about going out in the rain.

"I'm goin' to a movie," I said. "There's one just down the way."

"*Really?*"

So I walked down to the theater and got on line.

This is 1958 now. I'm in the big leagues for a few years, remember? I put my money down.

"One, please."

"We don't serve blacks."

"What?"

"We don't allow blacks in the theater."

I take the money back, and now I'm really pissed. I go back to the hotel, open the door, and Brooks Lawrence takes one look at my face and starts laughing so hard he falls off the bed. He's just howlin'!

He *knew* it. He just didn't tell me.

I got all over him. All over him.

"Why didn't you tell me?"

"Hey," he said, "sometimes you gotta learn the hard way."

It left a bad taste. Seven years after that, when I learned I'd been traded to Baltimore, that moment came right back to me. All I could think was, I've got to move to Baltimore, and I'm not gonna be able to go to the movies.

BILL GREASON

◆◆◆

I PLAYED WITH Willie Mays on the Birmingham Black Barons team that got to the Negro League World Series in 1948. When the Black Barons would leave Birmingham to go on the road, we were always clean and dressed right. We looked out for each other. We didn't come into another town lookin' like tramps. If one of our players didn't have the proper clothes to wear, we'd chip in and buy him a suit. People respected us everywhere we went.

We might hear *nigger this* and *nigger that*, but *we* knew who we were.

After Jackie went up to the Dodgers, I was called to Korea. When I came back, I was the third black player signed in the Texas League. It was 1952, Oklahoma City, Double-A ball.

Now, let me tell you, nobody was buyin' anybody any suits in the Texas League. It was dog-eat-dog. A pitcher on your own team wouldn't help you. A catcher wouldn't help you. But I was 9–1 with a 2.14 ERA, so I was doin' okay.

We had a huge crowd one night when I went up against Dave Hoskins—another black pitcher—down in Dallas. People don't realize how Jackie affected the attendance at baseball games all over the country, even in leagues he wasn't playing in. Soon minor league teams that *didn't* have a black ballplayer weren't drawing all that well.

At the end of the season, the Yankees and the Red Sox both offered $100,000 and a couple players for me. But Oklahoma City was an independent, not a farm team of some major league team, and the owner had seen the crowds that clubs with black players had been pulling. So he said no to the Yankees and the Red Sox. He figured he'd be able to get more for me the following year.

He got greedy, and he paid for it. A year later, the talent pool of black players must have been bigger, and he only got $25,000 and four players for me from the St. Louis Cardinals.

The Cardinals sent me to Columbus, Ohio. The Red Birds, Triple-A ball. I was moving up, and I was sharp. Had pretty good heat, pretty good breaking stuff. Johnny Keane was managing the club, and one day he told me I was being called up to St. Louis.

This is going to sound crazy, but I didn't want to go. I'm serious: I did *not* want to go. Not in the middle of the season. Not with Eddie Stanky being the Cardinals manager. Everybody knew that Stanky didn't like black players. The team was in fifth place. The timing was all wrong. Better to start at spring training. Get the feel of everything. Be around the players in a fresh setting.

But Johnny said, "They want you. You have to go."

So I went up to St. Louis, and when I get there, this front office guy sticks a contract in front of me. Nine hundred dollars a month. I said to him, "Look, I was making $1,200 a month in Triple-A. And now you're offering me $900 to play in the major leagues? Why did you bring me up here if this is what you're gonna do to me?"

The guy said, "If you stay 30 days, we'll give you a little more."

Honestly, I don't know why they brought me up. My best guess is they wanted a companion and roommate on-the-road for their first black player, a guy named Tom Alston. Tom was a great prospect. First baseman. Real tall. Outstanding hitter. But there was so much pressure on him that he'd go 0-for-3 or 0-for-4 and get real down on himself. The Cardinals brought me up to make Tom more comfortable.

The reception I got was cool. There was no overt hostility. But the worst feeling you can sometimes get is that you're being ignored. People don't speak to you, don't look at you. Things were cool enough in Columbus, but St. Louis was like goin' from the refrigerator to the freezer. Any white guy who might have wanted to be friendly to a black ballplayer was in a spot; he had to worry about being ostracized by his own.

◆ ◆ ◆

BUT THE WORST part was that for the first two weeks after I was called up I didn't throw the ball. They wouldn't let me. You couldn't go to the bullpen unless they told you. I don't know if race had anything to do with it. That was just the way things were.

I'd go out and run before games, but that was about it. Maybe if you came out early enough they might let you swing the bat at batting practice. Other than that, the only thing I could do was sit on the bench and watch. Man, when you're a pitcher, you've got to keep throwing to stay sharp. Two weeks without throwing—you know what that does to your confidence?

I knew about confidence. I learned all about it in the Marines. They instill a self-confidence in you that allows you to tackle anything. If they say, "Go knock that pillbox out," you believe you can do it.

You know how much talent it takes to be a pitcher? Talent's only about 15% of the deal; 85% of being a pitcher is mental.

It comes down to what you believe about yourself. You may have the talent to throw a baseball, but you've got to *believe* that you're going to throw it by somebody or you ain't no kind of pitcher. How can you believe that when you aren't allowed to pick up a ball for two weeks? In anything you engage in, if you don't believe in yourself, you're beaten before you begin.

Finally, they gave me a start against the Cubs. I got roughed up pretty good. Then I started against the Phillies. Same thing. Next I pitched a scoreless inning against the Giants. Turns out, that was it for my major league pitching career.

Stanky spoke to me only *one* time the whole time I was up with the Cardinals. One time. I was pitching batting practice one night in Philadelphia, and I was wild—stands to reason, seeing as I hadn't touched the ball in a while. Stanky came out to the mound and said, "Get the ball over the plate." I said to him, "What do you think I'm trying to do?" He just looked at me, turned on his heel, and walked away. That's all he said to me the whole time I was there.

I stayed about seven weeks. Let me tell you, I was happy to get out of there.

So that was my cup of coffee. I played five more years in the minors and then gave it up.

Never did get to go to spring training.

◆ ◆ ◆

JIM "MUDCAT" GRANT

◆◆

THE INDIANS SENT me off to play minor league ball in Fargo, North Dakota, in 1954, and I won Rookie of the Year. I had just turned 19. When I got back to Lacoochee, Florida, everybody welcomed me home.

Some guys that I had played with over in Brooksville, the next town over, wanted to get together, so a friend and I hopped in his car and headed over. It was about 17 miles away, and on the way there we stopped off at this juke joint along the road.

Just before we got there, a bunch of guys had been causing some trouble, and somebody had called the police. The guys who'd been causing the trouble hightailed it. Just about then we showed up. So it was just the two of us sitting in this place drinking Coca-Colas and not knowing what had gone down earlier when the sheriff and his deputy arrived.

Now, the person who made the phone call had to give the sheriff some reason for making it or he'd get on her, so she pointed to us.

So they walked over to where we were sitting, and the sheriff says, "Where you boys from?"

I say, "Well, my friend here's from Brooksville. I'm from Lacoochee."

"You been making trouble?"

I say, "No."

The minute I said it the deputy kicked me from behind—right in the back.

I turned around real fast-like. I just reacted. I wasn't thinking where I was. I guess the time I'd spent in North Dakota had made me forget the way things were back home, made me think I had freedom or something like that. As I turned toward him, the deputy put a .38 in my face and said, "Say, 'No, *sir*,' nigger."

I didn't say anything, not a word. So they handcuffed me and took me off to jail. My friend went and called my mother.

Now, we have a park down in Lacoochee called Jesse Stanley Park. It's named after Jesse Stanley, who was a local constable, a *white* constable, and he was a great man. Never arrested anybody. Just *told* people to go to jail. Used to say, "Just go on over to jail and tell 'em I sent you." Never carried a gun. Mr. Stanley was one of these white guys in the South who actually believed in justice.

My mother went to talk to him, and he drove my mother over to the jail in Brooksville. Mr. Stanley walked up to the front desk there, and he said, "Y'all got a guy in here named James Grant?"

The sheriff said, "Let me look."

"You just arrested a black kid," Mr. Stanley said, real slowly now. "His name is James Grant. He also got kicked. I want him out of here. Now."

The sheriff said, "We got written down here that he was drunk."

Mr. Stanley said, "That's a damn lie. I know his mama. I know him. And I know *y'all*. I want him out now, and I hope the Cleveland Indians sue the hell out of you."

One of the deputies said, "Uh-oh."

So Mother and Mr. Stanley got me and took me home. By the time we got there, I'd remembered where I was.

AL DOWNING

◆◆

THE HISTORY YOU read about in school is about George Washington and the Declaration of Independence and the Revolutionary War. You never read about segregation.

When I signed with the Yankees, I was told to report to a fellow named Jerry Tollman at a hotel in Bartow, Florida. So I flew down to Tampa from my home in New Jersey and took a bus to Bartow, and I got a cab over to the hotel. It was 1961. I was 19 years old. At the hotel, they had this big flight of steps leading up to the main entrance, and I started walking up.

A guy in a doorman's outfit stops me: "Where do you think you're going?"

"I'm with the Yankees," I say, "and I'm looking for Mr. Jerry Tollman from their minor league club, the Binghamton Triplets."

"You can't come into this hotel."

"But I'm with the New York Yankees."

"I don't care who you're with. You just stay right here and I'll go talk to somebody."

I didn't think you had those types of problems anymore in baseball. If you were a New York Yankee, you could stay anywhere, right? This was *14 years* after Jackie.

After a few minutes, the guy comes back with a man who introduces himself as Jerry Tollman, the man I'm supposed to meet. About then, a black cab driver pulls up at the curb.

"Here's the thing," Tollman says, "you can't stay in the hotel. I'll explain it to you tomorrow. This cab driver will take you over to the McCoy family home, and you'll stay there."

I get into the cab, and I'm thinking, why send me to the team hotel if they knew I couldn't stay there? Why not have somebody meet me at the bus station and tell me where to go?

I get to the McCoy house. There were Latin players living there too. But nobody ever talked about the situation. It was like this unwritten rule. You tolerated it, and you did what you had to do on the ball field.

Over time, I realized that what I was going through was nothing in comparison to what the guys who'd come up from the Negro Leagues years before had to put up with.

◆ ◆ ◆

ONE OF THE great things about spring training was meeting all the other black players. The Yankees were still training in St. Petersburg back then, and all the black players on teams with camps in that area would get together and eat in the black section of Tampa.

That's where I first met Henry Aaron, in a restaurant in the black section of Tampa, during spring training.

Every spring, especially those first few years, I'd spend night after night listening to those guys talking. Bob Thurman used to say stuff like, "If I had the money, I'd get an all black team and put it in the major leagues. And here's who'd be on it . . ."

I just soaked it all in. I mean, I was living stuff that they started writing books about years later.

One of the big things I learned was how self-sufficient the black community was throughout the South. Be it in Richmond, Atlanta, Jacksonville—even Little Rock. People had their own businesses. Your funeral director might also serve as a CPA—maybe not the best combination—but those services were available. In the South, you did what you had to in order to survive, and you built your community around your own people.

Another thing was the history, and that cut a lot of ways. When I got to the minor league club in Richmond, I came home one night to the family that put me up, and I said, "Mr. Banks, why do you have so many monuments in Richmond?"

"Sit down, son," Mr. Banks told me. "Don't you know that Richmond was the seat of the Confederacy? All those statues on Monument Boulevard are of Confederate generals."

"Oh . . ."

◆ ◆ ◆

I NEVER WENT back to the hotel in Bartow with all those stairs. If I couldn't stay there then, why am I going to stay there now? I'm not bitter about it. Everybody approaches it differently.

Ever hear of Willie Gary? Well, Willie's the Johnnie Cochrane of class-action suits. Willie grew up in a family of sharecroppers. Lived in different towns in Louisiana, Florida, Georgia, South Carolina. Once, when he was a kid, his family was living in Fort Pierce on a block with a hotel on the corner. He could work in the hotel. But he couldn't stay in it or eat in it.

Anyway, I lived down in Florida from 1999 through 2001. One day, Don Newcombe called me up and said, I'm coming your way, and I want you to meet me in Fort Pierce. We'll go to Willie Gary's birthday party.

We went. And that's when I found out that Willie Gary had bought the hotel and turned it into his offices.

DICK ALLEN

◆◆

THE ARKANSAS TRAVELERS had never had a black player until I went there to play. This was in 1963. I was 21.

When Little Rock had been ordered to integrate its public high schools a few years earlier, the Arkansas governor had said, "Not on my watch." He refused to do it, and President Eisenhower had to send in troops to make it happen. When you heard that, it got you to thinkin'.

I grew up in Wampum, Pennsylvania. As a kid, I learned to play baseball with a broom handle and rocks. If you hit the rock over the tree, it was a double. If it went over the barn, man, it was a homer.

The Phillies signed me in 1960. After two seasons in the low minors—

Class-C and Class-D, back then—I went up to Class-A ball in Williamsport, Pennsylvania. Going into the last day of the 1962 season, I was in the race for the batting title. I went 4–for–6. Jim Ray Hart went 6–for–6 and won it.

All in all, things were lookin' pretty good. I got married and I was invited to spring training in 1963. I was told I was going to go north with the big team, but on the last day they changed their minds. They took a guy much older than me, a guy named Wayne Graham, and they sent me down to Little Rock.

There was no preparation for Little Rock. Back then, you didn't get a chance to talk to the team's management and say, exactly how we gonna do this?

I probably signed the same sort of contract that Jackie signed. It read something like, "Contract negotiations are solely between uniformed player and parent club." Once you signed it, you were stuck. If they said you were going to Little Rock, you were going to Little Rock. My wife and I decided it was better that she stay back home.

So they sent me to Little Rock. There were three of us of color down there. Ferguson Jenkins was a Canadian; he didn't know anything about racial tensions. Ricardo Quiroz was from Panama. He didn't know anything either.

The team flew from Florida to Little Rock, and when our plane landed, they wanted to parade us through town in convertibles. One of those "Here's your Arkansas Travelers" deals. You know, sit on the back of the convertible and wave. I wouldn't get in. Just a feeling . . .

They had changed some of the rules by 1963. They let me stay in the same hotel that the white players stayed in. The Marion. Like with every minor league team, you'd arrive in town at the beginning of a season and get three days in the hotel on the club. Three days to find a place to stay.

They let me stay there, but they wouldn't let me eat there. So I ordered room service, and pretty soon I get this knock on the door, and I yell out, Come on in. Well, the door swings open, and this guy starts to roll his cart into my room, and when he sees me, he pulls that cart right back out the door.

A teammate, Joe Lonnett, was walking down the hall to his room, a toothpick stuck in the corner of his mouth, and he saw that guy yank the cart back out. Oh, jeez, Joe raised some hell. Cussed that guy out. Then Joe dragged me to his room. He ordered room service for me. He said he didn't realize it was like that.

Well, how would he know? He was white.

So I ate in Joe's room or in the back of the kitchen at the bus station. There was a little table against the wall. I came to learn you didn't want to eat where you weren't wanted in the South. They might let you in, but jeez, you'd find spit in your food.

I found myself a place on the black side of town, 1121 Cross Street. Ain't that something? Address is still in my mind. The man who rented it to me, one of his kids had integrated that high school. I got myself an old piece of car for 100 bucks so I could drive back and forth to the ballpark.

◆ ◆ ◆

OPENING DAY. I'M an infielder—third base, some first, but mostly third. One of the coaches tells me before pregame workout to go out to left, that they're going to use me out there. I'm not too comfortable out there to begin with, and they have this terrace out there in left. Sort of like what they had at Crosley Field in Cincinnati.

But hey, I'm in the lineup and I'm gonna get my swings.

Well, the first thing a defensive player is supposed to tell himself is *I hope this pitch is hit right at me! I hope this pitch is hit right at me!* You know, so you can make a play and break the ice.

Only I'm not really a leftfielder, so when I go out to leftfield and hear *Play ball!* the first thought that goes through my mind is *Please don't let that first pitch be hit to me!*

Sure enough, the first batter hits a fly ball to straightaway left. Straight at *me.* I start backing up and backing up, and then I come to that terrace, and I fall down flat on my ass, and the ball drops right next to me.

Oh, did that get the crowd started!

You come out of high school, where all you've been hearing for three years is cheers from friends and family. Now you're playing professional baseball, and you're still hearing cheers, alright—*cheers* with a J on the front: *jeers.*

You'd have thought my name had been changed to *Chocolate Drop* or *Nigger.* That's all I heard coming down from the stands. *My* stands.

Anyway, they'd announced before the game that a local shoe store was offering a new pair of Florsheim shoes to the Traveler who got the first extra-base hit of the season.

My first at-bat, *Bam!* Safe at second.

Cool. A new pair of shoes just for hitting a double. Only when I went to get those shoes, they wouldn't even let me in the door of the store. The shoe store didn't serve blacks.

But the Chamber of Commerce got into it, like they sometimes do when mistakes like that are made, and they swept the whole thing under the rug. The next thing I knew, a brand-new pair of Florsheims was waiting for me in my locker at the ballpark.

A lot of hate mail came to that locker. I'd be sitting there reading that shit and wondering, Who the hell is sending me this? Why didn't he have the balls to sign it?

I'd go out to the parking lot after the ball game and find my windshield covered with pieces of paper stuffed under my wiper blades. Remember how they used to put those fliers on car windshields in parking lots in the old days to advertise stuff? Well, mine had messages printed by hand like, "We Will Kill You On The Field!"

Your eyes see that kind of stuff, and it puts something in your mind. Then you get strange phone calls, and now it's in your ears. You go out to play ball, and you're really not playing ball. You're lookin' around, checkin' things out, wonderin' where it could come from . . .

◆ ◆ ◆

WANT TO KNOW what nerves can do to you?

Ferguson Jenkins was a control pitcher. One of the great control pitchers of all time. Fergie could put that slider down and in, right in the same spot every time. But his first few pitches in Little Rock, Fergie missed the catcher. Missed everything. The balls would go way up the screen.

Same thing with Ricardo Quiroz: wild as a March hare.

Season before, they both had something like 1.00 ERAs. In Little Rock, they can't throw a ball for a strike.

After a while, Jenkins and Quiroz got sent down to Miami. All the way from Triple-A down to A-ball. The Phillies front office had to be thinking, *Maybe we made a mistake.* Yeah, and that mistake was sending young players of color to Little Rock in 1963.

With Fergie and Quiroz gone, that left just me. I began to talk less and less. I'd sit around trying to figure it out. Why did they hate me so much?

They don't even know me. And I just got quieter and quieter.

One really hot night, I couldn't sleep, and I was thirsty. So I went out to get a soda. There was this soda machine in front of a store a block away from the place I stayed, so I went down and got my cold drink and headed back. I was jogging along the street with this soda in my hand when all of a sudden a squad car pulled over. These two cops got out and put me up against the wall. One of 'em pulled his gun. They wanted to know if I'd stolen the soda. I said no and they asked me, "Then why were you runnin'?"

They let me go, but a thing like that, it doesn't leave your mind.

Get thirsty, and you just might take a bullet in your back.

◆ ◆ ◆

I THOUGHT THE Phillies would call me up within the first 30 days that year, but April turned into May, then May into June, and no call.

Well, I guess that figured. I wasn't hitting for shit with all that I was trying to deal with.

The year before, I'd almost won a batting title. Now I was hitting a buck twenty. Sometimes I'd wake up at night and hear gunshots. *Was that for me?*

Finally, I go to the pay phone with ten cents.

Call collect.

"Mom, I want to come home." (God rest her soul in peace.)

"Dickie! You put that phone close up to your ear!"

"Yes, Ma'am."

"Now, listen here. God gave you to *me.* Do you hear me?"

"Yes, Ma'am."

"*And* he's given you a talent. *And* a place to show it."

"Yes, Ma'am."

"If you quit and you come home, you're not being disobedient to me," she said. "You're being disobedient to *God!*"

And she hung up.

No shit.

Man, I'm by that pay phone all alone now. People are sayin' they want to kill me. I'm standin' there all by myself, and you know what I'm thinkin'? *My own mama's done turned against me!*

But then I thought about it some more.

Had it not been for baseball, I'd have been what my dad said: what the little bird left on the limb.

Had it not been for Jackie, would I have even gotten a chance?

Mama was right: I *was* lettin' the Good Lord down. He gives you a talent and a place to show it regardless of where it is. So what if it's a place like Little Rock? What am I gonna do? Go home and die? No! I'll stay and die right there in the batter's box.

The next thing you know, my rhythm started to come back. Pretty soon my timing returned. Not only did I weather the storm, but the Travelers fans voted me team MVP. When I got called up to Philly at the end of the year, I left Little Rock with more friends than enemies.

I love Little Rock now, because it made me a better man. I left with a diploma. And, believe me, I needed that diploma. That was just preparation for what I was going to go through in Philly . . .

Oh, yeah, man. They had some good shit waitin' for me there.

◆ ◆ ◆

CHAPTER SEVEN

A LOT
OF WAYS
TO HOPE

IT WAS HARDER than I ever imagined to hear the voices that make up this book.

I was shocked, when I began trying to reach ballplayers and others who had lived through the times, at how many ignored my messages, avoided me, or just told me point-blank that they had no interest in speaking to me.

Gradually I came to understand their reluctance. Many had been burned by writers in the past. Many couldn't trust a stranger to convey something so complicated and close to the heart. Many wondered why they should pour their personal pain into somebody else's book.

There was one name on my list that I knew I could count on, though: Mr. Cub, Ernie Banks.

Through my youth, Ernie Banks was the welcoming face of the Cubs franchise, baseball's pair of open arms, the game's embodiment of hope. Even *with* Ernie's 512 home runs, the Cubs never won a pennant during his 19 years playing shortstop or first base—in fact, they were often mired in or near the cellar by August. But even on the grimmest and grayest days, Ernie would smile and invoke his pet phrase: "Let's play two!"

I imagined him, when I explained my request, singing out, "Let's do *two* interviews!"

Sure enough, the first time I met Ernie, he flashed me that signature big smile of his. Call me anytime, he said. But before we got much further, he began peppering *me* with questions:

"Tell me, how many people of color do you work with?"

"How diverse is *your* company?"

"What about at the very top?"

It went on like that over months. Every time we spoke, he was all smiles and open arms. But every time I tried to arrange an interview about what *he* went through to carve out his place in baseball, he nudged the conversation elsewhere.

Once I found myself in the produce section of the supermarket, doing the family grocery shopping—and taking a call on my cell from Ernie. On that day and others he caught me, we talked about everything from the definition of the word *hope* to the significance of the Dalai Lama. But never about Ernie. "The stories have all been told before," he finally said. "There's nothing new to say."

One day, though, Ernie conferenced a third person into our conversation, a professor from the University of Chicago. "You know," the professor said, "before Ernie, the face of baseball in Chicago used to be Cap Anson."

I knew a little about Cap Anson, but not much. So I began to read about the man. Here's what I learned: Anson was a legendary first baseman who hit .333 over a 27-year major league career that began in 1871 and included 22 seasons with Chicago's National League franchise. He also was a shrewd, bellicose and successful manager who led Chicago to five National League pennants.

Cap Anson was the toast of the town. A larger than life figure across America—Babe Ruth before there was Babe Ruth.

And what did he do with all that stature and influence in baseball? He *bleached* the game for six decades.

See, baseball wasn't *always* segregated before Jackie. Back in the 1880s, about 20 black players were scattered among the white teams. One of them, a catcher named Bud Fowler, was credited with inventing the first set of shin guards by taping wood to his legs, after repeatedly being spiked.

Some people, of course, didn't like sharing a ball field with blacks. But it was a single incident that shifted history. On July 19, 1887, Cap Anson's Chicago White Stockings were preparing to play an exhibition game against the Newark Little Giants in Newark, New Jersey. On the mound for the Little Giants was a superb black pitcher named George Stovey, who would win a league-record 33 games in a season.

"Get that nigger off the field," Anson reportedly said before the game. Then he threatened to have his team walk off if the black man wasn't banished. The controversy was defused and embarrassment avoided by Stovey's feigning an injury and withdrawing from the game. Word spread rapidly, and in no time, blacks disappeared from America's professional baseball leagues.

I sat there, shaking my head as I read this, wondering how Ernie Banks had come to replace *Cap Anson* as the face of baseball in Chicago. That's when it dawned on me: Ernie hadn't done it the way so many of his black peers in the 1950s and 1960s had. He hadn't taken all his anger and distrust and funneled it, molded it, hardened it into a weapon to be wielded only on a baseball field. He wasn't like Henry Aaron, Frank Robinson, and Bob Gibson, men who kept their emotions under wraps and played the game with a tightly controlled fury.

Ernie's weapons—his tools, really—were his sunshine and his smile.

They were the tools he used to bring hope every summer to a city stuck in a marriage to a bad baseball team, and to bring hope to black kids across America who wanted to play ball. And here I was, asking him to lay down his tools and reveal his pain, to turn off the sunshine and show me the darkness. To show me the mess in the kitchen, when he just wanted to serve that warm apple pie.

Finally, I gave up asking Ernie Banks to bare his heart to me and just let him open his arms.

So here's the Ernie Banks chapter, without Ernie Banks.

Here's the section on hope, and how Ernie's peers managed to find it against some long odds—served up with the hope that I'm still conversing with Mr. Cub in the produce aisle for years to come.

◆ ◆ ◆

BILLY WILLIAMS

◆◆

WE WERE COMING back from a road trip to Victoria, Texas. The year was 1959. I was with the San Antonio Missions. All summer it had been the same old stuff. You stop at a restaurant and you can't go in and eat. You can't do this, because you're black. You can't do that. When we got back to San Antonio, I turned to my roommate, J.C. Hartman, and I said, "J.C., take me to the train station."

"What are you gonna do?" J.C. said. "Go home?"

"Yeah," I said. "I'm tired of this shit."

I knew this was the way of the world. But I felt I didn't have to go through it. It may sound strange since I came from Alabama, but I guess Mobile was a little different. I hadn't gone through that stuff where I was living. You knew it happened, but not where I grew up. You knew where you could eat. But there was no comfort zone in the Texas League. Once you got a real taste of the way it was, you just got fed up.

"If you don't take me," I told J.C., "I'm gonna go grab me a cab."

"You're serious, aren't you?" He was surprised, because I was really starting to swing the bat well.

"Yes," I told him. "Dead serious."

And I got a cab down to the train station and bought myself a train ticket and went straight home to Mobile.

Well, I'd been home about four or five days, mostly doin' nothin', when I looked out the front window of the house, and there was Buck O'Neil in his Plymouth Fury pullin' into the driveway. Buck always drove a Fury. I said to myself, "I'm in trouble now."

Buck understood people. He'd seen the situations of a lot of guys who played in the Negro Leagues, and so he came with a little plan. He said, "Billy, how you doin'?" As if nothing had happened, as if I hadn't left San Antonio and come home.

"I'm doin' fine," I told him.

He said, "Why don't you and me go down to the park tonight and watch some of these young kids play?"

That evening we got in that Fury and went down to the park. Everybody I went to school with came over and they're all saying, "Hey, it's Billy! What are you doin' back here? You're playin' professional baseball! That must be great. Goin' around the country. Gettin' meal money."

With all these people around idolizing you, it was hard to say, "Yeah, you get meal money, but you can't even spend it. Somebody else has to go into the restaurant and spend it for you."

Buck's plan worked, though. Without saying anything, he showed me that I was in a position that a lot of other people wished they could be in. Within two days, I said, "Buck, I'm ready to go back."

At the time, the minor leagues weren't set up like they are now. Now it starts with A-ball. Back then, you started all the way down at D-ball and there might be two Double-A clubs and two Triple-A clubs. San Antonio was Double-A, Texas League. All those players on all those teams were trying to get to the majors. And back then there were only eight teams in the National League and eight teams in the American. There were so many ballplayers, and only a few could get there.

And if you were black, the teams did everything they could to take strength away from you. The black player would be the first one the bus picked up in the morning and the last one to get dropped off home at night. And he had to perform twice as good as his white counterpart. There was an old saying: "You got to be a play-yuh." They weren't going to pay you $6,500 to sit on the bench.

When I was in Double-A ball, the Cubs front office sent Rogers Hornsby through the entire minor league system to see what kind of players they had. Rogers was one of the great hitters in baseball. He was a rough guy who played in the back in the '20s. I once heard a story about when he was managing. When he wanted to change a pitcher, he'd walk to the top step of the dugout, point at the bullpen, and say, "You, go in." Then he'd look at the pitcher and say, "You, come out." Wouldn't even walk out to the pitcher's mound.

He came to our club, and we all worked out for him. Afterward, he had us sit in the stands. He'd look at a guy and say, "You can go get a job right now. You can't play baseball." Then he'd look at the next guy. "You can't play." Ron Santo and I are sitting there scared stiff. Hornsby goes, "Santo, you can play some defense. You're gonna get some hits in the big leagues." Then he comes to me: "Williams, you can hit in the big leagues right now. You just need to work on your defense." I let out a breath, and Hornsby says, "All you other guys can go get jobs cause you can't play."

Here he was, this tough old white guy from the 1920s, but he didn't see color at all. He just saw me as a player who could possibly help the Cubs. And he wanted something to do with that, which was great.

We'd go to the batting cage, and he'd bring a chair and just sit and watch.

After a while, he'd say, "I want you to hit 10 balls hard in a row. If you don't reach 10, we start all over again." I'd hit, hit, hit, hit—then miss one, and we'd start all over again. Hit, hit, hit, hit, hit—miss one, start all over again.

He'd say, "Try to see the ball hit the bat." Now, you can never really see the ball hit the bat. But the closer you get to that point, the better you're following the ball.

Hornsby was looking at me about as carefully as one human can look at another and just not seeing my color. He only saw my swing. An old-school white guy. And he's helping *me* become what I can be in the big leagues. He's helping *me* take somebody's job. Those were the moments that gave me hope.

There was another moment. It happened when I first came down to spring-training in 1957. I looked around and saw Buck O'Neil carrying this clipboard, this chart of players. That made me comfortable. I figured, hey, this guy's got *authority* here. It was just a clipboard. A clipboard. But it meant a lot.

LOU BROCK
◆◆◆

IT COMES DOWN to a heartbeat—the passion to change things in America. But you're talking about heartbeats on both sides. Slavery would never have been abolished if somebody on the other side of the coin hadn't championed our heartbeat. The Underground Railroad—what do you think that was? People with a heart. It wasn't on our side of the coin. We couldn't have created an Underground Railroad. We wouldn't have known where to go.

JIM "MUDCAT" GRANT
◆◆◆

TED WILLIAMS IS responsible for the Negro Leaguers getting in the Hall of Fame. He noted their absence from the Hall in his speech when he was inducted. But let me tell you a story about him.

The Indians always used to play an exhibition game against the Boston Red Sox in New Orleans. I think this happened the last year Ted was playing. Could've been 1960.

When you flew into New Orleans, the white players and all the bags went on the bus. The black players, we had to make our own travel arrangements. They didn't want us in the airport. They wanted us to cross the airport to this grassy spot. We had to wait until a black taxicab would come and get us.

Now, this particular time was on a Friday. Black taxicabs in New Orleans are real busy on Fridays. So we had to wait an hour and a half or so. In the meantime, the white players went on to the hotel with all the bags.

The black cab finally came to take us to the black hotel where we were gonna stay. It was me and Vic Power, Pumpsie Green, and Earl Wilson. We knew the four of us couldn't go up to the white hotel to get the bags. So we pulled straws.

I was always lucky with straws. But this time I lost the pull, and I had to go into the white hotel to pick up the bags. Samsonite bags, with the Red Sox logo or the Indians logo. Your name was on your bag so you couldn't mistake it.

We got the cab, and the driver said, "I ain't goin' over there."

We said, "We're gonna pay you to go."

He said, "I *ain't* goin' over there."

I said, "We've got bags over there."

He said, "Bullshit. I ain't goin' over there."

We had to pay him three times the fare just to get him to go over there to the white hotel so we could get our bags. So we got there and now it was hours after the team had arrived. I walked up to this guy in front wearing a green coat and epaulets.

He said, "What do you want here?"

I said, "I'm one of the colored ballplayers, and I came to pick up our bags in the hotel."

He said, "Bullshit, you ain't got no bags in there."

I could see them. "You see those bags over there?" I said. "The reason they're not in a room is because you don't have us registered here. Those are our bags."

Now, Ted Williams was coming from dinner and he saw me and said: "Hey, Mudcat, how you doin'?"

I said, "Ted, I ain't too bad, but I got a problem. You know we can't stay at this hotel."

"Yeah, and it's a damn shame."

"Our bags are in the lobby and this guy won't let me get the bags."

"You know what?" Ted said. "He's right. You shouldn't be goin' over to get those bags. *He* should be goin' over to get those bags."

So I turned to the guy and said, "That's right, boy. Now go on over and get those bags."

The cab driver hears this and he's got his foot on the gas and he's ready to go. *Rmmmmmm! Rmmmmmmm!* When the bags were in the car, I flipped the doorman a quarter and jumped in that cab, and we were out of there . . .

All the way down the street, the cab driver was moanin', "He's got my cab number. He's got my cab number. Oh, no, I'm in trouble now."

BOB VEALE

✦✦✦

HUMOR HELPS SOMETIMES. A guy I know went into a restaurant and they told him, "We don't serve niggers here." And he said, "I hadn't planned on ordering any niggers. And I don't want no crackers, neither. All I want is a steak sandwich."

TOMMY DAVIS

✦✦✦

ALL YOU *COULD* do was laugh.

In 1958, the Dodgers sent me to Double-A ball in Victoria, Texas. I guess it was time to put me through the Jackie Robinson phase. You know, see how I could take the pressure.

Buzzie Bavasi, the general manager, talked it over with me. He said, "I know you're from New York City. But you've just got to understand it's a different way of life in the South."

Victoria was a tough little town when it came to making remarks. Nigger was an everyday word. One time, I'm playing leftfield, and a line drive hits the ground and goes right between my legs. I start running after the ball and I hear, "Nigger, don't even pick up that damn ball. Just jump over the damn fence and don't come back no more."

Even when I did something good they called me a nigger. Then it was, That's *our* nigger.

Anyway, there was a player in the league named Nat Peeples. He was an old time Negro Leagues ballplayer. He must've been 40 years old, but even at that age he was the fastest thing in the Texas League.

I forget what team he was playing for. But he's hitting singles and doubles and triples. We just can't get him out. Then, finally, someone saw something. Every time he got up to hit and dug in at the plate, his back foot would edge out of the batter's box.

The park only held 5,000 people. Sometimes, right before a pitch, it could get kind of quiet. When it was all quiet like that, you could sometimes hear one voice from the crowd. And this time, one voice really sounded out: "Mr. *Um*-piah! Mr. *Um*-piah! Can you please keep the nigger's foot in the box?"

I could hear it clear out in the outfield. All I could do was laugh.

Even as Nat Peeples kept hitting his triples.

MAURY WILLS
◆◆

WHEN I WAS going for the stolen base record in 1962, Sandy Koufax and I read each other's mail. His locker was right across from mine, and he'd open my mail for me, and I'd open his for him.

See, what with me being black and him being Jewish, we both got a lot of hate mail.

"Oh, you probably don't want to read this one," Sandy would say. Or "Hey, this one's okay. Some little kid wants an autograph." And sometimes, "*Oh, my God! You don't want to see this...*"

Every time he'd come across one of those, I'd always go, "C'mon, let me see it." And he'd say, "Nah, nah, it'll only mess you up."

So we had some fun with it.

We even got to the point where we could recognize the same guy writing different hate letters: "Look, he must use a ruler to get the margins so straight."

TIM McCARVER
◆◆

IT WAS MY first spring training. Curt Flood and I were at the batting cage. This was in the time of the pitching machines with a mechanical arm that would throw the ball, make a full rotation, scoop up another ball, then throw the next one.

Well, Curt would feed balls to the machine and I would hit. And then I'd feed the machine and Curt would hit. The two of us were responsible for the balls. We had to bring back the same number that we took with us.

There were trees not far off the field, and there were black kids who used to climb up in them and wait. When a ball was hit near them, they'd drop down, get it, and run away. Quick as can be. Well, one of our balls got near the trees, and one of the black kids dropped down, grabbed it, and started to run. And I yelled, "Come here, you little cannibal!"

And Curt turned to me and said, "Timmy . . ."

"Curt, I am so sorry," I said to him before he could go on. "I'm so, so sorry."

I felt awful. I was so narrow-minded when I left Memphis. I had never played with or against black players growing up. And I had all the stereotypes that everyone else had in a segregated society. I just didn't know any better.

That's not making an excuse. But if you don't know any better, how can you be any different? I don't think I was bigoted. In many ways, it was worse than that, because bigots have hate. I was just indifferent to the whole situation, and if you're indifferent you don't care one way or another.

So from my naïve indifference—or whatever you want to call it—I grew into a man who started thinking, How did this happen to me? How was I put in that situation? You have no control over it. You're brainwashed. You know what I mean?

The first time I played with or against a black player was after I signed and was sent to Keokuk, Iowa. My father asked me some really silly questions. Like: "You don't eat with those guys, do you?" Reluctantly, I said, "Well, yeah." And I felt guilty. I felt that he didn't approve. Not that I let him down. I just knew that he didn't approve.

There was just no attitude of social justice in Memphis in those days. You were taught blacks were inferior, plain and simple. When I look back, I can't believe some of the things that happened. After the games in spring training, the black players would leave—almost mysteriously, now that I think about it— and the next day we'd go to the park and they'd be there.

Years later, you think: God, how stupid we were! But you just didn't know. You had no idea of the ordeal that they faced.

I remember Bill White going to the execs at the brewery in spring train- ing one year and saying that it was an outrage for us to compete on the field together but then not be able to stay or eat together. That changed things.

The intelligence level was an important factor in our success. All of the black players connected to the Cardinals in those early years—Bill White, George Crowe, Curt Flood, Bob Gibson—were highly intelligent. I mean, not just okay intelligent, but off-the-charts intelligent. They got it. And they helped me get it.

George Crowe changed my life, certainly my life in baseball. He was a real influence on the Cardinals, particularly on the black players. And because he was such an influence on the team, they made him a roving instructor after he was released. I was in the minors, in Charleston, West Virginia, and George really helped me with my hitting. I had an open stance and I was choking up on the bat. George said, "You're losing all your power. If you close the stance, you get your power." My whole batting stance from then on was based on every-thing George Crowe taught me.

Bob Gibson had his own way of helping me make the 180-degree turn. Once he saw me drinking a bottle of orange pop and he said, "Can I have a swallow?"

There must have been a little flinch or a cringe, and then I must've tried to recover. I told him, "I'll save you some." But he was already laughing.

Another time, there was a guy outside the locker room waiting for Bob and I went to give him the message.

"There's a colored guy waiting outside for you," I told him.

Bob was taking off his shoes and he didn't even look up. "Oh yeah," he said, "what color is he?"

Not only did Bob help change me, he also affected my father. I remember Bob and I once went down to Memphis to shoot a picture for a milk ad. They gave us $500 bucks or something. After that, my father sent Bob a letter with-out me knowing it: "Whenever you're in Memphis, please feel free to come by our house to eat." To be honest with you, it kind of pissed me off that he would send that letter without letting me know. But he became a front-runner.

Bob and I worked through a lot. You've got to understand, the nature of catchers and pitchers going back and forth presents its own set of problems. Forget black and white, white and black, black and black, whatever. It doesn't matter. It's all about pitcher and catcher. You've got to bring together two minds. Because of that—and I've told Bob this—he was the toughest friend that I ever had to make. I mean, it's a bit of an understatement to say Bob Gibson is a man of strong mind and strong will.

Bob didn't want me coming out to the mound to talk to him in the middle of a game. One time, I walked out and he hit me with that famous line: "Get on back behind the plate. The only thing you know about pitching is you can't hit it."

So I didn't go to the mound for maybe four years. That's the truth. I can remember Johnny Keane, the manager, saying, "Go out there and settle him down." I'd say, "*You* settle him down."

The man had already told me how he felt about visits to the mound, so I wasn't going out there. It wasn't fear. I just knew him, and I just didn't want to hear that shit anymore.

It's funny. Whenever you hear the words "human nature," it's always in a negative context. You know: "That's human nature." And it's human nature to think of the bad pitches you've called and the bad pitches that are thrown more than you think of the overall success.

I remember a night in 1966 in Pittsburgh. It's a 1-1 game, runners are on second and third. A base hit drives in both runs. Roberto Clemente comes to the plate. There's a real hard infield at Forbes Field. Clemente hits one of these patented 10-hoppers, and for whatever reason, Julian Javier was positioned toward second base and the ball got through.

Bob was backing up home plate as the runs scored, and as he passed me on the way to the mound, he said, "You know, you've got more than one goddamn finger down there." He's saying I should have called a different pitch. So I said, "You can shake me off too!" Now, we're screaming at each other between home plate and the mound.

And the thing is, Bob is a pussycat. He's one of the sweetest, dearest men you can imagine. But at times he had an absolutely unharnessed rage.

In 1968, when he had that great year, he had two complete game 1-0 losses, and after the second one, in San Francisco, I went up to him—by this time we were close friends—and said, "Bob, you pitched great."

"*Great, my ass!*" he yelled back at me. "You guys ought to score some fucking runs every now and then. I'm out here busting my ass and this damn offense . . ."

I just go in and start shaving. And I'm pissed. Everybody's pissed. They're pissed that they didn't score any runs for Bob, and they're pissed at me for setting him off. Hey, all I was doing was telling him he did a great job. And this is what I get?

So, I'm over there shaving, and Bob has cooled down. He comes by and whacks me on the back. That was his apology. I mean, I was supposed to accept that. And if you didn't accept that—well, that was all you were getting.

That was Bob. "Don't worry about it," I said. The next day was a new day.

◆ ◆ ◆

TWO THINGS THAT really raised everybody's consciousness back then were the assassinations of Bobby Kennedy and Martin Luther King Jr. They were killed—what?—two months apart.

Dr. King was one of those people who was never appreciated in life like he was in death. There were a lot of white Americans who said he was a bad guy, a rabble-rouser, a Communist. Then he died, and clear-thinking Americans thought, You listen to his speeches, and you realize that this man was a saint.

I remember going to dinner and Roger Maris telling me, "Martin Luther King has been shot."

"He was in Memphis," I said.

And he said, "That's right."

I grew up four miles from the Lorraine Hotel. I used to deliver papers two miles from there. So I knew exactly where it was. I was in shock.

I remember tears filling my eyes talking to Bob about King and bigotry and prejudice and everything. I had come to understand and appreciate the changes I'd been through.

I think I appreciate where I am on this more than people who grow up in the North and say they've always been proponents of social justice. That's bullshit, you know what I mean? I've seen the other side. I know what it's like. And I think hypocrisy was flourishing in the North just as much as bigotry was thriving in the South. You know, there are no boundaries to racism. Racism is an attitude.

And so we're sitting on these stools in the clubhouse, and I remember saying, "You know, Bob, I was raised a Catholic in a state that was only 6% Catholic."

And he said, "Yeah, but you're white."

I never forgot that simple statement: "Yeah, but you're white."

Years later, I brought it up with him. I said, "Remember that day after King was shot, and we were talking, and you said, 'Yeah, but you're white'?"

And Bob said, "Well, it would have been hell to be a *black Catholic*."

BILL COSBY

◆◆◆

I REMEMBER AS a kid going to Shibe Park in Philadelphia to see Larry Doby and Luke Easter play for the Cleveland Indians. There was a white woman sitting behind us one day. Without caring that we were right in front of her, she said, "My goodness, they have *three* of them!"

One of the Philadelphia players hit a hard ground ball right at an infielder for Cleveland who had this habit—if a ball was hit slow enough—of looking in his glove after he'd scooped a ball up and studying it before he threw it. He did it this time, but then he threw high to Luke Easter at first base.

Luke stood almost 6′5″ and weighed about 240, and he jumped as high as he could for the ball. He caught it in the tip of his glove, but no way was he going to get down in time to tag the bag. So in the same motion, he swung his left hand down while still in midair and slapped that runner in the back of his head to tag him out.

Man! You knew those white people had never seen anything like that.

DICK ALLEN

◆◆◆

I'M A ROOKIE and we're workin' our way up north from spring training. We leave Clearwater and the Pittsburgh Pirates leave Fort Myers and we play each other all the way up. Two teams from Pennsylvania. Bragging rights, you know?

We play 'em in Atlanta. Then our bus follows theirs or vice versa, and we play 'em in Birmingham. Then we take it through Chattanooga, and then we get to Asheville, North Carolina.

Before the game there in Asheville, the Pirates manager, Danny Murtaugh, gets in the middle of a big argument.

Now, Danny was the kind of guy who usually just sat in the dugout chewin' his tobacco. Every once in a while, he'd spit. That was Danny Murtaugh. That was all he had to do. He had 'em prepared, and he just let 'em go out and play.

But this argument was really ragin', right out where we could all see what was goin' on. It was between Danny and this guy from the Chamber of Commerce. I can still see tobacco juice flyin' out of Danny's mouth and goin' all over this guy's shirt.

What Danny had done was, he'd penciled-in an all-minority lineup. And the guy from the Chamber of Commerce was out there to tell him he couldn't do that.

At first Danny said that he didn't know it was an all-black lineup till they told him. But he didn't want to change it, and that's when the tobacco juice started flyin', 'cause Danny just didn't give a shit.

Anyway, he did change the lineup. The Pirates played eight blacks that day. Danny put Bill Mazeroski back in at second base. Maz had a bad ankle, and he wanted to rest him. So Danny gave Maz one at-bat, and then Maz came out. So it was all black anyway.

That was 1963. Now flash forward to 1971. Pirates-Phillies again, only this time it was during a pennant race. Same Murtaugh, same deal.

Not long ago, I got an invitation to an exhibit commemorating it. Here's how the invitation started out:

On September 1, 1971, the Pittsburgh Pirates manager, Danny Murtaugh, prepared to oppose the Philadelphia Phillies by listing the following names on his lineup card.

1B:	**Al Oliver**
2B:	**Rennie Stennett**
SS:	**Jackie Hernandez**
3B:	**Dave Cash**
Catcher:	**Manny Sanguillen**
Outfield:	**Willie Stargell, Gene Clines, Roberto Clemente**
Pitcher:	**Doc Ellis**

That's an all-minority lineup. First time it was ever done in the big leagues. Those guys turned out to be the Lumber Company. They put some wood on your ass. They put more wood on your ass than Howdy Doody had.

Won them a World Series that year, too, am I not correct?

❖ ❖ ❖

CHAPTER EIGHT

LIFE AND DEATH

YOU DON'T THINK about death on your way to a funeral. You think about the meaning of a life.

Headlights linked a long row of cars crawling single file toward Forest Hill Cemetery in Kansas City on October 14, 2006. All other traffic was stopped.

If you're in that long row of cars, what you can't help thinking is that white people wouldn't let Buck O'Neil attend their high school 80 years ago. Now white policemen are blocking traffic for his funeral the way they did only weeks before for a visit by the president of the United States.

Eight months earlier, in his 94th and final year on earth, Buck O'Neil was surrounded by 200 people who had gathered around him expecting to celebrate word of his election to the Hall of Fame.

He came up just shy.

Buck had led the Negro National League in batting twice. He'd been an All-Star three times. He'd managed teams to two championships. But a special, 12-person committee commissioned to render final judgments on Negro Leagues and pre-Negro Leagues players determined that Buck's numbers weren't good enough.

Statistics, though, don't take into account the meaning of a life. There are no statistical categories for the number of Hall of Famers who might never have reached Cooperstown if it hadn't been for Buck O'Neil. Sitting at Bethel AME Church on that October morning were Ernie Banks, Lou Brock, and Billy Williams. Only they could truly know where they might have ended up if Buck hadn't found, signed, or mentored them.

No man was more responsible for keeping the memory of the Negro Leagues alive. The stories Buck told in Ken Burns' documentary *Baseball* turned the nation's eyes back toward those forgotten men in a way that made us all wish we could have been there to see for ourselves.

The stories went much deeper than the great or humorous

moments occurring on a baseball diamond. Underneath was the pride and unity the Negro Leagues brought to a group of people who had known separation since the day they'd been taken from their families on one side of an ocean and sold to strangers on another.

The divisions never ceased. By work—house servant vs. field hand. By color—light skin vs. dark skin. Between 1900 and 1930, as blacks migrated north in large numbers to cities like Pittsburgh, they found themselves further separated from each other by education and social class. It was the Satchel Paiges and the Josh Gibsons and the Buck O'Neils who, for moments, brought everyone together.

There's no denying the inequities and disadvantages in Negro League baseball. The players didn't even have formal written contracts and swallowed enormous indignities traveling across the South to play the game they loved.

So blacks would even part ways on how they looked at the Negro Leagues. Buck chose to bring out the bright side for millions. Just as, with a heavy heart, he chose to seek the light after he'd been denied entrance to the Hall.

He had not gotten the opportunity to go to high school, he told those 200 people, but at least he'd had the chance to be admitted to baseball's sacred circle.

O'Neil's living legacy is the Negro Leagues Baseball Museum on 18th Street and Vine in Kansas City, where he was the voice of the institution and chairman of the board. Coupled with a trip to Gates Bar-B-Q, a visit there makes for a great day.

The new ballpark in Pittsburgh features a special Negro Leagues exhibit called Legacy Square. There's now a foundation to help young people in the name of Josh Gibson, who was once buried nameless. Former players like Bob Veale and Bill Greason are trying to bring a museum to Birmingham that will make sure people can remember the Black Barons. The Yogi Berra Museum will add a new Negro Leagues gallery as part of a planned expansion. Historians now comb for information stacked in attics or crammed into trunks or stuffed into Bibles.

It's wonderful that America's finally holding memorial services for the Negro Leagues. But it's a funny thing, just like at Buck's and every other funeral. We get so busy remembering a life that we overlook the details of the death.

The passing of the Negro Leagues was as catastrophic for the African-American community as it was, on another level, beautiful.

The institution was one of the largest black businesses in America in 1946. Just imagine the impact on white America today if one of its largest businesses collapsed almost overnight. That, in essence, is what happened to black America the day after Jackie Robinson entered major league baseball.

◆　◆　◆

BUCK O'NEIL

♦♦♦

WELL, AFTER JACKIE, it killed the Negro Leagues, killed 'em plumb dead in the East. All the fans lined up to see Jackie and Larry Doby play.

Who it really hurt at first was the ballplayers like me. I'm in my 30s at the time. Josh Gibson's in his 30s, and Cool Papa Bell's in his 40s. The major leagues didn't want us. They wanted the young ballplayer. First they wanted the Don Newcombes and the Monte Irvins. Later they wanted the Ernie Bankses, the Willie Mayses, and the Henry Aarons.

Older stars in the Negro Leagues like Willie Wells had to go to Canada or Mexico or Puerto Rico or somewhere else to play, because the major leagues didn't want 'em and the Negro Leagues didn't want 'em anymore either.

The reason the Negro Leagues didn't want 'em is that they wanted to bring in the younger guys so they could sell them to the major leagues.

What they were hopin' was to become a part of the minor leagues. They were hopin' to link their teams up to the major league farm system. So the Negro Leagues let the old ballplayers get away, and the major leagues took away the great young ones.

At first it didn't hurt us all that much out in Kansas City. At the time the major leagues only went as far west as St. Louis, so we still had our fans. That's when we brought in Toni Stone and some of the other teams brought in their own women players to draw a crowd. A lot of fans wanted to see women play against the men.

But even that didn't last long.

Our league, the Negro National League, went out of business in 1948. The Negro American League hung on another 10 years or so, but it might as well have died when we did.

LOU JOHNSON

♦♦♦

WE'D PLAY FOR a percentage of the gate when I was playing Negro Leagues ball. And if we'd drive into a city and there weren't many people paying to see us, we would just drive on through to the next stop. Stop? *For what?* Who was going to pay for our rooms that night? How were we supposed to eat?

CHARLEY PRIDE

◆◆◆

I WENT TO try out for the Memphis Red Sox in 1952 when the Negro Leagues were going through some pain. The best players were being drained away. 'Course, there still was a quota in the minors. About two blacks was all the minor league clubs would have.

I didn't make the team right off, and a guy named Jim Ford took an all-black team up into Iowa. We were stationed in Andy Williams' hometown—Wall Lake, Iowa—and we played for a percentage of the gate.

The thing about Wall Lake was that it would be beautiful during the day and at night it would rain buckets so there'd be no game. Luckily, the Pop Corn King—a local guy, I forget his real name—took over the team and started feeding us. But I do remember pulling up weeds and chewing on a few of those.

BOB VEALE

◆◆◆

TAKE AWAY ALL the seeds from the field, pretty soon there's no more crops.

Instead of playing four times a week, it got to be only on weekends. Then it wasn't at all. You know, the Negro Leagues meant money for a lot of people, and rent wasn't that much in those days.

How many years did it take before the Negro Leagues folded for good? How many mouths weren't fed during that time?

SAM LACY

A longtime African-American sportswriter who crusaded all his life for the integration of baseball, SAM LACY (1903-2003) was inducted into the Hall of Fame in 1997. This is taken from an ESPN television interview the same year.

◆◆◆

PEOPLE SAID THAT the acceptance of black players from the Negro Leagues would eventually destroy the Negro Leagues and as a consequence put some 400 Negro athletes out of jobs. And there were people put out of jobs.

When Abraham Lincoln signed the Emancipation Proclamation, he put 400,000 Negroes out of jobs. It took slavery right out of there, and people had to find some other way of making a living. The Negro Leagues were looked upon as an institution, but they were also a symbol of segregation. And that symbol was one that needed to be eliminated.

SHARON ROBINSON

◆◆◆

I DIDN'T GET a very glorious picture of the Negro Leagues through my father. I got that from Buck O'Neil. My father was like, This is not just. This is not fair. We're not getting the same salaries in the Negro Leagues and we're not getting the same conditions.

The Negro Leagues *were* romantic, though. It was great baseball and great entertainment. It drew a lot of people, made money, gave ballplayers a place to exhibit their skills. The injustice was that you had no choice. It was Jim Crow baseball.

My father had been fighting against that since he was a little boy. He was always wondering, Why am I looking through the fence and seeing all the white kids swimming and we're not allowed in the pool? Do they think we don't get hot?

My father went on to play integrated ball. He played at the college level with whites. When he arrived in the Negro Leagues, he already knew there was another way.

PHIL DIXON

A noted baseball historian, PHIL DIXON has written extensively about the Negro Leagues and about the Kansas City Monarchs.

◆◆◆

WHEN BRANCH RICKEY signed Jackie Robinson, he didn't give the Monarchs any compensation—not a dime. At first the Monarchs complained, but what were they going to do?

So they decided they would sacrifice Jackie but that they'd protect everybody else. That's when they started signing their own players to contracts to stop theft in the future. The Monarchs started selling player contracts to the majors, and the Dodgers were the major league team with the most blacks in their organization. But the two weren't working in harmony.

The Monarchs were still so mad at Rickey that if you go back and look, you won't see another black player signed by the Brooklyn Dodgers from the Kansas City Monarchs. The Monarchs had their own little boycott going.

The goal of a lot of the Negro Leagues owners was to turn what they had into a minor league within organized baseball or do something that would keep them competitive instead of becoming a third-rate business without a product to sell.

But Major League Baseball was taking the best talent and pretty much sucking the Negro Leagues dry. That left the Negro Leagues constantly searching for new talent. And businesses like the Monarchs survived simply by getting good at finding players to sell to the majors.

For every player who reached the majors, there were probably five or six you never heard of who were sold to minor league teams. There was no intention of bringing those guys up to the major leagues because there was sort of a quota system in place. But those minor league teams now had a new product to sell and could use the black players as attractions of their own.

So white baseball took not only took the cream of the crop from the Negro Leagues—it also cleaned out everything just underneath the cream.

Then, when that got pretty much done, white baseball cut out the middleman—those Negro League teams that were doing the selling. It cut them out by hiring scouts who'd been in the Negro Leagues.

JERRY IZENBERG

◆◆◆

THE CLUB OWNERS in black baseball were very fearful of what the integration of the major leagues meant for them. What they really tried to do was to become a Triple-A league. They were willing to take that status and stay in business. But the major league clubs had no interest in that. All they wanted to do was steal ballplayers. This involved Monte Irvin. The year before Jackie came to the majors, Monte and the Newark Eagles won the Negro League World Series.

After a while, Branch Rickey called up the owner of the Eagles, Mrs. Effa Manley, and he said to her, "This is a great day for your race."

And she said, "Well, my race could use one."

Then Rickey said, "You'll be happy to know that we're bringing Monte Irvin to Brooklyn to play for us."

"Not only will I be happy but I'll be totally surprised," said Mrs. Manley. "I have a contract with Mr. Irvin. Are you telling me you want to buy it?"

"No, we don't want to buy it," Rickey said. "What are you telling me, that you're going to stand in the way of your people's progress?"

Mrs. Manley said, "I'm standing in the way of my bank account. And you're going to have to pay $15,000, which is what Mr. Veeck paid for Larry Doby, or you're not getting Monte Irvin."

So the next thing Rickey does is call a press conference for black writers. They're ecstatic. They've never been invited to Ebbets Field for lunch. And wouldn't you know it, they start vilifying Mrs. Manley in their newspapers.

But she holds her ground, and finally Rickey realizes he ain't getting anywhere and he calls up Giants owner Horace Stoneham and says, "Horace, I've got a great idea. We already have a great rivalry, but can you imagine how great it would be if we got a whole new audience to tap into it at the same time?" Stoneham sees where Rickey's going, and he says, "I don't know any black players."

And Rickey says, "There's a guy over in Newark who really would be ideal for you: Monte Irvin. Call Effa Manley and make a deal for him."

Stoneham did just that, and got Irvin—and for only $5,000. Now, Monte goes to her and says, "Mrs. Manley, I only think it's fair that I get a piece of the sale price. I came back from Mexico for you."

Mrs. Manley says, "Monte, there's a lot of truth in what you're saying. Let's sit down and talk about it. There's a guy in Newark who's done all our legal work who's never been paid. I want to give him $2,500. Do you think I should cheat him out of that?"

"Oh, no, Mrs. Manley," Monte says. "I think you should pay him. But you still have $2,500 left."

And she says, "You're right about that, Monte. But, you know, there's a fur store I walk by a lot, and I've noticed a stole in the window. I've never had a mink stole. You think I should get that mink stole?"

Along about now Monte's seeing where his piece of the sale price is going: "Well, Mrs. Manley, I guess I don't think you should deprive yourself."

"Well," she goes on, "that mink stole costs $2,500. Now, let's do the math. You know, I don't see where your bonus is coming from."

Okay, years go by, and a group of Negro Leaguers and major league owners are at this posh private party thrown by some company. Effa Manley walks into the room. She's in her 70s, and she's gorgeous—a really stunning woman—and dressed to the nines. She's got the stole on.

She runs into Monte Irvin, who tells her, "Oh, Mrs. Manley, you look great."

"Monte," she asks him, "do you remember this stole?"

"No," he says, "I don't think I do."

"Well, this is the stole I bought . . ."

"Oh, yeah," Monte says. "I remember that stole. And you're still wearing it! You got a good deal."

And Mrs. Manley says, "No, Horace got the good deal."

◆ ◆ ◆

MAX MANNING PLAYED for the Newark Eagles. Good pitcher. They used to call him Dr. Cyclops. He had these big, thick glasses. He'd come in to warm up, and the first thing he'd do was throw the ball over the catcher's head, just to deliver a message.

Before one game, a scout for the New York Giants called him over and asked him, "Hey, Manning, you want to pitch for the Giants?"

That was like asking if he wanted to go to heaven, so Manning said, "Are you kidding?"

"Okay, here's what you do," the scout said. "There's a tavern around the corner of the ballpark. You meet me there after the game and we'll work out the details."

After the game, Manning went around to the tavern and sat down with the scout at a table in the corner.

The scout said, "You're probably going to have to go to the minors for a month or so. But there's no question that before this year is over you'll be pitching with the Giants."

"That's great," Manning said. "I can't wait to tell Mrs. Manley. You talked to her, right?"

"No, I haven't," the scout said. "We're not going to talk to Mrs. Manley. You want to pitch for the Giants or not? We're not buying your contract. If that's not acceptable, well, there are a lot of guys out there we can get."

Max Manning walked out. Talk about a reason to be bitter. Max was loyal to his employer. So he never got to play in the major leagues.

BUCK O'NEIL

◆◆

WHAT WAS EVEN sadder about the crowds drying up was you could see what it did to places like the Streets Hotel.

Anybody who was black who was somebody who came to Kansas City stayed in the Streets Hotel. Ballplayers. Jazz musicians. We traveled the same circuit, and we all stayed in the same hotels because they were black hotels. See, a lot of the black musicians performed at the big hotels downtown but they weren't allowed to stay there.

The Streets Hotel was an outstanding hotel. You'd head down for breakfast and Louis Armstrong or Duke Ellington or Lionel Hampton might be sitting at the next table. The restaurants on 18th and Vine served the best food in the country, because during that time the best cooks in the world were black. The Streets was the place to be.

After big league baseball integrated, things got a whole lot tougher for hotels, restaurants, and other businesses in the black community. The musicians who were performing at the big hotels downtown began to stay in them. The Streets lost all that business and it became hard to compete. Fans from out of town weren't making the trip into Kansas City to see the Negro League games anymore, so they weren't staying at the Streets.

It was quite a change. Before, money made by the black community had always been spent in the black community because it was just about the only place we could spend it. When integration started, we started to spend it somewhere else.

In Kansas City, blacks began moving farther south where they hadn't used to be able to live before. All the doctors and lawyers started moving out with their clientele. Truth is, the death of the Negro Leagues just about killed the center of the black community.

◆ ◆ ◆

ROB RUCK

ROB RUCK is a senior lecturer in the Department of History at the University of Pittsburgh. His books include *The Tropic of Baseball: Baseball in the Dominican Republic* (1999) and *Sandlot Seasons: Sport in Black Pittsburgh* (1993). He is a member of the Hall of Fame Negro League Election Committee.

◆◆

ON A NATIONAL scale, other than the black insurance companies, the Negro National League was one of the first black institutions to emerge after slavery.

By their own account, the Negro Leagues were a $2 million-a-year business during World War II. That may not sound like much now. But back then, they were one of the largest black enterprises in the country. And they were at the center of the black economy because they were tied together to the black press and the numbers game.

Numbers were the poor people's lottery. If you're a poor person, you're never going to accumulate much money trying to save a nickel or a penny a day. But if you played your number and hit it every now and then, you had a nice payoff.

Look at Gus Greenlee, owner of the Pittsburgh Crawfords. Nobody ever called him a thug or a racketeer because he ran the numbers. This isn't to say that there was no racketeering connected to numbers game. But in many ways, Greenlee was like a banker for the black community.

In Pittsburgh, after the collapse of the black-owned Steel City Bank in 1925, it was hard for a black person to get a loan from a white bank to build a business or buy a home, and efforts to form a black bank collapsed until New World National Bank was established in 1975. So if you're excluded from a loan by the white bank because you haven't built up the equity or the capital or the credit history, the numbers man is going to be very important.

Greenlee was the source of many a loan to help somebody with a doctor's bill, to get a load of coal, to send a kid to college. If you look around the Negro Leagues, you'll see many of the clubs were either owned or backed by the numbers men, because that's where the money was.

So you've got the numbers holding together the community in one way and the black press connecting it in another.

A black newspaper like the *Pittsburgh Courier* would be distributed by Pullman porters on trains. These porters were the disseminators of information for black people living all over the South. Newspapers like the *Courier* helped black people down South make decisions about where they might want to migrate to up North.

There was a symbiotic relationship between the black newspapers and the Negro Leagues, the same way there is for all sporting teams and the press. Sports sell newspapers and newspapers promote sports.

The *Pittsburgh Courier* and the *Chicago Defender* had long been big boosters of black baseball. They'd be involved in the selection of players for the Negro League All-Star Game. They helped make players like Satchel Paige and Josh Gibson legendary at a time when these players got meager attention from the white press.

The black newspapers got caught up in the drive to integrate American society after World War II, and Jackie Robinson's major league debut in April 1947 became the most positive symbol of that movement.

Black fans traveled in groups to see Jackie, and the black press did the same thing. Black reporters followed Jackie's every footstep. The noted black newspaperman Wendell Smith not only covered Jackie during spring training, but he lived with him in Florida. If Jackie got a head cold, there was a story about it.

As Larry Doby and Satchel Paige made it to the majors, there was huge coverage in the black newspapers. And there was a corresponding decrease in coverage of the Negro Leagues.

When you look back at the last Negro League World Series ever played, in 1948, you'll see the coverage in Pittsburgh's black press is almost nonexistent.

LARRY LESTER

Historian LARRY LESTER has written extensively about baseball.

◆◆◆

BACK THEN, THERE would probably be just one big sportswriter on a black newspaper, and so now he was divided. Was he going to cover the Negro Leagues or was he going to follow Jackie Robinson?

A little later, as the Satchel Paiges and the Willard Browns came into the major leagues, the writer was curious: Was the Negro League player as good as the writer always thought he was?"

◆   ◆   ◆

ROB RUCK

◆◆◆

IF YOU DON'T have the newspapers' attention, it's going to be hard to draw fans. And if you can't draw fans, it's going to be hard to stay in business. The overall impact on the Negro Leagues of breaking the color barrier in baseball was pretty much summed up by Buck Leonard: "After Jackie, we couldn't draw flies."

A year after Jackie integrated baseball, the Negro National League called it quits. And the Negro American League was really reduced to barnstorming mode, which meant relying on showmanship that drew on racial stereotypes and old-style minstrel buffoonery.

What happened in the newspaper industry followed naturally enough from the integration of baseball. If you were a top black sportswriter like Wendell Smith, and you placed a huge value on being part of an integrated America, then you felt beholden, morally obligated, to take part in that integration once the walls begin to fall.

So Smith left the *Pittsburgh Courier* in 1948 and took a job with one of the white newspapers. And he took a lot of his black readers with him.

Integration posed very stark choices for African-Americans. A lot of things became either/or propositions. Black people were let in the door a little, but power was held nearly exclusively by whites.

Integration brought the best young black players to major league teams. It brought the black fans into major league stadiums. But it did not bring black institutions or black leadership into society.

Black newspapers, black-owned hotels, black-owned sports teams, and black-owned businesses of all sorts had benefited from segregation because it gave them a clientele. In an integrated society, they couldn't compete. The small black pharmacy just didn't have the capital to compete with the large white one downtown. So once there was integration, a lot of these black-owned businesses went under.

And what eventually happened to the numbers game? Well, look at who runs the lottery today—the state.

◆ ◆ ◆

THE HILL DISTRICT of Pittsburgh was a very integrated community well into the 1930s. But in the 1950s and 1960s, the black professional and middle classes were able to take advantage of economic and social changes and move to the suburbs. The community that was left behind is now segregated not only by race but also by class. In a couple more decades, deindustrialization began to wipe out the black working class.

And so we come to the Hill today: an impoverished underclass, living in wretched, deteriorating housing projects.

BOB KENDRICK

BOB KENDRICK is the director of marketing for the Negro Leagues Baseball Museum in Kansas City.

◆◆

WHAT WE'RE TALKING about reminds me of that old adage: Be careful what you wish for—you might get it.

That certainly rings true when you look at what integration did to the infra-structure of African-American communities.

There's always a cost for progress. But many people in the black commu-nity back then saw the words "integration" and "equality" as synonymous. They felt that if they got access they'd be treated equally. That wasn't the case, of course. And in the process of change, a great deal was lost.

PHIL DIXON

◆◆

THE BLACK COMMUNITY's hope for integration was just not realized. Twenty years later, Martin Luther King Jr. was still marching for basic rights. To me, the broken dreams of the integration period sparked by Jackie were partially behind the riots of the '60s.

JIM BROWN

◆◆

ALL THE GANG warfare you have now, all the crime, all the overcrowded pris-ons, all of those things are based upon a dysfunctional lower class. The country suffers for the failure to bring African-Americans into the mainstream of American life.

The Negro League All-Star Game used to draw about 40,000 black fans every year. Forty thousand people dressed in suits and ties watching a baseball game. *A beautiful sight.* When we were working together because of necessity, we were doing better from the standpoint of black businesses and black families.

Then we had integration and deindustrialization in the North. A lot of black small businesses got killed by the spread of suburban malls. Black-owned banks failed or were absorbed as the banking industry consolidated. Once we gave up that kind of economic power, we really got lost. We never had a large enough capital base in the black community to draw from, so we never could create ownership in industry or technology that could be competitive.

Basically, in the last third of the 20th century we regressed on a lot of fronts. There was a void. Drugs were the economic force that filled that void. A lot of the young people got caught up in drug problems, and the family structure was attacked.

There's a big difference in the family now and the way it was back then. In the South, there was a strong sense of family, a sense of being, a sense of belonging. There was a sense of the father holding together the family. Now, we have no fathers in these dysfunctional areas.

Today, young men have no idea what happened or what's happening to them.

◆ ◆ ◆

CHAPTER NINE

SYMBOL OF INFLUENCE

PERHAPS YOU'VE SEEN the famous film clip of Jackie Robinson stealing home in the 1955 World Series against the New York Yankees. It's an image that's always misled me.

Every time it flashed on the screen, I figured it must've been the winning run in a critical game, perhaps the play that won the Series. As I grew older, I began to assume it symbolized something more: Jackie as an innovator, bringing speed and the stolen base to baseball.

But when I looked into it, I found out that Jackie's steal occurred in the *first* game of a seven-game Series, with two outs in the top of the eighth inning and the Dodgers behind 6-4. The Yankees held on to win 6-5. For all practical purposes, the play had absolutely no impact at all.

What's more, the record book indicated that Jackie wasn't even remotely an innovator on the base paths. The most bases he ever stole in a single season was 37 (1949). Not only was that 59 fewer than the record at the time—Ty Cobb's 96 (1915)—but it was also the only time in Jackie's career that he stole more than 30. Stealing home? Ty Cobb did it far more often than Jackie.

Yet, when I heard Kareem Abdul-Jabbar speak at a gala for the Jackie Robinson Foundation in 2006, he spoke of that play as one of the highlights of his childhood. The scene was depicted on a mural in the streets of Philadelphia half a century after it took place. It's become the single most-enduring image of Jackie Robinson on a ball field.

Jackie died in 1972, so I couldn't ask him to explain the significance of that moment. That left the other guy in that image, the catcher trying to tag Jackie out, a guy renowned for his insight and wisdom as well as his baseball talent. A guy who has said, among other things:

If you come to a fork in the road, take it.
Nobody goes to that restaurant anymore, it's too crowded.
The future ain't what it used to be.
Half the lies they tell about me aren't true.

So I went to see Yogi Berra at his museum in Montclair, New Jersey. I wanted to view the footage with him because, as Yogi has pointed out, *You can observe a lot just by watching.*

I followed Yogi into the auditorium, and we relaxed in seats from the original Yankee Stadium. Grainy black-and-white images of the Yankees and the Dodgers filled the screen. "I love watching these old films," Yogi said. "You forget what you can remember."

I nodded and licked my chops, confident that understanding was just around the corner.

Yogi pointed out that the pitcher on the mound, Whitey Ford, is giving Jackie a slight advantage by going through a full windup. That was the practice in those days with a runner on third. Nowadays, a lefthanded pitcher would work from the stretch. Being positioned sideways on the mound in stretch position allows him to monitor the runner's every move and keep him close to third base, making it less likely that he'll score on a ground ball.

On the other hand, Yogi said, Whitey's pitch will have a little more velocity coming from a full windup, more to his advantage against the hitter.

Anyway, there goes Whitey, rocking back to start his windup, and here comes Jackie down the line.

Jackie's not a sleek speedster. He's a football player in a baseball uniform, a churning locomotive. Something that football legend Jim Brown told me suddenly makes sense. Brown said that Jackie wasn't a natural baseball player the way Muhammad Ali, say, was a natural boxer, and Jackie was no one-sport wonder. He was, Brown said, one of the five greatest all-around athletes of all time. Jackie could play any sport at the highest level. He simply chose to focus his talents on baseball.

Up on the screen, quicker than a blink, Jackie's there. His slide sends up a cloud of dust as Yogi slaps down the tag. The umpire signals safe, and immediately Yogi hops up and down in protest as if he's just gulped 26 cups of espresso.

I looked over at the 81-year-old Yogi sitting beside me. He was shaking his head. "He's out!" he growled. And before I could ask him about the deeper meaning of that play, he was leading me around the museum to a gigantic photo of the tag that detailed the exact position of the cleats, the catcher's mitt, and home plate, all the while still arguing the particulars of his case.

But, Yogi, I spluttered, I'm trying to see the big picture here, and you're just showing me the small picture blown up into a big picture.

Then I chuckled at the words I was stumbling on, wondering if Yogi was somehow contagious. But his flipping my mind upside down like that, in a funny way, actually helped.

When Yogi departed, I looked at the picture again and asked myself what was really happening here: *A black man is stealing home plate in a World Series game.* Just saying those words made me begin to glimpse the big picture.

Yes, Jackie had stepped on the field as the first black man, and that was the historical breakthrough. But what did it really mean, allowing an African-American on a ball field—or inside an office or a classroom, for that matter—if he just stayed in the background, kept silent, kept his eyes on the floor, remained invisible.

What Jackie was doing in that image was the single most-brazen thing on a ball field that a man could legally do: stealing home in a World Series game.

Imagine the confidence that it took to do that, with every eye in America upon him. Imagine the confidence that it seeded in every black man, the challenge and invitation to be free in a much truer sense than the donning of a major league uniform.

So Yogi, even if Jackie was out, he scored.

◆ ◆ ◆

KEN BURNS

◆◆

THE GREAT SUB-THEME in American life has always been race.

How could it be otherwise?

We were founded more than 200 years ago on the most noble principal yet advanced in human kind—that all men were created equal—but the man who wrote those words owned more than 200 human beings and never saw fit in his lifetime to free them.

Thomas Jefferson set in motion an American narrative that was not only bedeviled by race but also ennobled by it. And I can think of no more potent moment in the history of this dynamic in sports up until that time than when Jackie Robinson trotted out to play for the Brooklyn Dodgers on April 15, 1947.

You simply cannot overstate the importance of Jackie.

First, you've got to place him in perspective in the nascent civil rights movement. When Jackie Robinson played that first game in Ebbets Field, Martin Luther King was still in college. There hadn't been a woman refusing to move to the back of the bus. There hadn't been lunch counter demonstrations. The term sit-in hadn't been coined. There were none of the signposts of what we think of as the civil rights movement, which makes Jackie's example one of the first real signs of progress in civil rights since the Civil War.

Now, just think about everything that happened in the wake of his arrival . . .

BILL COSBY

◆◆

A LOT OF people think that racism is sort of an individual thing. It's not that simple. It's very important for you to understand that it got started as a group thing. It was a group thing because this country set up slavery according to law. It was lawful to own slaves.

Well, slavery was abolished. What happened? We got new laws. Jim Crow laws. When Jackie Robinson came along, a black man couldn't use the white bathroom. He couldn't drink out of the white water fountain. He might have to pay a tax to vote. So you've got to look at the laws.

◆ ◆ ◆

JIM BROWN

◆◆◆

WHEN SOMEONE BREAKS through a barrier for the first time, he becomes a great symbol. Jackie was that symbol. You know, like Roger Bannister was a symbol of the four-minute mile. It was seen as an unbreakable barrier until Bannister broke it. Then a lot of people broke it. It takes an individual to accomplish something that most people don't think can be accomplished, and then that frees up many people to soar to new heights.

WALTER CRONKITE

◆◆◆

IT'S A TERRIBLE story, just terrible. But it allows you to gauge the impact Jackie Robinson had on America.

When I was a boy, my dad had been lured to Houston to teach at the dental college and share an office with a wealthy dentist. We came down from Kansas City. On our second or third day, we were invited to this dentist's fancy home for dinner. At the time, there was no air-conditioning in Houston. It got quite warm, and electrical refrigeration wasn't usual. So you'd finish dinner, call over to the drugstore for ice cream, and it would be delivered.

After dinner we were sitting on the front porch, rocking on wicker chairs, awaiting this delivery. We could hear the *pop-pop-pop* of a motorbike. Then we saw this delivery boy shine his flashlight along the curb and toward the sides of the house. He was obviously looking for a way to the back door. There was an alleyway, but it was partially hidden, and he couldn't find it. So he finally gave up and began to walk to the front porch with this ice cream.

The dentist stopped talking, and he stopped rocking, too. With each step the delivery boy took toward the porch, the dentist inched forward in his chair. I could see the delivery boy, who was black, as he put his foot on the front step.

Suddenly, the dentist jumped forward, drew back his fist, and hit the delivery boy with all his might right in the middle of the face. The blow knocked the young man down the stairs and into the bushes. The dentist said, "Nigger, this will teach you to never step foot on a white man's front porch."

My dad got up and said, "Come on, Helen. Come on, Walter. We're leaving."

As we walked away, the dentist called after us, "Wait a minute. Why don't you stay? Come on, have your ice cream." He didn't even know what was the matter.

Aside from the obvious prejudice, what you must realize is that in those days delivery boy was the sort of job open to blacks. For the most part, good jobs weren't available to African-Americans.

After Jackie Robinson came along, we began to see African-Americans playing professional baseball, football, and basketball—and, slowly but surely, working in every other walk of life.

We clearly haven't achieved total equality in any area of work—except, perhaps, in some areas of education—and we have a long way to go. But after Jackie entered the major leagues, that's when the picture started to change.

LASALLE D. LEFFALL, M.D.
Dr. LaSalle D. Leffall is the first African-American president of the American College of Surgeons and of the American Cancer Society.

◆◆

I THINK WHAT happened is that after Jackie Robinson integrated baseball, people in practically all professions started asking themselves an obvious question: *Is there something we should be doing in our area?*

Let me give you a single example of what I mean.

Jackie entered the major leagues in 1947. In July 1949, Dr. Jack White was the first black to be accepted at the Memorial Sloan-Kettering Cancer Center. Later on, it was Dr. White who suggested to me that I go to Memorial Sloan-Kettering for training. And it was Dr. White who helped me gain admission.

Now, I have no way of proving a connection between what happened in my profession and Jackie. All I know is what *did* happen.

ERNEST WITHERS
◆◆

JACKIE WAS EVIDENCE that African-Americans could do the same thing as anybody else. He cleared the atmosphere for mental acceptance.

It was the mood that came after Jackie Robinson that gave people in Atlanta the idea to hire black police. We had a racial problem in Memphis, and it was decided to try to unify the city by hiring black police.

I was in the first group of Negroes to enter the Memphis Police Academy. There were 14 of us. Nine of us finished. We were stationed in the black community, not in the white community.

Since that time, Memphis has had four black police directors.

LOU BROCK

WHAT CAUSED BLACK people in America to start moving toward education? A law. See, there was a law passed way back that you had to be in school until you were age 16. Prior to that, people where I came from might be out of school at age 8, or whenever they were physically able to work in the fields. That law had a huge affect.

My mom, her mom—they only got to grade five or six. Why? Because the law didn't protect them. People were working 90 hours a week and had no rights.

You're also talking about people affected by the Jim Crow laws. Jim Crow laws say "separate but equal." But there is nothing that's equal. Just separate. And therefore, you're not even human.

A law said you were inferior. A law said that you weren't welcome. A law physically separated you. Can you imagine being an 8-year-old kid growing up and hearing that?

How do you survive under this system that is constantly pounding at you? Under this system, a man could be hung on a tree limb. You know where I heard the word "picnic" came from? *Pick a nigger and let's have lunch.* It was a hanging ceremony. I don't know if that's for sure true, but that's the way I heard it growing up. Think about it. You go to the park and have a picnic. Well, the park used to be the hanging place. Pick one, go out, sit around and eat, and enjoy the view.

My family was in the same position as Monte Irvin's father when he went to the store and tried to get change for his purchases. My mother would add up one plus two and get three dollars. But the white clerk was always adding one plus two and asking for five dollars.

It was a great inspiration to study math in school. I went to school in a one-room shack with one teacher who taught all grades. I didn't need to take math to prove that the numbers were wrong. I already knew that they should have matched up. But you wanted to know. You had to know. You needed to know. You knew it wasn't in your favor. But you didn't know the *degree* to which it wasn't in your favor. Otherwise you're just walking around. You're not challenging. It didn't matter if you didn't seem to be challenging at the moment, your mind was working different now. That gave you hope for a ticket out of there.

What Jackie Robinson did was make all the arithmetic match up. He could be seen and appreciated for his work by everyone and that performance would no longer be hidden away. Now, one plus two equals three for everybody.

GREGG GONSALVES

A former Jackie Robinson Foundation Scholar, GREGG GONSALVES is a partner and managing director at Goldman Sachs, the New York-based investment-banking firm.

◆◆

I TRY TO make sure my kids understand what Jackie went through, because as you get further and further away from it, it's harder to comprehend.

I didn't grow up with segregated bathrooms, so frankly, I'm even a bit distanced from it.

I've done between a half dozen and a dozen billion-dollar deals. I can't imagine what it would be like to go to work under a similar pressure. A lot of people wouldn't be able to get the job done under those conditions. And even if they could, they wouldn't want to put up with the hassle.

Somehow, Jackie was able to get beyond all that and *still* be able to play so well.

SPIKE LEE

◆◆

SOMETIMES I WONDER if today's African-American athletes could have gone through what Jackie did, what Joe Louis did, and what Jesse Owens did. (Hey, three J's—just thought about that.)

Maybe I'm wrong. And I do love Derek Jeter. But I don't know whether there are many—if any—present-day athletes who could go through what the three J's did.

◆　◆　◆

BILL COSBY

◆◆

So HERE COMES Jackie stepping into the "national" pastime. This wasn't about a boxer knocking people out three times a year. This was about Mom's apple pie. The *national* pastime.

Remember, the word was out. The word was out on our race. We can't play this game as well as the whites. No, you can't play.

Why?

Because you're not bright enough.

Because we don't want you next to us in the shower.

That was white voodoo. It was also a form of insanity, one that makes people become entrenched with these kinds of thoughts and want to do damage to other human beings, whether it be physical, economic, or emotional.

So this man comes before us. There is no question of the tone of Jackie Robinson's skin color. The man is *black*. This is a trial to find out if a whole race of black people, including the ones in Africa, has not only the physical ability but also the *intelligence* to play the "national" pastime.

A trial. An entire race is being judged on whether Jackie hits the ball through the hole for a single, whether he catches the ball, whether he has the nerve, the guts, and the intelligence at a time of extraordinary tension to rise to the standard of the game's champions. Not to the standard of its mediocre players, but the standard of its champions.

TOMMY DAVIS

◆◆

EVER SEE THAT great photo of Jackie Robinson in a rundown? It was a mob scene. Jackie's on the third base line about 25 feet away from the bag, with five guys from the other team spread along the line trying to get him out. And they can't get him!

Usually, you run a guy down, fake a throw to stop him in his tracks, and then tag him. Simple. But Jackie just kept going back and forth, back and forth, and they couldn't tag him. It would happen a lot. Back and forth, back and forth. The more times you have to throw the ball, the more chances for screwing up. One of the fielders gets nervous or something and throws the ball away.

In that picture I'm talking about, that's *exactly* what happened: Jackie scored.

CHARLES RANGEL

◆◆

WATCHING JACKIE RUN those bases . . . Let me tell you, there was a part of every black man in every run he scored.

BOBBY BRAGAN

◆◆

THE CONVERSATION LASTED five minutes at the most, and it changed my life.

There were a few of us Dodgers who expressed displeasure at playing with a black. Me. Dixie Walker. Eddie Stanky. And Carl Furillo, which was a surprise, because he was from Pennsylvania. Dixie was the only one who put it in writing.

It may be hard for someone who's young to understand how it was back then, because there's a world of difference today from when I was growing up in Birmingham, Alabama.

I had a wonderful mother and father. My family went to church every Sunday—my parents, seven boys, and two girls. My mother cooked 30 biscuits every morning. The ones we didn't eat, we put peanut butter and jelly on and took 'em to school. All I knew was that blacks had a different water fountain in town and a different restaurant and a different school.

I've heard all that stuff about a petition going 'round against Jackie playing. I never saw any petition. But we did let our dissatisfaction be known.

We were in Cuba for spring training in 1947 because of Jackie. Mr. Rickey called in the guys who'd expressed dissatisfaction. Each of us met with him individually. He just said, "You know, it looks like Jackie Robinson is going to make this team. Would you like to be traded?"

I said, "Yes, Mr. Rickey, I would."

"All right, but if I don't trade you, are you going to play any different just because he's on the team?"

"No, sir," I answered, "I'll play just as hard."

That was basically it. Nothing drawn out or unpleasant. It was very respectful and honest. And that honesty was the start of a great friendship between me and Mr. Rickey.

We used to travel by train back then, and when the Dodgers went on our first road trip, for 12 days, nobody wanted to sit with Jackie in the dining car.

But later we all got to know his character, and the longer we got to know him, the more respect we had for him. He became like one of the guys.

Now, when I got back home to Alabama, I had a couple of brothers who used the n-word. But there wasn't much talk about me playing with a black man. The conversations were about me being in the World Series.

Jackie and I became good friends. But I don't think we discussed the beginning of 1947 much. When Mr. Rickey died in 1965 in Columbia, Missouri, I flew in from Fort Worth for the funeral, and Jackie flew in from New York. We sat right next to each other in the second pew. That was satisfying.

That first five-minute conversation I'd had with Mr. Rickey led to many others. One day in 1948, he called me into his office and said, "Bobby, you've been on the bench so long they're starting to call you Judge. Would you like to go down to Fort Worth where you can be the player-manager?"

Sure, I said, and that's what I did. Pretty soon there was a joke going around the organization that the biggest contribution I made to the Dodgers was being sent down to Fort Worth so the team could bring up Roy Campanella.

But it was the start of my managerial career. Going through the experience with Jackie really helped me down the road. It came out in my relationship with Maury Wills and Hank Aaron and Felipe Alou and a lot of others.

And it really made a difference.

MAURY WILLS

◆◆

I HAD JUST about let go of my dream. I had started to think I wasn't going to make it to the majors. Okay, I told myself, I'll just try to be the best Triple-A shortstop I could be.

Then Bobby Bragan took over the team in Spokane. He embraced me. I think I was a chance for him to make amends. He said, "Maury, I've been watching you. You've got a lot of talent. You can run, you can throw, and you can field. But you're afraid of the curve."

If there's any fear in baseball, it's of getting hit with a pitched ball in the head. I was a righthanded hitter, and when that righthanded pitcher was coming around with that arm, I was shying away.

So I knew I was afraid of the curve, even though I'd never admitted it to anybody. People had said it to me before, and I'd denied it and wanted to fight them about it. No man wants to be told he's afraid of something. For some reason, when Bobby said that to me, it was as if God had just put his hands on my shoulders and said, "Son, keep quiet and listen."

"Did you ever think of switch hitting?" Bobby asked me. "You know, you've got nothing to lose. If you turn around and bat left against a righthander, you won't be bothered by his delivery. And if you can just hit the ball in the hole, with your speed the shortstop'll never throw you out. C'mon out tomorrow and I'll throw to you."

Bobby threw to me for about 20 minutes with me hitting lefthanded, and he taught me how to bunt. The same way Bobby taught me how to bunt is the way I teach it today. And I've taught it that way to players on 17 different big league teams. Two or three days later he came up to me before a game and he said, "They've got a righthander going today. As of now, you're a switch-hitter."

We were the visiting team, so I was the first batter of the game. I went up there like Bobby told me and tried to hit the ball to deep shortstop. First pitch was a fastball over the plate. I chopped at it, the bat clipped the top of the ball, and the ball hit home plate and bounced 50 feet in the air. Before the ball was in somebody's mitt I was already on first base. Stole second. Stole third. Scored a run. Came into the dugout.

"Hey, way to go, Wills."

"Thanks, Bobby."

Couple innings later, I got up again and tried to hit the ball to the right of the shortstop. I swung, hit another chop, and once again the ball hit home plate and went 50 feet in the air. By the time the ball came down, you know where I was. Stole second. Stole third. Scored another run.

My teammates came down to shake my hand, and I was beginning to feel like a baseball player again.

I said, "Bobby, can we keep working?"

"Oh, yeah," he said. "Oh, yeah."

A little later that season, Don Zimmer broke his toe. The Dodgers started calling around the league looking to trade for a shortstop, but they couldn't find anybody.

Once again, Bobby Bragan came to my rescue. He called down to LA and said to Buzzie Bavasi, "You guys lookin' for a shortstop, right? Well, you got one right here in the organization."

"Who?" Bavasi asked him.

"Wills."

"*Maury* Wills?" Bavasi said. "The guy's been around forever. He can't play."

And Bobby goes, "Oh, yes, he can. He's a different man now. He's a switch-hitter."

JIM "MUDCAT" GRANT

◆◆◆

JACKIE DIDN'T TALK like the average black guy. Being from California, he talked different. He was very crisp in his delivery. You could put Jackie behind a curtain, and if you just heard his voice you didn't know he was black.

Negro League players knew that if they got to the majors they might have to talk different. They were always joking around and saying, "We don't want to mess up the King's English." They'd be at a train station, for example, and the train'd be comin' around the corner but still out of sight, and one guy'd say, *very* crisply, "*He-yuh* comes the train."

Somebody else would then ask, also very crisply, "Well, how you knew?"

And the first guy, trying to sound like some English lord or something, would say, "I heard it *blew*."

It was just having fun. But things were really happening with language and voice about then. I'm not sure that Elvis' music would have been the same if it hadn't been for Jackie Robinson. The Elvis we all know might not have existed if there hadn't been a Jackie Robinson.

CHARLEY PRIDE

◆◆◆

I HEARD THIS story about a meeting that took place between Rickey and Jackie in 1946, after Jackie had a great year in the minor leagues up in Montreal.

Seems that Rickey called Jackie into his office, and when Jackie entered, Rickey said, "Sit down, n-word." Well, he didn't say *n-word*, of course. You know what he said.

Anyway, Rickey paused and said, "You wondering why I called you that?"

Jackie looked him in the eye and didn't say a word.

And Rickey said, "Well, you had a great year up in Montreal. And you're going to hear that a lot around the league when you're playing for the Dodgers.

Now what are you going to do when you hear people call you that?"

Another little pause.

"I'll tell you what you're going do when you hear that word," Rickey's said. "You're going to do nothing. You're going to hit, and you're going to field your position, and you're going to run the bases. You're going to play baseball. Nothing else. Because if you don't make it, nobody of your race is going to follow you."

That's the way I heard it. The slight difference between me and Jackie is that nobody sat me down and said, "Sit down, n-word, we're gonna have you sing country music."

See, RCA just put out my record. They didn't release any pictures of me. They let the record speak for itself.

Early on, I'd shocked a few people walking onstage in small venues, maybe 400. But they didn't have any idea what kind of reaction it would get when a black country singer came out onstage before 10,000 white people.

There was this big show up in Detroit. Flatt and Scruggs, Red Foley, Dick Curless, Merle Haggard . . . and Charley Pride.

As the show approached, the promoter started getting a little antsy. Backstage, the emcee said to me, "You want me to say something? You know, so as not to shock them when you come out."

I said, "No, just go out there and announce me as Charley Pride with RCA records."

My time comes. I'm still offstage, and I'm hearing the emcee say, "Our next entertainer has three singles movin', up the charts including the big hit "Just Between You and Me."

That brought a nice little round of applause.

"Now, ladies and gentlemen, put your hands together for a rising star from RCA Records, *Charleeeeey Priiiiiiiide!*"

I went out to all this applause, and then all of a sudden it was like someone turning down the volume so you could hear a pin drop.

But I had seen how it worked in the little venues, so I said, "Ladies and gentleman, I realize it's unique me coming out on a country music show wearing these burgundy pants."

When I said that, there was some laughter, and then a big round of applause, and I just hit it. From that matinee show to the 8 o'clock show that night I signed autographs. They had to assign a team of ushers to hold people back. And it's been that way for 40 years.

I'm sure that Jackie Robinson had something to do with that moment.

A little earlier, you know, Elvis got a lot of static—from black people as well as white people—for trying to sound colored. "Who's he think he is, trying to sound like us," black people would say. "Who's he think he is, trying to sound like them," white people would say.

But you know what? After Jackie, you listened to the radio and sometimes you didn't know. I heard the Righteous Brothers or Sam the Sham and the Pharaohs and at first I thought, Yeah, that's us. I was surprised to find out different.

And I was doing the same thing, only in reverse.

RACHEL ROBINSON

In 1956, we were looking for property in Stamford, Connecticut. One broker took me out to funny places, and I said to her that this was not really what I was looking for.

She finally said, "You'd be better off not looking in Stamford."

I think in some ways discrimination and racism were more insidious in the North, because you thought you were free but you really weren't.

So you see, it wasn't over for us just because Jack made it into baseball. When we finally located a place there, two or three families moved off the block.

It's very hard to fight an attitude. And these attitudes still exist today. You hear people say, "There's lots of opportunities, but *they* are lazy. *They* aren't working hard enough." Whatever. There are still barriers that haven't been removed.

But we did move in, and Jack started to think about things like mortgages. He came to see solutions in terms of politics and economics. It's not enough to be able to walk in a restaurant and be fed. It's not enough to get on the bus and sit wherever you want. The next step is ownership and investment. That's where Freedom National Bank came in.

If you're going to have economic development in a community, you've got to have a lending source that allows you to make the changes you want to make. You want to buy a house. You want to start a business. You can't if the bank is redlining your neighborhood in an unfair system.

Jack got very intrigued by the economic possibilities.

LOU JOHNSON

BACK IN THOSE days, you used to see pictures of Jackie and Rachel hugging and holding hands. You didn't see too many pictures of black people like that in those days. There's an emotional thing that goes along with that. Think about that.

Think about Rachel Robinson. If you buy a car and it ain't got no motor, it ain't gonna run. And that's what Rachel was—the motor of that relationship. If you ain't got a home, you ain't got nowhere to go. And that's what Rachel was—Jackie's home. She done seen the pain. She done been *in* the pain, man. That's what I look at.

And after Jackie died, Rachel carried the torch. She magnified what her husband had done. It doesn't get any better than that. Do you understand?

AL DOWNING

I'LL TELL YOU what opened my eyes. Remember, at the end of Jackie's career, when the Dodgers traded him to the Giants?

Jackie told them he'd retire before he'd play for the Giants.

That rankled a lot of people. A lot of people said, How could he do that? How could he stop playing baseball? But, of course, he could. He could do whatever he wanted to do within the law.

Jackie showed them that he could make his own decisions and control his own destiny.

TOMMY DAVIS

I *LOVED* HIM when he said he wasn't going to the Giants. *Vice President* of Chock full o' Nuts. Show me somethin', baby! Show me *somethin'*!

◆　◆　◆

SHARON ROBINSON

I CAN REMEMBER begging my father to support Kennedy in the 1960 election.

I was a 10-year-old girl, and in my school all the kids were supporting Kennedy, and their parents were too.

My fifth-grade teacher asked us to go home and ask our parents who they were supporting. I didn't know the difference between Kennedy and Nixon or a Republican and a Democrat. For me, it was all about saving face with my friends at school, because I hated being different anyway. I was already the only black kid around, so I said, "Dad, could you please support Kennedy!"

My father said, "I'm sorry, but I have to do what I believe in."

He didn't want the lumping of black people with a particular party. He wanted to look at each of the candidates, examine the record, and see who could be the most helpful.

Even when Nixon didn't take his advice about Dr. Martin Luther King Jr., and he realized this was not the guy he really wanted to support, he stuck with him through the election because he'd made a commitment. If my father was mad at Nixon, he could express his feelings directly to Nixon, but he honored his commitment.

But he didn't go with him in the *next* election.

JIM BROWN

WHEN A BLACK man supports a Republican, most people don't understand it. So there was controversy about Jackie working for Nelson Rockefeller as his special assistant for civil rights. He was also a friend of Richard Nixon. But so was I. We've got to tell the truth here.

Nixon was a great sports fan and was always reachable. So I think Jackie probably thought like I thought. If you were a Democrat or a Republican, that didn't really matter. If you were gonna get things done, you had to find a way to get to the White House and deal with who was there. So he was of that mind. To get inside and do something, rather than verbalize on the outside but never be able to put things into action.

There were people who didn't like his position because it was opposite that of Malcolm X.

But if you look at what Jackie was saying, he wasn't taking the position of an Uncle Tom. He was taking the position of an intelligent man who understood that the emancipation of black people had to come through working a certain way. That's why Freedom National Bank was such a great symbol. That's what Jackie had in mind.

One of the things that you have to do is work with the system. You can't work against the system, because you can never, ever destroy the system. So you must find people and ways to do that. Maneuvering among giants—or even having the understanding of that sort of politics—that's a whole different kind of ball game that Jackie was playing.

What Jackie was saying is this: If you slowly build and put systems in place, you'll get results. If you work hard, apply strong family values, and use education, economic power, and political power directly, you can damn near deliver yourself.

SHARON ROBINSON

DURING THE WHOLE Black Power movement, my father came off looking conservative in comparison to the revolutionaries, who were saying, *Let's get the weapons out there.*

Dad told me, "Sharon, black people shouldn't be picking up guns and going out there and doing battle. Why lead them in that direction?"

So he looked like he was conservative, and he was conservative in comparison to the revolutionaries. He didn't believe in a fast change like that. He knew it was going to take a lot of long, hard, ongoing, consistent work—and he was doing it. He was doing it in economic development. He was always doing it himself. He wasn't just talking.

TOMMY DAVIS

AFTER A WHILE, Jackie got involved in the civil rights marches. He was marching—and I was impressed. You know, he stood up against a lot of people. He spoke his mind.

Jackie had a message. Baseball was just part of the deal.

LEE ELDER

A longtime (1966-90) member of the PGA Tour, LEE ELDER in 1975 became the first African-American to play in the Masters.

◆◆

WE WERE BOTH on the same road, but Jackie was ahead of me, and I really wanted to know how he conducted himself in certain situations.

I'd been called nigger several times at exclusive places where you didn't really want to rock the boat. The thing was, I really wanted to play in tournaments, and so I didn't want to do things that would alienate people. But what do you do when the place where you're playing the tournament at won't let you in the clubhouse? What do you do if they won't let you eat with the players you're competing against?

So I asked Jackie how I could make it easier on myself. Discipline, he said. And that's what's what we talked about: discipline.

Jackie told me that the thing about being confronted with a situation you have no control over is that you have to use your best judgment. You have to decide how valuable the position you're in really is. I distinctly remember him saying. if you want to really accomplish something, a lot of times you have to look the other way.

I know that helped me prepare for going back to play in Pensacola. I had made the statement that I would never play in Pensacola again because in a tournament there in 1966 they refused to let the black players come into the clubhouse to eat. But I did go back in 1974, and I won the Monsanto Open there, and that was what qualified me for the Masters.

Jackie was gone by the time I got to Augusta, but he was definitely with me.

VIOLET PALMER

The first female NBA referee, VIOLET PALMER is an African-American.

◆◆

IT HIT ME a few years ago when I was on the phone with a friend and she said, "You know, you're like the female version of Jackie Robinson."

And I said, "Huh?"

"Think about it, Violet," she said. "You're doing something that no other woman has ever done in the entire world. Ever."

I was aware that what I was doing wasn't exactly ordinary. When I first started, I'd walk into the arena and everybody would be staring. I used to get the whispers: "Oh, we have the lady tonight." And they weren't saying it in a way that meant they were happy to see me. They were saying it because they thought I was an oddity.

People don't realize the effect that can have on you psychologically. You're a rookie to begin with. Plus you're uncomfortable knowing the microscope is on you. But you just work through it. You don't really know what an impact you're having, because you're just trying to get the job done and be successful.

A couple of years passed and the whispers stopped. Now every time I walk into the arena, it's just, "Hi, Violet."

Then you hear yourself telling little girls, "There's a glass ceiling up there. And I'm living proof that if you really want to you can break through it. Nobody can tell you what you cannot do. If you have the desire and the willpower, you can have your dreams."

And then one day your friend calls up and mentions you in the same sentence as Jackie Robinson.

I actually had to sit down and take a deep breath.

CARL ERSKINE

◆◆◆

WHEN MY SON Jimmy wins a gold medal in Special Olympics, I think Jackie had something to do it. I truly believe it was the momentum that Jackie started that brought handicapped people into the mainstream of society.

MAURY WILLS

◆◆◆

JACKIE ROBINSON BREAKING the color line wasn't something just for African-Americans. What about the Latin Americans who were black?

JOSÉ CANÓ

JOSÉ CANÓ is the father of New York Yankees second baseman ROBINSON CANÓ.

◆◆◆

I NEVER SAW Jackie Robinson play. In the Dominican Republic when I was kid, not many people had a TV. My family didn't. We had a radio. All the time on the radio I was hearing, Robinson this . . . Robinson that . . . Robinson, Robinson, Robinson. Jackie Robinson. The *great* Jackie Robinson.

I thought to myself, When I have a son, that's the name I'm going to give him. And I did.

Robinson isn't a common first name in the Dominican. When my son started to talk, we told him why he got his name. And he said, "I like it."

I didn't have any idea how things would turn out.

Now I turn on the TV and watch my son leave the dugout and run out to play second base for the New York Yankees. Sometimes it's hard to believe.

My son, Robinson Canó.

◆ ◆ ◆

CHAPTER TEN

RED LIGHT, GREEN LIGHT, CHA-CHA-CHA

I**T'S BROAD DAYLIGHT.** The 1950s. A man with dark skin crosses a street in St. Petersburg, Florida, against a traffic light. A policeman watches.

You guessed it. This story is headed toward the local jail. The twist in this tale is that the dark-skinned man is not from America. His name is Vic Pellot, he plays first base as well as the position has ever been played, and he comes from Puerto Rico.

At the police station, the captain asks Vic Pellot why he broke the law.

Pellot speaks little English. But he does his best to explain that he's come to the United States to play baseball in the Yankees organization, and he's simply confused by all the strange customs and rules.

When he wants to get a drink of water, he's been told, he must drink from the fountain opposite the one from which the white people drink. When he needs to go to the bathroom, he understands, he must go for the door that says "Colored" instead of "White." So when he saw the light turn green and all the white people on the corner crossed the street, he thought it only natural to wait until it turned red before *he* crossed.

Unfortunately, we'll never know what the police captain thought of this explanation or how the story ended because Vic Pellot isn't alive to finish it.

The 12-year major leaguer died in 2005. But his unique perspective left us all something to think about.

The trail that Jackie Robinson blazed was soon coursing with a different sort of traffic: black Latino ballplayers. These men weren't stepping out from the shadows like the black players in America. They came from the sunshine of the Caribbean. To their astonishment, they suddenly found themselves in a land where their flesh color made them inferior, their personalities made them suspect, and their language left them bewildered.

Vic Pellot learned how to solve the black man's age-old lodging dilemma in the new land. He once slept in a black funeral home. When the pronunciation of his last name sounded like a vulgar description of a female body part—to the ears of the French Canadians in the minor league town in Quebec where the Yankees shipped him—he adapted by changing his name from Vic Pellot to Vic Power. He figured out how to hit a Triple-A curveball well enough to hit a league-leading .349 in the American Association.

Glovework? His was out of this world, so easy for Vic Pellot—sorry, Power—that he flicked his glove like a Venus flytrap at pop-ups and leaped to catch shoulder-high throws to first just to add some spice for the fans.

But that flair created the one impediment he couldn't sail over: the stereotype of loosey-goosey nonchalance that would be held against nearly every Latin ballplayer who came to America. That, along with one too many white women being seen in the passenger seat of Vic's orchard-green Cadillac, meant that he was not destined to become the first black man to wear Yankee pinstripes.

The Yankees traded him, and when Vic Power eventually got to the majors, and as he bounced from Philadelphia to Kansas City to Cleveland to Minnesota to California, he collected seven Gold Gloves, once stole home twice in a single game, and smiled through it all.

Were Vic Power to arrive on the scene today, when one in three major league players is Hispanic and the game's highest-paid name is Rodriguez, there might be a chain of restaurants named after him.

Latinos have pushed past the initial barriers and blended into baseball so seamlessly that when one looks today at the love affair between the city of Boston and Papi Ortiz it's hard to imagine that the Red Sox didn't have a player of color for 12 years after Jackie—and that the beat writer for the *Boston Globe*, Bud Collins, once had his head smashed into a plate of beef Stroganoff by the Red Sox general manager for dwelling upon that fact in print.

It would take a book, not a chapter, to chronicle the rise of Latinos in major league baseball from the instant Jackie opened the door. Jackie's old boss, Branch Rickey, would play a huge role once more, siphoning Roberto Clemente and other Latin talent at bargain-basement prices in his new job with the Pittsburgh Pirates.

Such a book would show the gradual acceptance of Latino eccentricities like Juan Marichal's mesmerizing high kick, and Luis Tiant's corkscrew motion, which left batters shaking their heads and Fenway Park fans chanting, "Lou-*eee!* Lou-*eee!* Lou-*eee!*" It might mention the flood of calls that Orlando "Cha Cha" Cepeda received from people in the best of neighborhoods when he was traded to St. Louis and the Cardinals announcer, Jack Buck, let the public know over the air that the first baseman was looking for a home. It might even have a comment from my own brother, who, at the age of 13, sat on the front steps of our home and wept when he heard that his favorite player, Roberto Clemente, had died in a plane crash trying to bring supplies to hurricane victims in Nicaragua on New Year's Eve in 1972.

The book would bring us forward to Édgar Rentería's game-winning hit in the 1997 World Series and Ozzie Guillen's breakthrough as the first Latino manager to win a World Series when he led the White Sox to victory in 2005. And it would certainly include the incredible dedication to the craft of hitting by Albert Pujols, a man who hustles to the clubhouse after each at-bat to study his swing on video . . . and shatter the last vestiges of that old stereotype of the loosey-goosey Latin player.

Now there are baseball academies spread all over the Dominican Republic and legions of children dreaming the dream. Pellot and Clemente, Cepeda, and Marichal, Tony Oliva and Tony Pérez, Felipe Alou and Matty Alou and Jesús Alou, and so many others have paved new roads for the young Latinos thronging these shores. Roads with only green lights.

◆ ◆ ◆

TONY OLIVA

◆◆◆

ONE THING THAT helped develop my eyes was corn.

In Cuba, out in the country, we grow a lot of corn. If you get an ear of corn, and you take the kernels off, and you break the cob up, you can throw a chunk of it like it's a ball. It gives you all kinds of movement.

Let me tell you, if you can hit a piece of corncob or a bottle cap with a stick, you can hit any kind of pitching.

TONY PÉREZ

◆◆◆

WHERE I COME from in Cuba—the region is called Ciego de Ávila—we used to make baseballs out of cigar cartons. We'd start with a rock. Slice up the cartons, get the paper wet, and wrap them around the rock. Then we'd get some string and wrap it around to make it a little harder. Then we taped it . . . if we had tape.

JUAN MARICHAL

◆◆◆

YOUR BAT IN the Dominican Republic was often a piece of the branch off a tree—we call it the *vácima* tree. When you set it in the sun to dry, it became lighter, and you would trim and rub the handle until it became smooth.

TONY OLIVA

◆◆◆

I DIDN'T KNOW nothing about professional baseball. The first contract I got was for $250 a month. I do know one thing. You live in Cuba in the country in the 1950s, sometimes you don't make $250 a *year.*

So you go, and sure, you miss your family. You don't know anybody. You don't understand the people. You don't know if you can go in the restaurant or if they'll serve you.

Even the eating was hard. The way they make rice in Cuba is very soft and full of flavor. The way they make the rice here, it's stuck together. You can pick it up and throw it against the wall and it'll stick.

Finally, after I was in the States for a while, a guy from Puerto Rico gave me a piece of paper just before a road trip. It said: "Ham and eggs in the morning; fried chicken at night." I ate ham and eggs and fried chicken every single day for a long time.

TONY PÉREZ

"HAMBURGER." THAT WAS a hard word to say. To this day, it's hard for me to say hamburger. Then I learned the word "chicken." Chicken was easy. So it was chicken every day.

ORLANDO CEPEDA

WE LIVED IN Puerto Rico without a refrigerator or telephone. When I arrived in Miami with four others to try out for the New York Giants, I was 17. About the only word I knew in English was *béisbol*.

The Giants signed me after the tryout and sent me to Salem, Virginia. Then, the day before the season opened, my father died.

My father was a baseball star in Puerto Rico. But often he gambled away his paycheck. I used the $500 I got for signing with the Giants for his funeral and flew back to Puerto Rico. I had to change planes to get home. I wonder now, How did I change planes? I was alone. I couldn't speak English. It was confusing. How did I do that?

I didn't want to come back to America. But my mother said, "You told your father that no matter what, you were going to make it."

My brother was in Korea, and we needed the money. So after the funeral I came back to Virginia. I was miserable, crying every night.

Everyone knew the kid from Puerto Rico was lonely, and word reached this white guy who played for the Kingsport Cherokees. One day, he came over to the black side of town, where I was staying, just to say hello to me. I was staying at Mrs. Davenport's. And so when this white guy knocks on the door and asks for me, they come to me and say, "Orlando, the police are looking for you." That's the only reason a white person ever came to the black side of town in Salem, Virginia.

The thing is, the manager's daughter liked me. She was about 15. And she came over to Mrs. Davenport's looking for me. The next day, the team found out and shipped me out.

Actually, I didn't know it but the team released me. The guy who wrote my autobiography with me found out a lot of things I didn't know. I didn't really understand what was going on at the time. But I've learned as a Buddhist that one thing leads to another, good or bad. At just that time, the guy who played third base for the club in Kokomo, Indiana, got hurt, and they needed a third baseman for 10 days.

I wanted to go home. But the guy who signed me said, "Go to Kokomo, stay there for 10 days, and then bring the money back to your mother."

Kokomo, Indiana. The Ku Klux Klan was strong there, had been for a long time.

But the manager in Kokomo, Walt Dixon, took care of me. I've been so lucky to meet some very nice people. You know, I don't remember the bad people. The bad people don't deserve to be remembered. But I'll never forget the good ones.

Walt Dixon said to me, "You're gonna hit cleanup, and you're gonna play every day. The rest is up to you."

I hit .393.

My father always said that real ballplayers are born with the tools. We always have them with us. So wherever we are, all we need to do is figure out how to use them.

FELIPE ALOU

◆◆

I REMEMBER WHEN I first went to the minor leagues. Lake Charles, Louisiana. The Evangeline League.

First game, this guy hit a ball clean over my head. Now, I was a track-and-field guy—fresh from the Pan Am games—and I could really run.

The ball was a line drive and I went after it. It had rained, the ground was very wet, and that slowed the ball when it hit the ground. I caught it on the first hop with my back to home plate.

If you were at home plate, it must've looked like Willie Mays' famous catch. And there were no fans in the outfield to see that I caught it off the hop.

I turned around, looking for someone to make a relay to. But the umpire thought I'd caught the ball on the fly, and he gave the out sign. My teammates were all running out toward me to congratulate me on this fabulous play—you see, it turned out to be the last out of the game and we won.

The other team ran out onto the field to argue. But there was nobody who could say they saw what really happened.

I was trying to apologize, to say what really happened. But I couldn't speak English, and nobody understood!

So I was a hero. And it was the only time I was a hero, because a new rule was passed in the Evangeline League that blacks couldn't play, and they wouldn't let me on the field much after that.

If you look in the record books, you'll see I got only nine at-bats in over a month in Louisiana. My teammates in Lake Charles were beautiful people. One time, as we were going into a stadium, all the white guys bunched together and tried to hide me in the middle. But the people at the stadium saw me and said I couldn't come in. And I was pulled out of the group.

MANNY MOTA

To us in the Dominican, Felipe was really The Man. He was the first. He went through a lot, and he told us what to expect.

We knew that we weren't going to be served in some restaurants because Felipe told us.

"You're going to feel bad because that would never happen in our country," he told us. "But you're in a different country with different rules. You have to obey the laws."

You don't ignore the situation. But there's nothing you can do to change it. It was a very big adjustment, learning to control your emotions.

TONY OLIVA

It's hard to imagine that anybody would want to intentionally hit somebody in the head or kill somebody. I didn't know if they really wanted to throw at me or if it was just the kind of baseball they used to play. I know I spent a lot of time on the ground.

Minnie Minoso ought to be in the Hall of Fame. He came up from Cuba not long after Jackie. He spent more time on the ground than me. And that says a lot. Because when I came up, I spent more time on the ground than I did standing up.

Sometimes the other team's manager would to go to the mound and talk to the pitcher. The next pitch would be right at my head.

In Baltimore, early in the 1964 season, Steve Barber hit me right in the center of the helmet. Right on the TC logo for Twin Cities. They took me to the hospital to be checked out, and I missed the game the following day. The day after that, I played both games of a doubleheader and hit a home run. I was lucky.

The more they threw at me, the better I got.

FELIPE ALOU

◆◆

WE WERE UNDER the impression that once we made it to the big leagues we walked around with some kind of tag that let everyone know we were big leaguers. But that was false. We were rejected and denied food at many a place.

They never told us up front they wouldn't serve us. But we'd sit at the table and no waiter would show up. Meanwhile, all the people who came in after us would have water set in front of them as soon as they were seated, and they would get their food as soon as it was cooked.

There was a time we played in Pittsburgh. After the game, Orlando Cepeda and I put on suits that we'd just bought. You know, ballplayers don't dress up anymore. But back then it was always suit and tie. Very sharp.

So we dressed up in our brand-new suits and went to eat at a restaurant one block from the hotel. When we got there, all the other people coming through the door were led to a table. But not us. We knew they saw us. You're talking about two well-dressed men in their mid-20s. So finally, a guy from the restaurant comes over and he says, "What are you guys lookin' for? We don't have any open jobs right now."

That was just another way of telling us we weren't wanted. So Orlando and I went back to the hotel. And we ate room service in our brand-new suits.

◆ ◆ ◆

ORLANDO CEPEDA

WE HAD A lot of talent on the Giants. We had a lot of guys with great numbers. But we were never a unified team. We had whites. We had blacks. And we had Latinos. On the road, each group dressed in a different area of the clubhouse. The manager, Alvin Dark, only separated us further.

One day, Dark called all the Latin ballplayers behind second base and told us we had to stop speaking Spanish in the clubhouse. He said the other guys were complaining that they couldn't understand us. I didn't believe there were complaints. And if there were complaints, why didn't the players come straight to us?

I said, "Look, I'm from Puerto Rico. I'm proud of my heritage. These guys from the Dominican Republic are proud of theirs. We're not going to stop speaking our language."

I had a portable record player that I carried around. I loved to listen to Latin music. Alvin didn't want me to carry my record player. He said I was too loose. He thought that I was too happy or something. His solution for that was to make the game miserable for me.

It got to the point where going to the ballpark was like going to hell. This was 1961, 1962, 1963. I had good seasons, but think of how good they could have been. I led the league in home runs in 1961 with 46. And that was playing in Candlestick Park. Do you know how many the wind blew back against right-handed hitters? Just ask Willie Mays. Plus, playing with all that tension . . .

Years later, Alvin Dark sent me a note, something he wrote from deep inside, asking me to forgive him. I'm not bitter about it. Looking back, maybe I was too sensitive for my own good. But there's a big difference when you come to the park and you feel like you're treated with respect, and when you know you're not.

Have you ever heard of Ino Rodriguez? He was from Colombia. We played together in the minor leagues. One of the best players I've ever seen. He died not long ago. But he didn't like the way he was treated in America and he just said, "I don't want to play here anymore." He went home. That's why you never heard of him.

When I was traded to the Cardinals, I realized what a team could do when there was mutual respect in the clubhouse and everybody got along. In 1967, we won the World Series.

FELIPE ALOU

◆◆

I LOVE ALVIN Dark. Love him now. I sure didn't love him when he was my manager. But after that, he changed. He understood that he had been wrong.

I would say probably because of lack of knowledge. There have been so many mistakes made by men and nations because of lack of knowledge. Lack of knowledge leads to lack of respect, because you really don't know who you're dealing with.

Alvin Dark was a guy who, at 39, had never managed at any level, and was given the team. I don't know if he brought some of his feelings from the year before when he was a player, and he had some black teammates. Who knows? But he changed with time.

When he was finished as a manager, and when we were finished as players, he came to us. He apologized to every one of us that he ran into. He apologized after he understood that what he did was out of ignorance, not knowing us, and not knowing himself.

When you find the truth out about anything, you can change. There have been many men in this game who were wrong, and then found out the truth, but they were stubborn and they wouldn't change. They wouldn't back off their stance because of pride or whatever.

I was elated to see this man who once was my boss, this tough guy, come out to meet me and be so humble. To me, that is what the truth does to a man.

We found out what a nice man he was. And he found out what a beautiful man he is.

MANNY MOTA

◆◆

THERE WERE MANY misunderstandings because of the differences in culture.

One time when I was with the Pirates, we were playing in Chicago. I was in leftfield, and Don Kessinger hit a line drive in my direction. As I started to go for the ball, I lost my balance. So I put my glove hand down to stop my fall and—I don't know how it happened —but my foot stepped on the glove. The glove came off my hand, but there was no time to pick it up. Forget about the glove! I had to react to the ball. So I ran down the line drive and caught it with my bare hands.

Kessinger got really, really mad. He thought I did that to show him up. Light-hitting shortstop. You know, I don't even need a glove. "Why did you do that to me?" he said to me after the game. "And you made it look so easy on purpose!"

So I explained what happened and told him, "Don, the only reason it looked so easy is because that's how I learned to play. In the Dominican, nobody has any gloves."

TONY PÉREZ

YOU COULDN'T EXPLAIN a lot of things. It was more than the language barrier. You couldn't explain to the white players the bond between the Latinos. We could be from Cuba or the Dominican Republic or Puerto Rico, it didn't matter. We all came from places where family is everything. Even though we played for different teams, we were like family.

We loved to talk. Marichal would always tell me, "You're never gonna see a fastball from me. I'm gonna throw you a lot of different stuff." We used to joke around about it all the time, and then one day a funny thing happened.

Marichal threw me a fastball, and I hit a home run. I started running around the bases. And he came after me. He was running side by side with me, screaming, "You're never gonna get another one. You'll never see another fastball from me as long as I live. Never again!"

He went all the way to third base with me, screaming the whole time, and then he walked back to the mound.

Now, Juan Marichal wanted to win as much as anybody. But we had the kind of thing you have as kids. It's hard to describe. It's very Latino.

I got back to the dugout and all the American guys were asking, "What happened? What he'd say?"

How can you explain?

OZZIE GUILLEN

I KNEW IT was special. It was like God had come to my country. But there was no way for me to realize *how* special. Because there was no way for me to know that it would be the only time I'd get to see Roberto Clemente play.

I was very young when Clemente came to Venezuela. He was playing in the Caribbean World Series. I was in the stands at the game when Puerto Rico was playing against the Dominican Republic. Just watching him walk out to the outfield was amazing. Every eye was on him, the way it is when Miss Universe walks on the *pasarela*.

I wish I could remember everything about that day. It was impossible to get another ticket when he played against Venezuela. Completely sold out. We had to listen to the game on the radio. People would take a break from whatever they were doing when it was coming time for him to hit. That's what I remember.

I was only 8 years old when he died. It was New Year's Eve 1972. New Year's Eve is always a big party in Venezuela and the family gets together.

Roberto had just gotten his 3,000th hit that season. When we heard about the crash, I remember my father shaking his head and asking, "Why now?" It was impossible to understand. It was mysterious.

There was an earthquake in Nicaragua. He gets on a plane to help bring in supplies. The plane crashes. Then he's gone.

Nobody had the opportunity to bury him. Nobody had to the opportunity to go to the cemetery and pray for him. We don't know where he is. It happened so quickly.

Roberto Clemente was proud to be a black Puerto Rican. That was really important, coming at that time when there was so much hatred because of color. He treated people with kindness. But he never kissed anybody's butt to conform. He was never a hypocrite. He said what was on his mind. He opened the door for so many of us.

Last summer I was in Pittsburgh, Roberto's town, managing the American League All-Star team when Major League Baseball honored his memory. His widow, Vera Clemente, was there on the field for the tribute.

Roberto Clemente was being honored like Babe Ruth or Jackie Robinson. I knew how special the moment was.

There were tears in my eyes.

◆ ◆ ◆

TONY PÉREZ

◆◆

FOR A LONG TIME, I never thought there'd be a baseball stadium in Miami. I never saw Miami as a baseball town.

When I look back, I realize I came up at just the right time. All the problems that Jackie Robinson and the others had to endure were almost over by the time I got up to the minor leagues in 1960.

It was a different world by then. In the South, I used to come up to bat and people would scream: "Hey, Pérez, where's your green card? Go back to Cuba!" But that was about it. It was a different world than the 1940s and the 1950s.

Then came the great days in Cincinnati with the Big Red Machine. We were family. We knew each other like we'd been together all our lives.

Not too many people in baseball had the career I had. All-Star Games. Two World Series rings as a player, and another World Series as a coach for the Reds. Then I came down to Miami as an executive with the Marlins, and we won two World Series.

A lot of great players don't get to one World Series. I've got five different World Series rings as a player, coach, and executive. I don't think there's one person who has it all like I do.

People ask me: Anything else?

I put a baseball in my son's hands before he could even remember. And I saw him play in the major leagues. What else is there? Now, I just have to make my wife happy.

◆　◆　◆

CHAPTER ELEVEN

THE SOUND OF SILENCE

ONE SUMMER NIGHT not long ago, a minor league owner named Mike Veeck held a baseball game where no one could cheer.

The fans covered their mouths with duct tape and held up signs saying "Yea!" "Boo!" and "Hey, Beer Man!" at appropriate times. The concessions workers were dressed as librarians. Ushers decked out as golf marshals held up signs that demanded "Quiet, Please!"

Veeck called it "Silent Night."

As the son of Bill Veeck, Mike came by his audacity honestly. Gagging the audience was just a gag, of course. A sports fan's inalienable right to cheer his lungs out could never actually be taken away. Or could it?

Yes, it could, and Jimmy Carter, the 39th president of the United States, could tell you about the day he witnessed it: June 22, 1938.

There were no televisions back then in Plains, Georgia, where Jimmy grew up, and only a few radios among the poorer households. So black farmhands from all over the area gathered near the Carter house that evening, desperate to hear the radio broadcast of Joe Louis' heavyweight title defense against Max Schmeling.

With the world marching towards war, more than a title belt was riding on the fight. Max Schmeling was a German, held up by Adolf Hitler and the Nazi propaganda machine as physical evidence that the Aryan race was superior. Joe Louis was an African-American, held up by blacks all across the United States as physical evidence of what a dark-skinned man could accomplish.

Two years earlier Schmeling had smashed his right hand through a flaw in the Brown Bomber's defense and knocked him out in the 12th round for the American's first defeat. Louis regained the championship against another fighter, but he had to beat Schmeling now to make his title authentic.

As hard as it is to believe today, a lot of the kids in Jimmy Carter's all-white school, along with their parents, were rooting for

Schmeling. Remember, this was the segregated South.

Earl Carter was a decent man. He agreed to place his radio in the front window of his home so the black crowd could listen in from his yard. The blacks were grateful . . . and careful.

The bell rang for Round 1 and Louis left his corner like a focused storm. He backed Schmeling up, pummeled him, paralyzed him, hit him so hard in the liver that ringsiders could hear the German scream. Three times, Schmeling went down. The fight was stopped after only 2 minutes 4 seconds.

During those 124 seconds, when the wildest hopes and dreams of all those black farmhands were being realized, they didn't make a sound. When the broadcast concluded, they said, "Thank you, Mr. Earl," then walked in silence back across the railroad tracks. Free black men, *Americans*, their emotions and voices were strangled by their fear of the possible response of white Americans if they were heard cheering for an American knockout of a German. It was only when they'd all squeezed into a shanty a few hundred yards away that they let out a roar, one that didn't stop until dawn.

If that seems so far in the past, fast-forward to the mid-1960s and consider what it was like for African-American ballplayers when the civil rights movement heated up. They were in a rare position. Men with microphones and pads and pencils approached them and asked for their opinions and feelings. Millions of fans who admired them on the field would be able to read or listen to what they had to say.

Nearly all of these men responded as if they were on Jimmy Carter's front lawn the night of June 22, 1938. "We were handcuffed," said Billy Williams of what he and other black ballplayers felt when asked for their thoughts on the civil rights movement. That's how it is when the price of speaking out might be the end of your livelihood.

Muhammad Ali spoke out, refused to be inducted into the Armed Forces during the Vietnam War, and lost his ability to earn a living for three and a half years. Martin Luther King was assassinated in April 1968. Then sprinters John Carlos and Tommie Smith showed their solidarity with the Black Power movement by raising black-gloved fists on the victory stand at the Mexico City Olympics—and were immediately whisked away and vilified. That summer, riots broke out in inner cities across America.

When you listen to ballplayers like Dick Allen and Lou Johnson reflecting on those times, you realize the value of a voice, what can happen when it's taken away, and what a man might have to do to get it back or even find it for the very first time.

◆ ◆ ◆

JAMES EARL JONES

◆◆◆

VERY FRANKLY, WHEN I came out of the Army after the Korean War, I expected there to be a race war. President Truman made a great effort to integrate the Armed Forces, and in the service we had pretty much solved it. But in civilian life we were far from it, especially in the South. This created a huge problem. You had young black soldiers who were used to being treated like men in the Army coming home and being treated like shit.

When the race war didn't happen, when we had opportunities to explore other ways of solving our social problems, I thought that God had smiled on the whole nation. That whatever happened afterward was supposed to happen and should have happened sooner.

One of the great ironies was that when President Lyndon Johnson pushed through the Civil Rights Act in the 1960s, it was then that things really got ugly. That's when the riots started.

To understand that, you've got to understand how much pain and how much anger people had swallowed up to that point. Once there was a glimmer of hope, that's when the anger found an outlet. It sounds very self-destructive, but it was natural to me. It was a release.

Every African-American male in the country was saying to himself, Why did I swallow all that shit over all those years?

DICK ALLEN

◆◆◆

THERE'S A DIFFERENCE between *muhfuhgger* and *sonovabitch*. A brother says, "Hey, muhfuhgger," and he don't mean anything by it. It's a way of saying, "How you doin'?"

Me and my wife have kids, that makes me a muhfuhgger. But I can't be nobody's sonovabitch. You're callin' my mama a dog. White guys take it for granted. They call everyone a sonovabitch. But if there's one thing a brother detests, it's being called a sonovabitch. Say it, and you're playing with your life.

The fight happened in my second full season in Philly. I was at third base fielding ground balls during batting practice, and Frank Thomas was in the cage, hitting. Frank's nickname was the Big Donkey. But I used to call him Lurch. Remember the butler on *The Addams Family*?

Johnny Callison came over to joke around, and he wanted to have some fun with Frank. The night before, Frank had struck out trying to bunt. So Johnny waits for Frank to take a big swing and miss, and he yells, "Hey, Lurch!"

"You rang?" Frank answered him.

"Why don't you try to bunt instead?" Johnny yelled.

But Frank didn't come back at Johnny. He came back at me: "What are you trying to be, another Muhammad Clay, always running your mouth off?"

Now that I'm older, I wonder if maybe he was just trying to play and didn't know how. What was in his mind, I don't know. But I'd seen him offer brothers a soul handshake, then bend their thumbs way back. I'd seen him toss a quarter in the air and ask a brother for a shoeshine. And I'd told him I don't go for that kind of stuff. This wasn't Little Rock, 1963. This was Philadelphia, 1965.

So I walked down to the cage and said to him, "Say that again and I'll hit you right where those words come from."

He kept going on and on, saying something like, "You'll get a meal out of me, but I'll get a sandwich out of you." Something like that.

I said, "What's all that about? We're wearing the same uniform. And I asked you not to do that."

And he went, "Ahhhh, you sonovabitch . . ."

"What did you say?"

"Sonavabitch . . ."

Bam! Left hook. He went down, and the next thing I know it seemed like everyone was grabbing me, you know how they do when they're trying to break up a fight.

Everybody was holding me but nobody was holding Thomas. "Richie! Richie!" I remember hearing Ruben Amaro's voice. "Richie! Richie!" Frank had picked up the bat. Now he was swinging. I turned around, swung Ruben around with me, and got in a position to block it. *Bam!* The bat comes down hard on my shoulder.

Now I'm firing. Left hand, right hand. It was like they were all against me. I fired at every fucking thing that touched me. Left hook, right hand, bob and weave. Didn't care. Didn't care. I was fightin' for my own spirit, man. I've got kids. I don't have to eat no shit, and they don't have to eat no shit. I fired at everybody. *Everybody.* Then I heard the voice of our catcher, Pat Corrales: "Get off of him! Get off of him!"

And just like that, everything came back into focus.

There I was, that little kid from Wampum, Pennsylvania, who'd learned to hit with rocks and a broom handle. *And now, coming to the plate, No. 42, Jackie Robinson . . .* All that Jackie had built up for everybody to carry, I'd just torn down. Oh, jeez, I felt *so* small. Exactly what Jackie would never have done, I'd just done. Can you have any idea what I felt like? I'm still so ashamed of it today.

My shoulder swelled up but I played anyway. We lost 10-8. Frank hit a home run.

Man, we were wearing the *same* uniform. After the game, we were over it. I shook his hand and apologized. But I said to him, "If you do it again, I'll do it again. I'll respect you as a man if you'll respect me as a man."

Gene Mauch, the manager, called me into his office. He picked up the phone and called upstairs. Called John Quinn, the general manager. Mauch said it was either Thomas or me. And he wanted Thomas out.

Gene came out of his office and said to the guys, "I don't want to hear or read a thing about this. If a single word is spoken to the press, it'll cost you $1,500. And $2,500 for you, Allen."

They released Frank immediately. That hurt me bad. Now he needed a job. Fortunately, he hooked up with Houston. He had a bunch of beautiful kids. A while back, I was in an old-timer's game, and Frank's son came over to say hello. Mark. A priest.

See, I *like* Frank. It's important that you understand that. We send each other Christmas cards. I know how good a man that experience made of him. And now I have the respect of his children and his grandchildren. He didn't want his grandchildren to make the same mistake just 'cause they didn't know.

Well, now they know.

◆ ◆ ◆

BACK THEN, THOUGH, I couldn't even tell my side of the story. I wasn't allowed. It didn't really matter what I had to say. If you were black, where could you get a soapbox to stand on so that anybody could hear you?

They say that I was controversial. Well, you need two sides to make a controversy. But there weren't two sides. It was one-sided. It was their story, and I became the villain.

When I say that it was their story, I mean that if you talked to the guys at *The Philadelphia Inquirer* or the *Philadelphia Daily News*, it would still come out the way they wanted it. It was still *their* story. The columnists used me as a punching bag and a pawn. One would try to one-up the next. After a while, I didn't want to talk to anyone.

See this scar on my hand? I got that a couple of years after the Thomas fight. It was a rainy night, and my car wouldn't start. I was pushing it, and I slipped, and my right hand went through the headlight. Oh, jeez. Blood was everywhere. My mother was at the house, and she ran out with a towel soaked in water and tied it around my arm. Saved my life. I was in surgery for five hours. Came out with a cast up to the bicep, and missed the rest of the season.

But here's the thing about it. All kinds of stories started circulating, stuff like me being knifed in a bar or by a jealous lover. That's what happens when you're the villain.

I worked hard to get my hand in shape. When I got back the next season, I could hit. But I had some trouble throwing, and believe me, I heard about it from the Philly fans. Maybe the whole thing would have been different if we'd been winning. Even when I was Rookie of the Year, in 1964, we had that meltdown in September and lost the pennant to the Cardinals.

So you had a team that wasn't winning, and you had a ready-made villain on it making the big bucks: me. In 1968, pennies began to fly at me from the bleachers at Connie Mack Stadium. Then bolts and batteries. I had to wear a batting helmet on offense *and* defense. Some of the guys on the bench cracked up when they saw me wearing it in leftfield. That's where the nickname Crash came from. Started out as Crash Helmet. Then it became Crash. I just made up my mind. I don't care what they throw at me. I'm not goin' down.

Campy used to say there's got to be a lot of boy in the man. Maybe, but that was all gone for me. If I could have played without all that stuff I had to put up with, what it was all doing to my head . . . well, let's just say I'll never know what I could've done. I don't know if I'd have made all those stops at the bars. I just don't know. There's a lot of things we'll just never know . . .

You know what the irony is? In a lot of ways, I was the type of player that the old-school fan could really appreciate. But the folks in Philadelphia stopped noticing that I could run the bases. They stopped noticing that I could bunt, move the runner over, do all the little things that make up the game within the game. I was the villain.

You may have heard all the stories about the tension between me and Gene Mauch—and, yeah, we had our arguments, and he fined me a lot of money over the years. But we were both really trying to do the same thing: win. It's just that when you're not winning, everything you disagree on becomes a confrontation, gets blown out of proportion.

I remember once when I started growing an Afro and facial hair. One day Mauch came over to me and said, "Clean it up." I looked down at my uniform to see if I had gotten it dirty. He's talking about my *hair*? Shit, I thought I'd come to play baseball. I didn't come to win any beauty contests.

Then you start to look around and realize there were no Afro combs in the clubhouse for the black players. The way they work it in the big leagues, you'd give the clubhouse guys fees for amenities, and they'd put the supplies in your locker. But there wasn't shit in there for us black players. You'd pay the same money as everyone else, but you never saw an Afro comb in your locker. Nothing in there for *you* to use. Well, there was a razor. But the brothers, man, we got pimples and shit. We used Murray's Magic Shave. So we went to the clubbies and asked them to get it for us, and they came back and said, "No, there ain't two sets of rules here, one for the whites and one for blacks." Isn't that something? Arguing about Afro combs and Murray's Magic Shave?

They used to call Connie Mack Stadium the House of Gloom. The booing never stopped. So one day I wrote "Boo" in the dirt with my cleats at first base. I started to write a lot of messages. I even traded messages with one of the umpires, Lee Weyer. It was fun. Then he got orders from the league office to stop, and if I wrote in the dirt again he's got to run me out. I'd never been run out of a game in my life.

Everything became a confrontation. I remember one game, the big signs above the bleachers caught my eye: Philco . . . Cadillac . . . Coca-Cola. Something clicked. And I thought, Here they are, telling me to stop writing in the dirt, but it doesn't seem to be against the rules to do a little advertising. So I wrote "Coke" in the dirt. Next time up, I told myself, I'll try to hit that Coca-Cola sign in left. That's what I'll do. Maybe that'll shut everybody up.

Next at-bat, *Bam!* The ball went *over* the damned Coke sign. When I got back to the dugout, everybody was talking about how far the ball went. Me, I was pissed that I didn't hit the sign.

People sprayed "Nigger Go Home" all over my new house. I'd come home and find out that my kids were hearing it at school. The whole town seemed to be eating me alive.

Finally, someone threw a brick through the picture window in the front.

Right where the kids played. The kids weren't there because a dear friend of mine, Clem Cappazolli, was taking us out for lunch. We came back home and the place was bombarded. Clem went crazy.

How could I go on the road anymore? My mind was . . . well, you can guess where my mind was.

Then there was the time in 1969 I was late for a game and got suspended. My fault. Had one of my horses goin' at Monmouth Raceway in Jersey. We had a twi-night doubleheader against the Mets, and I got caught in traffic tryin' to get out to Shea. I heard I'd been suspended on my car radio and went straight on back to the hotel. But I didn't hear from the manager, Bob Skinner, or anybody in the front office, so I didn't bother going out to the ballpark for the second game. I thought to myself that maybe my baseball days were over.

Later, Skinner asked me, "Why didn't you come to the ballpark?"

I said, "You suspended me."

He said, "Yeah, but that was only for one game."

Why didn't someone tell me? If you screw up, they take you to the principal's office, don't they? But nobody contacted me. Instead, they told the world that I was suspended. That's like telling the world they don't want me there.

It was time to go. At the end of the season, the Phillies sent me to St. Louis in a seven-player deal that brought Curt Flood to Philadelphia. Or would have, except Curt said that the buying and selling and trading of people ended a hundred years ago, and that he wasn't going to be traded. Remember, the Dodgers tried to trade Jackie Robinson to the Giants, and Jackie said, No, I'll retire first, and he did. Curt went Jackie one better: He sued baseball over the reserve clause.

So I went to St. Louis, and it was like night and day. First-class operation all the way. My first at-bat there, the fans give me a standing ovation. I tip my hat, but the cheers don't stop. I step out of the box and tip my hat again, but still they keep cheerin'. Man. Tears were in my eyes. I was young again. After all the boos for all those years in Philadelphia, I could relax and swing the bat. I was happy.

We went to Philly for a series, and the first game, I hit a home run. When I got to home plate, I lifted my fist in the air. Some people interpreted it as some kind of racial statement, a Black Power salute. What I was really saying was that all I had ever wanted to do was win and be happy.

I got voted a starter for the National League All-Star team. I hit 30 home runs in 102 games heading into August. The Cardinals club record for a season was 43. And I had all of August, September, and October to go. Then I tore a hamstring sliding into second base. I went back to Pennsylvania to heal it. I knew my body. I'd healed my hand. But the club didn't want me to leave St. Louis. They weren't happy. But I knew what was best for my body. So I stayed at home.

I came back at the tail end of the year. The Phillies were moving to Veterans Stadium the following season, and I wanted one last chance to play at Connie Mack. I shouldn't have been out there, but I begged Red Schoendienst to put me in the lineup. I came up for what would probably be my last time at Connie Mack. *Bam!* Fastball into the leftfield seats. As I went around the bases I looked up at the crowd, the press box, the Coke sign. Then I stepped on home plate and just kept going. I was dressed and gone before the Philadelphia writers could ask me for a comment or anything. This was *my* story, not theirs. And that home run was all I had to say.

A few days after the season was over, I was traded to LA. *I get it!* Now, I'm seen as some kind of quick fix. I had a good year, not a great one, with the Dodgers. And then there were three good years with the White Sox, playing with Chuck Tanner. My first season there, I was named the AL MVP. But even then, what did you see on the cover of *Sports Illustrated*? A picture of me smoking a cigarette in uniform.

I'll never know what my life would have been like if I'd had a smile on my face in every picture you saw of me.

LOU JOHNSON

◆◆◆

I WANTED TO be on that floor. But there wasn't no way in the world for me to get on that floor without putting on a white jacket. So I put on the white jacket and got a latrine brush. That identifies you as being part of the janitorial service. I must've been 13 years old. That was my pass to see a University of Kentucky basketball game.

See, in the South back then, you learned *Yes* and *No*. Weren't no *Maybes*. *Yes*, you can. *No*, you can't. And if you were black, this wasn't even a question. You were not getting into that arena when the University of Kentucky played basketball . . . unless you were wearing that white jacket.

I wanted to play basketball at the University of Kentucky badder than anything. And I got to go where I wanted. I got to the floor of that arena. Got to the floor with that white jacket. But I had no voice. I cheered silently.

I turned a *No* into a *Yes* the only way I could, the only way that was open to me. Psychologically, I paid a price for that. When you were black in the South back then, you learned to succeed by lying. Society was set up to make us liars.

And the ego part of it was that I'd go out to a pickup basketball game on Sunday and tell everyone I'd seen Kentucky play.

Man, you ain't been nowhere!

But I *was* there. Now, I was a star. There was a future in that, I could tell. The future was just being in an arena of stars. See, that's how you set plans. Now I know what to look for if I get the chance. You can become this or you can become that. This goes here and that goes there. But you need to be on that floor to get the idea what it looks like.

When I was in high school, two white boys in a car called over to me and asked me where so-and-so was. I put my head forward to answer them, poked my head in there, and they punched me right in the face. Hit me right in the face and drove off.

But there was some traffic that slowed them down, and I outran their car. I outran their car, pulled 'em out, and beat the fuck out of 'em. I didn't care. I vented myself and it felt good, real good. I had a voice. But it wasn't *my* voice. It was anger.

Our high school basketball team won the state championship. Same year, the white high school in Lexington won the state championship. We followed them around all summer, and finally got them on the court, and just beat their asses.

To this day, people don't know I could play basketball. There was no chance for me to play on that court at Kentucky. Adolph Rupp as the coach? Give me a freakin' break. People know I could play baseball. But baseball was never, ever, *ever* on my mind back then. My dream was to be a star on the basketball court at the University of Kentucky.

Baseball became my job.

I played for the Yankees in Olean, New York. I played for different teams. Bounced around the Negro Leagues. Released. Released. Released.

In the minor leagues, we had it worse than the guys in the majors. They had New York and Chicago. We had Don't Stop Here, Mississippi, and Keep Going, Georgia.

Nigger. Black dog. I heard everything. You don't let them see the hurt. You don't show emotion. You don't let the white person see you cry. That's a sign of weakness. So we laughed. Laughing was my tears. Go back to what I told you about lies.

I used to think I didn't move up in baseball because I was black. I know now that I wasn't prepared technically. But it was confusing because I could hit.

I'd be hitting .300 and they'd take me out of the lineup and put a white boy in—that made me angry. I'd see that lineup card and didn't even wait for the manager to get to the office. I'd go straight to him and let him know what I thought. Wouldn't even let time water it down.

They called me an angry man. Guy asked me one time, "Why is it the black ballplayers attack the ball so hard?" And I told him, "It's white."

I'd call my mother. I'd be burdened and all tied up inside, and I'd just call her up to hear her voice.

She'd say, "What's wrong?"

"Nuthin', Mom. I'm fine."

She'd say, "No, you've got your hands in your pockets."

She always told me that in order to receive the gifts, you had to keep your hands open.

You know who suffers the most when you're angry and lashing out? *You know who?* Your family. Your livelihood is in jeopardy, and you put that anger inside, but it comes out. It comes out all over your family. I've been married four times, and I'm just getting my kids back in my life.

You know where I saw opportunity? Venezuela. That's where I learned to play. Color don't make no difference there. I was one of the crowd. We had freedom to go anywhere at any time. Learned to eat. Give me some cornflakes *con leche*! Oh, man, I was totally relaxed. When you're relaxed, that's when the game comes. Hey, I was a *big* man in Venezuela. I'd finally arrived. But it was a lie. Remember what I told you about lies?

I'd go back to spring training and it would start all over again. You can't go there. You can't go here. And I'd get angry all over again.

I was traded to the Dodgers before the 1964 season. They had won the World Series in 1963 and I was invited to spring training. They had a good team, and I was sent out to Spokane, Triple-A ball. Came close to a batting championship. Then I went to Puerto Rico to play winter ball and won the batting championship *there*. So that was almost two batting titles in a single year. Now, the 1965 season is coming up and the Dodgers don't invite me to spring training!

I cussed the farm director out. I didn't know what I was gonna do. I was getting up in age. Thirty-one years old. If I didn't get a chance soon . . .

My wife and I were wondering if we should go back home to Kentucky. But the kids had a comfort zone in Spokane. And I was making a little money now.

Two months into the season, I get a telephone call from Peter O'Malley: "You're going to Cincinnati."

"Peter," I said, "I'm *not* going to Cincinnati."

Cincinnati had Vada Pinson and Frank Robinson. With the outfielders the Reds had, that meant I was going to be sent to another Triple-A team in another town, and I'd have to start all over. At least I had a home in Spokane. At least my family had a comfort zone. I didn't want to go to Cincinnati. So I hung up.

He called me right back: "Why did you hang up?"

"Peter, I . . . "

"You're going to join the Dodgers in Cincinnati."

I was dressed before that phone hung on the hook. Gathered up my wife and kids. Ain't it amazing? I end up with the team that, had it not been for that one person, Jackie Robinson, I wouldn't be here today.

◆ ◆ ◆

I WENT TO the Dodgers, and I was home. You know that saying, "Died and gone to heaven"? Well, I walked in the front door to heaven, and there in the clubhouse was Sandy Koufax. He shook my hand and said, "Welcome." Anybody could have done that. But it was *Sandy Koufax* who did it.

Everyone was saying, "You've got some big shoes to fill." See, they called me up because Tommy Davis had broken his ankle.

I said, "I wear size 9."

They said, "Tommy gave us size 12."

So I gave them a 13. I had myself a year, man. If you look at the statistics in September, when we won 13 games in a row, you'll see I was right in the middle of it with clutch hits.

My swing put a new sound to my voice. It was my voice that gave me my nickname. During an interview, I answered a question with six words: "Sweet Lou can do it all." Next thing I know, I was Sweet Lou Johnson. What you have to do when that new voice starts to come out is you have to learn to live without so many lies.

Two hits. After all was said and done, two hits are the reason you're reading my words right now. You never would have remembered me if I hadn't got those hits, and I never would have gotten a job back with the Dodgers years later.

The first hit came on September 9, 1965. Sandy was pitching against Bob Hendley of the Chicago Cubs. They were both throwing perfect games until the fifth inning. I walked, got sacrificed to second, stole third, and when the catcher overthrew the base, I scored. We had a run, but still no hits. I got a double later in the game. And that was the only hit. If I hadn't gotten that hit, there would have been a double no-hitter in a single game.

And Sandy's was perfect.

The second hit came in the seventh game of the World Series that year. I hit a home run in the top of the fourth. Gave Koufax a 1-0 lead. That's all he needed, and we won the Series.

Sandy said "Welcome" to me.

And I said "Thank you" to him.

◆ ◆ ◆

SEE THIS CHAMPIONSHIP ring? Now, that's truth. It's verification. Athletes can talk a lot of shit. They can make a lot of money. But if they don't get that ring . . .

Back home in Lexington, Kentucky, that fall, they gave me a huge parade. Gave me the keys to the city. Had me speak to the crowd.

But I had no voice.

What do I mean by that? Well, let me tell you. You treat me a little different because I'm an athlete, you put me up on a little pedestal. But what about that garbage man? What about that janitor? ESPN doesn't send nobody out to talk to no janitors. C'mon, now! How many times does *that guy* get a chance to have a voice? So we were fightin' for that guy.

But I wasn't speaking for that janitor. Not when the riots came. The riots had nothing to do with baseball. They didn't stop the games. But they scared the hell out of a lot of ballplayers. Do you know what it's like to see your own people get slaughtered in your own backyard? You can't lose for talkin' about it now. But you could lose for talkin' about it then.

We had a chance to make a good living. And we had sense enough to know one thing: Be as big a man as you can, but don't disrupt the family. Make the money for your family.

Because they're just waiting for you to say something . . . they're just waiting. It was like Jackie when he got on that field and had to take it all at first in silence. You had no voice.

You had to have a law written in the United States of America so I could sit down wherever I wanted and eat a sandwich. You had to pass a law for me to go to a hotel to sleep. You had to pass a fucking bill for me to sit in the front of a bus.

I didn't say that then. I didn't have a voice. But I'm telling you now.

Everywhere I went, people knew Sweet Lou. I'd helped win a perfect game and a World Series. My wife could be 20th in line at the bank, it'd be, "C'mon right up here, Mrs. Johnson." Materially, I was well-off.

The Dodgers traded me after the 1967 season. It was like losing my home. I played two more years, and then the Angels released me in 1969. When I lost baseball, my life was through. The baseball bat wasn't in my hands anymore. Using that bat to hit was about all I knew how to do.

What you gotta learn when you lose the bat is you gotta be a winner in another ballpark. I didn't know how to turn the bat into something comparable outside the game.

I had to be out there by myself without a bat, and I found something on the outside that took care of that. It's called alcohol. The alcohol keeps the bat in your hand. You think it's another bat. But it's a lie. Remember what I told you about lyin'.

I became a menace to me. My own worst enemy.

My name got me into the dope houses when I had no money. After a while, there was nothing more important to me than the dope. The championship ring on my finger? I didn't need that ring. I needed another bat in my hand. The dope was another bat. The ring could get me that other bat. So I handed my 1965 championship ring over to the dealer and he handed me the dope. The dope dealer had the ring. I couldn't even call the police to get it back.

Some things you just take with you. Some things you're never gonna tell. Nobody leaves everything behind. That's why the best books are fiction. Nothing's held back in fiction. Dig what I'm sayin'?

I had one foot in the grave and another on a banana peel when Don Newcombe grabbed hold of me. Peter O'Malley and the Dodgers were right behind him.

When you go through the rehab process you come to realize that we stuff our feelings with drink. That's why you keep drinking, man. Everybody in therapy had a disease, and we all got stripped down. And when I got to the bottom of me, I got to the question that, to this day, nobody has ever given me an answer to: Why did the pigmentation of my skin have to be hated so much?

To this day. To this fucking day. Nobody has given me an answer.

The people in therapy had a disease just like I had a disease. When they talked, I listened. And when I talked, they listened. They were just like me. I wasn't being judged. For the first time in my life, I had a voice.

I got my life back together through the Dodgers. I got another bat. I got another swing at the ball.

The ring turned up in a safety deposit box. They were cleaning out this safety deposit box in Washington for lack of payment of the box rental, and my ring went to unclaimed properties. A man saw it with my name in the center: Lou Johnson, 1965, Los Angeles Dodgers.

He called Ron Fairly. Ron had played with the Dodgers in the 60s. At the time, he was an announcer for the Seattle Mariners.

Took two years. They had to go through the process. But I got the ring back. But what really mattered to me is I had a new life by then. I don't drink today. You could give me a million dollars, it won't mean shit to me if I lift a beer.

Who knows what turned it around for me? I can't pinpoint it. I guess there was something for me to do on the other side.

In 1992, I went home to Lexington, and a friend took me to a University of Kentucky basketball game. I didn't even know what was coming. But at half-time, they announced me to the crowd. I didn't even have to step on the court. The spotlight came to me, and I got a standing ovation. That was deep. Really deep. I was crying. The tears were flowing silently, and there were a lot of 'em.

When you release those feelings, the spirit puts you in a place where every time you think you've got a roadblock, you go right past it.

The other day I was at my mother-in-law's funeral and there was a kid who was wearing a jersey with No. 42 on it. He had no idea what the 42 meant. In the heart of the hood, and this kid had no idea.

I put my arm around this kid and I showed him my world championship ring. I said, "It was No. 42 who got me this ring."

And then I told him about No. 42.

◆ ◆ ◆

CHAPTER TWELVE

FLOOD OF MONEY

NO, THERE'S NO way to prove this. But those player contracts that are so large you wonder how so many zeros could possibly be spent might all be traced back to a dirty uniform in a heap on a clubhouse floor between games of a minor league doubleheader in 1957.

Curt Flood must have thought he was beyond tears by the time he entered his second year of minor league ball in the South. After all, he'd seen and overheard a large white fan teach four little boys just the right way to scream *"Black bastard!"* at him from a front row box throughout a game in High Point, North Carolina—with no usher or member of his team's management making any motion whatsoever to stop them.

But his voice still quivered when he told the story of that uniform four decades later.

After the first game of a doubleheader, Flood peeled off his uniform like all the other players on his club and threw it into a pile on the floor. The clubhouse manager's job was to pick up the uniforms and have them washed and dried so they could be reused in the second game.

But the white clubhouse manager couldn't bear the thought of touching fabric that had rubbed a black man's flesh. Instead he used a long stick with a nail on the end to carefully pluck each piece of Flood's uniform, right down to the jock strap, out of the pile. Then he sent it all to the cleaners on the black side of town rather than contaminate his washing machine.

The white players' uniforms were ready before Flood's uniform could be returned. He watched his teammates dress and leave for the field to warm up as he waited, stark naked.

Whatever Flood was thinking in those lonely moments surely stayed with him. You can see it in his eyes and hear it in his voice when he tells the story in Ken Burns' documentary *Baseball*. One thing is certain: His thoughts were unlike those of any other ballplayers in the clubhouse that day.

Maybe it's a stretch to link those lonely moments to the day 12 years later when he received a perfunctory phone call telling him he'd been traded from the St. Louis Cardinals to the Philadelphia Phillies. But maybe it's not.

Flood won seven Gold Gloves, hit over .300 six times, and helped the Cardinals win two World Series in 12 seasons as the St. Louis centerfielder (1958-69). He had an elite salary: $90,000. But he was still thinking differently from all the other players around him. Curt Flood didn't want to go to Philadelphia. He wanted the same freedom enjoyed by most every American. He wanted to live and work where *he* wanted to, not where an aging beer tycoon and a Dupont heir—Cardinals owner Gussie Busch and Phillies owner Bob Carpenter—had decided he should. A letter he wrote to baseball commissioner Bowie Kuhn started out as if baseball were a plantation and he were a slave.

"After 12 years in the major leagues, I do not feel that I am a piece of property to be sold irrespective of my wishes . . ."

Many people misunderstood the furnace within Curt Flood that drove him to test a baseball rule dating to the 19th century called the reserve clause. "God profaned! Flag desecrated! Motherhood defiled! Apple pie blasphemed!" That, Flood wrote in his autobiography, was how America responded to his challenge to Major League Baseball. Many writers believed his refusal to accept the trade was a ruse to get a bigger contract. But Curt Flood walked away from a sweet salary at a time when his career was starting its downward arc. When Flood decided to stand up against the rule that gave a team owner the rights to a player's services for as long as the owner wished, he was as alone and naked as he had been in that minor league clubhouse in 1957.

Flood eventually sued baseball, and the case eventually landed in the Supreme Court. On the day he was scheduled to testify, a respectful hush filled the courtroom as Jackie and Rachel Robinson entered in support. "I would be remiss," Jackie would tell Curt, "if I didn't share these burdens with you."

The burdens were heavy. The Supreme Court voted against Flood, 5-3. His outside businesses went belly-up. He tried to return to baseball a couple of years later, but it wasn't in him anymore, and he left the Washington Senators after 13 games. He would open a café in Spain, have problems with alcohol, and eventually die of throat cancer.

Six years after Curt Flood pushed baseball to the brink, an arbitrator ruled in favor of two white players seeking the right to play where they wished. Since the birth of free agency, neither the spiraling salaries nor the bittersweet twists have stopped.

◆ ◆ ◆

MAURY WILLS

♦♦♦

THE FIRST THING you've got to understand about Curt Flood is that he was some kind of ballplayer.

When you're playing outfield at the same time as Willie Mays, Mickey Mantle, Roberto Clemente, Frank Robinson, and Hank Aaron, it's easy to get lost in the shuffle. But the ballplayers of his day had a full appreciation of Curt Flood's talents.

TIM McCARVER

♦♦♦

CURT COULD CATCH a fly ball with anybody who's ever played the game.

Nobody ever got a better jump on the ball. And he was smart. I mean *smart*. When I think of Curt Flood playing centerfield, I think of a pitch outside and, in the background, I think of him moving three steps to his left. He was always in position, always in the game, always ready to make the play.

BILLY WILLIAMS

♦♦♦

NEXT TO WILLIE Mays, he was the best centerfielder I ever saw.

TIM McCARVER

♦♦♦

TO GIVE YOU an idea how conscientious Curt was, let me tell you something Johnny Edwards once told me. Johnny was a catcher, and he was traded from the Reds to the Cardinals before the 1968 season. He played with Curt and me for only a year. And he told me something about Curt that was very revealing.

Johnny said, "I've never been on a team before with a guy who goes 0-for-4 and is still cheering for his teammates." He was exactly right. When guys are 0-for-4, they don't yell for their teammates. They've got their head in a towel cussing themselves and their sorry luck and the guy on the mound, and maybe even the day they were born. The same guys, when they're 3-for-4, that's when you see them yelling for their teammates.

You know when you would hear Curt Flood yelling loudest? When he was 0-for-4 and had failed to get a runner in from third.

BOB VEALE

◆◆

MY GRANDDADDY HAD a third-grade education. He didn't let nobody walk over him. He figured like this: Better to go through life as a lion for one day then to go through an entire life as a sheep.

That was Curt Flood.

He was made to feel like a piece of chattel to be moved when the boss man says it's time to go: "You can do what you want to do when I say we're finished with you."

That can make a man bitter. But, you know what? Bitterness is just like manure—you spread it around. And manure isn't all bad, either. It can help you grow some pretty good vegetables.

CURT FLOOD

From his 1971 autobiography, *The Way It Is.*

◆◆

FREDERICK DOUGLASS WAS a Maryland slave who taught himself to read. "If there is no struggle," he once said, "there is no progress. Those who profess to favor freedom, and yet depreciate agitation, are men who want crops without plowing up the ground . . . Power concedes nothing without a demand. It never did and never will."

TIM McCARVER

◆◆

YOU HAVE TO understand what the structure of the game was like back in those times. At the time the players union hired Marvin Miller as executive director, in 1966, we were more concerned with our pension plan than anything.

To a lot of the older players, the pension plan was the only thing that mattered. It's kind of funny looking back at it. But our 1967 winter meetings were in Mexico City. And we were told to bring a list of all the grievances that we had against the owners. I mean, guys were coming up with some comical stuff. But the best was Milt Pappas, who was a player representative for Cincinnati at the time. And his grievance was that there weren't enough hair dryer outlets in Forbes Field in Pittsburgh.

Marvin said nicely that he was really talking about grievances on the playing field—not your hair—and there Milt was with his blow-dried hair and it was pretty funny.

I mean, in those days at the winter meetings, the general manager might get together with the player representative. And the owner might be saying something like, "You know what? We ought to give you guys another $2 a day meal money." So it went from $8 to $10. With the Cardinals, we received $8 a day meal money, but if we ate on the plane we had $4 deducted because we'd already eaten. And we just accepted it. We got a packet with $48 for six days. If $4 was deducted, we still had $44. So, I mean, come on, we're in the big leagues.

We were just so dumb and ignorant. Then Marvin came in and started listening to us and explaining things to us.

And we were like, "*What?*"

MARVIN MILLER
◆◆

WHAT I KNEW was that it would be impossible not to succeed.

The players were not the lowest-paid workers in America, of course, but they were the most exploited. There was a huge difference between what they were worth and what they were being paid. It was the greatest gap I'd ever seen, greater than that affecting Cesar Chavez's grape pickers.

And the issues went beyond salary.

The players were owned lock, stock, and barrel as property.

TIM McCARVER
◆◆

MONEY WASN'T THE issue with Curt. If money had been the issue, he would have signed. He wouldn't have done what he did, give up his livelihood, and yet what's remarkable is how many of the sportswriters in those days wrote that he was only after the last buck.

In many ways, Curt was ahead of us. It took somebody like Curt to open our eyes and see things the way they really were. Curt took it many, many, many, many steps further than anybody would have up to that point. Think of it: In two years, we go from Milt Pappas' grievance over hair dryer outlets to Curt Flood's wanting to overturn the reserve clause.

MAURY WILLS

I DON'T KNOW how Curt Flood had the courage to do what he did. I knew he was a different kind of guy. He wasn't an everyday baseball player walking down the street. He just looked at life a little different than we did. To me, baseball was everything. It was life itself. To Curt, there were things more important than baseball.

He had an inner strength. I looked up to Curt Flood. I thought he was a better man than I was. He had something I wish I had. There were plenty of times when I could've stood up for my rights but I gave in, because I came up that way. Not Curt.

BILLY WILLIAMS

WHAT HE WENT through as a ballplayer had a lot to do with why Curt Flood made his stand. See, he equated the experience with slavery, with somebody selling you to somebody else.

I was with Ali when his boxing license was taken away because he refused to be inducted to the Army. It was in Houston. We were playing the Astros, and Ernie Banks and I took a cab over to the Americana hotel. We spent two days with Ali. That was about his religious beliefs. A lot of people thought that was fake. But it wasn't. He simply said, "No, I don't want to go."

It was very much like that with Curt Flood. He walked away from a lot because of what he believed in.

◆ ◆ ◆

TIM McCARVER

◆◆◆

I WAS INVOLVED in the same big trade that would have sent Curt to Philadelphia. The general manager, Bing Devine, called me and told me I was going. You feel a certain betrayal when something like that happens because, you know, you sign with an organization, and they tell you you're part of the family—and all of a sudden you're not part of the family anymore.

So ever since, I've said, don't give me that family shit. Let's make it clear that this is business. You know, like Don Corleone. Nothing personal.

But don't tell me I'm part of the family. I know better now.

BOB VEALE

◆◆◆

NOBODY WITH WHITE skin was going to challenge the reserve clause.

JUDY PACE

Actress JUDY PACE is CURT FLOOD's widow.

◆◆◆

WHEN YOU THINK about it, it's not surprising that a black man did this. A white man was not going to have that consciousness. A white man was not walking around thinking, My rights are always being penalized.

That's what Curt called it—the penalty of being black. There were always penalties for being black. If you never had that inflicted on you, then you might think everything was okay.

If you were a white baseball player, you might think, I'm doing something that some people would give their second child for—a chance to play major league baseball. Why stir things up?

TIM McCARVER

I CAN REMEMBER telling Curt, "There's no way I'd do anything like what you're doing. I've got a family to support."

And he said: "Timmy, I've got a family to support too."

"Curt," I said, "I just don't have the courage to do that."

"You know," he said, "I appreciate that. But I have convictions more than I have courage. My convictions are stronger than my courage."

You could see that he had really gone over this thing. And it was a hard decision for him. He didn't come into the players association saying, "Now, dammit, I know I'm right."

Curt came in cautiously. When questioned by his fellow players, he was firm with his answers, but he was cautious. That was a very lonely decision to make. I mean, God almighty, how do you make a decision like that with your life being affected so dramatically from a financial standpoint? I mean, he was giving up $90,000 a year, which was a huge salary in baseball back then.

And on top of that, he was turning himself into a baseball outcast.

MARVIN MILLER

BEFORE THE SUIT was filed, I wanted to be absolutely certain that Curt understood what he was about to do.

I said to him, "Curt, you're past 30. The odds are you won't be able to play for at least a season, and it may take much longer to fight the case through. Even if you're out for a year, it might be impossible to come back at your age."

He didn't hesitate. He said, "I'm prepared to make this the final fight of my career. I really don't want to play for those people."

JUDY PACE

CURT WORE NO. 21. Half of 42.

Jackie was Curt's hero from childhood. Curt wore 42 in the minor leagues. But 42 wasn't available when he got to the Cardinals. So he took 21.

The moment that Jackie and Rachel walked into the courtroom for Curt's trial—well, that was one of the high points of Curt's life.

To have Jackie Robinson tell him, "Young man, I respect you. What you're doing is right. You have the courage to stand up. I am here for you."

That brought Curt almost to tears.

◆ ◆ ◆

TIM McCARVER

◆◆

IN MANY WAYS, Curt was sacrificed. The players association paid the legal expenses. But we didn't have a Curt Flood fund to help make up for his lost income, which, in retrospect, would have been the right thing to do.

SPIKE LEE

◆◆

CURT WAS WHITEBALLED. I don't like to use the word blackballed. The owners were in cahoots, as they always are, and they said, "This guy's not playing anymore." End of story.

TIM McCARVER

◆◆

WHEN I GOT to Philadelphia, there was some commotion around the fact that Curt didn't come. But it seems to me there should have been more. I think the writers interviewed me for a day or two. Then it was gone.

Looking back, I'm surprised that it disappeared so quickly. It ceased to be a big story. A lot of the press at the time were . . . well, they weren't on the owners' payrolls, but they were chummy with management. The press hated Marvin Miller, really hated him.

And the owners made sure the press hated Curt as much as they could. So I'm sure they snuffed that story and squelched it as soon as they could.

Howard Cosell stood up for Curt in typical Cosellian fashion. But there were many more negative articles than positive.

What you've got to realize is that there would have been just as much opposition to what he did if he had been a white player. The real issue to the owners was a player breaking away from the ranks and, in effect, trying to end baseball as everyone knew it. Their position was pretty simple, really: "He can't do that. The players have got to remain indentured servants. He's trying to take my servants away."

It was colonialism in its purest form.

The Supreme Court voted against Curt two years later, and it was news for three or four days. And then—boom!—it was gone.

JUDY PACE

◆◆

THE INTERESTING THING about Curt's lawsuit is that people say that he stood up and he lost. Well, let's look at what really happened. He didn't go to the Phillies. Later on, it was worked out so that he could negotiate a new contract with the Washington Senators. With that contract he got a raise. That contract also stated that he couldn't be traded without his consent. And it also stated if he wanted to leave after the first year, he could. So he got the first free agent contract ever, even though it wasn't perceived that way.

He got precisely what he said he wanted for his fellow players. He set the stage. Curt refused to put on a uniform that he didn't want to wear. He got clauses in his contract that no one else ever had. He got what he wanted. It just didn't work out in Washington.

Curt was coming back from a layoff, and he wasn't playing up to his standard. But he left the team and the country because he thought he was going to be killed. There were all these letters: *You're a dead nigger . . . We're going to kill you.* When he got to the clubhouse for the last game he would play with the Senators, there was a black wreath in his locker. A large black wreath.

Now they guard a clubhouse like they guard Fort Knox. I mean, you just don't wander in with something like that. Scared the hell out of him.

If Curt's reaction strikes you as extreme, you have to remember that he'd seen a lot. He'd marched with Jackie Robinson in Jackson, Mississippi, in 1962. Medgar Evers was the host for that event. The following year, Medgar Evers was shot and killed. People were getting killed for wanting to vote. Churches had been bombed and little girls had been killed. Martin Luther King had been assassinated. Curt had seen brothers dying all around him. He just felt people were a little too crazy. So he felt he had to leave.

MONTE IRVIN

◆◆

CURT WENT TO live in Europe. He was a talented artist. But he hit hard times and had to come back home. He ran out of money. The last time I saw him—I never will forget it—he had nothing and he was sick.

◆ ◆ ◆

SPIKE LEE

◆◆

IT KILLED HIM. Like Jackie, Curt died prematurely. He was only 59. I definitely feel that you can bring that stuff upon yourself. Heartbreak can turn into illnesses like cancer.

BILLY WILLIAMS

◆◆

THE STRANGEST THING about it is that if you asked players today who Curt Flood was, 95% of them would say he was a disc jockey or a rapper or something. A lot of people don't know who he was. A lot of people don't know who Marvin Miller is. These are two guys who changed the face of this game for the players who came after them.

I heard Curt Flood once walked into a clubhouse in the mid-1990s. He stood there for a while, and nobody came over to talk to him.

Nobody knew who he was.

SPIKE LEE

◆◆

I GOT TO know Curt, and I think toward the end of his life he had some bitterness. That was understandable. He knew what he'd done, and he knew how people benefited from it, and yet the players who came after him had no idea. They were ignorant. They felt that players had always made the big money, that they always had the freedom to move about. As if there never had been anything called a reserve clause.

All these cats makin' all this money today? They should send a check to Judy Pace with a note that says, "Thank you."

TIM McCARVER

◆◆

WHAT I WOULD like to see is more of an appreciation for what Curt did.

Joe Torre's playing career and his managing career combined are going to put him in the Hall of Fame. His playing career puts him close, but not quite there. He's on the underside of the bubble. But with what he's done as a manager, he's a shoo-in.

What Curt did in his playing career, combined with what he did in raising the consciousness of the people involved with the game, ought to put him in the Hall of Fame.

It'll never happen, but I think Curt ought to be there.

LOU BROCK

CURT AND JACKIE were two different things. Jackie Robinson showed you how not to live in the shadows. Curt Flood showed that you could take your talent and market it to anybody you want to.

Curt was an expansion of Jackie because his message went out to other sports. If Curt Flood hadn't tested the reserve clause, Brett Favre might still be playing football in Atlanta today. He wouldn't be working in Green Bay. Curt opened the doors so that players could take advantage of the free market system, just like other Americans.

That changed everything.

JUDY PACE

THEY PREMIERED KEN Burns' documentary about baseball at the National Theatre in Washington for the president and the Congress. Bill Clinton was sitting two rows in front of us. Here's the president of the United States, waving at Curt.

There was a barbecue. They put up a batting cage on the White House lawn, and Hillary was in there hitting. She was pretty good. It was kind of surreal. A lot of the guys from the Negro Leagues were there. Guys who could never get through the gate to play in the major leagues were eating barbecue at the White House.

The year after Curt passed away, Congress eliminated baseball's exemption from antitrust laws in labor matters. That happened in 1998. Bill No. 21. The Curt Flood Act.

Curt would have been tickled by that. His name is now part of the law of the land.

BILL RHODEN

A columnist for *The New York Times*, WILLIAM C. RHODEN is the author of *Forty Million Dollar Slaves: The Rise, Fall, and Redemption of the Black Athlete.*

◆◆

THE SIGNIFICANCE OF Curt Flood is that he made a racially neutral statement. What he did is free *everybody*. When he started saying, We're *all* on the plantation, there were a whole lot of white ballplayers who couldn't even conceive of such an idea. They'd been so polarized that they couldn't imagine they were in this together with the black players.

Curt was rooted in the Martin Luther King mentality: If the system enslaves anybody, it enslaves everybody. None of us is free until all are free.

The irony is that the pot of gold Flood helped lead athletes to has had a boomerang effect. It's become sort of like hush money. A player really has to think twice before he makes any kind of protest so as not to be perceived as a troublemaker, or he hurt his market value.

JIM BROWN

◆◆

YOU ALWAYS RISK losing money when you speak out. Those who spoke out risked everything. So you had a choice of opening your mouth and maintaining your dignity or closing your mouth and keeping your money.

A lot of guys were Johnny-come-latelies. After their careers were over, they started raising their voices. It's a lot easier to stand up and speak your mind when your career is no longer in jeopardy.

BILL RHODEN

◆◆

BACK IN THE '60s, the racial issues were clear-cut and in-your-face. The black athletes just needed the courage to step out.

Today, because of integration, racism has gone underground and taken different forms. There is very little on the surface to react against. At the same time, the money has now put the athletes in a position to act—and act aggressively—if they're motivated to.

In this era, you don't have to do a lot of yelling. The money speaks for itself. You build a bank. You develop movie theaters like Magic Johnson did. That's the challenge now: mobilizing and organizing the financial clout that Curt Flood made possible to provide a much-needed economy for the large number of people on the periphery.

The twist in all this is the money has opened a Pandora's box and created a disconnect between the athlete and the average fan.

BRYANT GUMBEL

THERE'S A HUGE divide in the world of sports today, and money makes it even more difficult to bridge that gap.

I'm not blaming anybody. But it's naïve to think that a 60-year-old white sportswriter who's making $60K a year is going to understand, empathize, and converse on mutually comfortable footing with a 20-year-old athlete who's making $15 million. That doesn't make either one a bad guy. I'm just pointing out the gargantuan gap between the two of them.

So when that 20-year-old black athlete feels the need to dance, express his jubilation, and put on a show on the field, and that 60-year-old white writer takes a dim view of it, it doesn't make one a showboat and the other a racist. It simply means they're coming from different worlds. They're playing to different audiences and serving different constituents. They don't understand each other.

The white guy doesn't understand why the black guy is putting on a show. The black guy doesn't understand why the white guy has a problem with it.

They're talking different languages. The money aspect only separates them further.

I feel for both sides.

◆ ◆ ◆

CHAPTER THIRTEEN

BLACK POWER

BASEBALL DELUDES US. The crack of the bat, the majestic flight of the ball, the slow, regal trot around the bases. We rise to our feet and roar. We think we're seeing *power*.

But we're not. Baseball is a business, and in business, true power reveals itself in a room to only a select few after a door has been closed.

Before the last home game of the 1974 season, a man who would hit 586 career home runs, a black man known for his power, was called to just such a room. There, Frank Robinson got a lesson in power.

He was in his 19th season as a player, he'd been traded to the Cleveland Indians only three weeks before, and he was looking forward to playing a 20th. When he got word that the Cleveland general manager wanted to see him, his first reaction was to wonder where he'd been traded to this time.

It was a long climb from the field up to the general manager's office at Cleveland Stadium. Frank had just hired an agent, who happened to be with him that day, and they walked together.

Once the door closed behind them, Indians general manager Phil Seghi made an offer that Frank Robinson couldn't have anticipated: "We'd like you to manage the club next year."

Frank blinked, unsure if he'd just been stroked or gut-punched. He wondered if maybe the Indians were trying to tell him they thought it was time to hang up his cleats.

"But I have a contract for next year as a player," he said.

"We'd like you to be player-manager."

Frank swallowed hard. No black man had ever managed in the major leagues. He asked for a moment to speak with his agent.

Phil Seghi had known Frank for 16 years. "Of course," he said. The general manager said they could use his office, and he left the room.

"This is a great opportunity!" the agent exulted. "Do you want to manage?"

"Yeah, one day," Robinson said. "But I don't know if I'm ready quite yet."

The agent stared at him, not even needing to voice the significance of the offer. "Well," he said, "the opportunity might not come along again."

The men looked at each other. All sorts of things ran through their heads, the first of which was this: *No black man had ever before been given this chance.* They called Seghi back into the office.

"Phil," Frank asked, "how much are you going to pay me to manage the ball club?"

"Two hundred thousand dollars," Seghi said.

"Well, I've never been very good at math," Robinson said. "But I know I've got a contract to play next year for $172,000. Correct me if I'm wrong, but that would mean you're only going to pay me *$28,000* to manage this club."

"That's right," Seghi said. The general manager liked Robinson, but what he said next made it clear that he thought he had him over a barrel. "That's our offer."

Anger flashed in Frank's eyes, and the agent saw it. "Phil, Phil!" the agent said, turning to Seghi. "Give us another minute."

This time, Frank and the agent walked outside. Frank's head was swirling. Two years before, at a celebration of the 25th anniversary of the integration of baseball, Jackie Robinson had walked to the center of the diamond in Cincinnati before a World Series game and told the crowd and a nationwide television audience that what he truly wanted to see was "a black man as manager."

Nine days later, he died.

Now, given a chance to fulfill one of Jackie's last wishes, Frank Robinson agonized. A white man had the freedom to argue the unfairness of being asked to manage a mediocre team with a million dollars worth of headaches for a mere $28,000. But Frank Robinson was chained to his race. Imagine the damage it would cause if word got out that baseball had held out the golden apple to a black man—and the black man had walked away.

Frank and the agent walked back in Seghi's office. The door closed behind them.

"Okay," Frank said. "Okay."

That's how Major League Baseball got its first black manager.

◆ ◆ ◆

FRANK ROBINSON

◆◆

THERE WERE ABOUT three weeks to go in the season when I got to Cleveland, and I thought maybe I could help put the team over the top. But when I arrived, I couldn't believe it. No way was this team going to win. The division of players was unbelievable.

The manager, Ken Aspromonte, sat on one side of the dugout with all the white players, and the black players sat on the other side of the dugout with Larry Doby, one of the coaches. And you couldn't mistake this because the old park in Cleveland had a big dugout. I thought to myself, Wow, this can't be.

But that's the way it was. So I just tried to stay in the middle and play as hard as I could. I didn't try to get everybody to blend by saying anything. I just led by example—by the way I conducted myself before the game, and then, once the game started, by going hard into second base, sliding headfirst, playing hard all the time. That's the way I'd always led.

I remember Luis Aparicio once saying to the press, "Here's a superstar who's always throwing his body around. We felt like if Frank could play that way, we could play that way." My idea was that just by being myself, I could maybe get people to come together.

But the team was losing, losing, losing, and there was a whole lot of negative stuff in the air.

I had trouble with Rico Carty at one point. Rico thought I was there to take his job, and that led some people to think I didn't get along with Latino players. Then I had a little dispute with Gaylord Perry.

One day, I picked up the morning newspaper and read that Gaylord was saying that he hadn't been rewarded properly and that the Indians shouldn't be paying me for all I'd accomplished in my career, that they should be paying me for what I can do now. The message was that he was earning his money but I wasn't earning mine.

I walked into the locker room, and he was sitting on a stool in front of his locker. I picked up the paper and held it out right in front of him: "Did you say this?" Over the years, I'd learned that just because you saw somebody quoted in the paper didn't necessarily mean the person had actually said it. But Gaylord said, "Yes, I did."

I said to him, "Look, I don't mind you using my salary as a negotiating tool.

But don't do it publicly. Don't drag my business out in the street. I don't drag your business into the street."

Gaylord had won nearly 60 games over the last three seasons. He said, "If they can pay you that, why can't they pay me what I deserve?"

"That's not my fault," I told him. "That's your fault."

He stood up, and it got loud. A lot of writers wrote that we went at it, but that was an exaggeration. What broke it up was Aspromonte's coming in and calling for a team meeting. That's when he announced that he'd be resigning at the end of the season.

A lot of people accused me of knowing what was going to happen when I came there. But I had no idea that Aspromonte was in trouble when I arrived. I can look anybody in the eye and say that the thought of managing the Indians never crossed my mind.

As soon as I accepted the job, I knew one thing: I had to get rid of the negative vibe in the air. I had to clean up the coaching staff. I had to bring in a fresh outlook.

Larry Doby thought that he was going to get the manager's job. He deserved it. He was upset when he didn't get it. And he was really upset when I didn't rehire any of the coaches on the staff. We didn't speak from the day I told him I wasn't going to rehire him until the day he was inducted into the Hall of Fame. That was 24 years later, and it was by accident.

I was in Cooperstown for the induction ceremonies because I went every year. They had a golf outing, and I went into the pro shop to get some balls. It was fairly empty. Then I spotted Larry over in a corner. I said to myself, This would be a good time—just go over and congratulate him, break the ice, reach out.

So I walked over and said, "Larry, I know we haven't talked in a long time, but I just wanted to congratulate you. It's well deserved and long overdue."

He said, "Thank you very much." That was the entire conversation.

So you learn that you're going to get in tough situations with all kinds of people when you get into this business of managing. But when I took the job in Cleveland, there was little time for me to think about repercussions. I made the right move, though. The barrier was broken, and if I'd passed up that opportunity, nobody knows when that door would have opened again.

◆ ◆ ◆

OPENING DAY IN 1975 was against the Yankees in Cleveland. I got to the park early and dropped by Phil Seghi's office to say hello. He wanted to know if I was going to put myself in the lineup.

"No way," I said.

"You ought to, you know" Phil said. "I've seen you rise to the occasion in situations like this."

I went downstairs and thought about it. Dang, how can I do that? We had a good designated hitter in Rico Carty, and I sure didn't want to be out on the field at first base. I was 39. I was too old to be out there.

But when I sat down in my office to write out the lineup card, I penciled in Boog Powell at first base, and I put myself down as DH, batting second. Why second? Because if the leadoff hitter got on base, I could show the rest of the guys that I'd bunt or do whatever it took to advance the runner.

The game started, and as the leadoff hitter walked to the plate, there was a horde of photographers packed between the dugout and the on-deck circle. It was cold. I remember having a hot water bottle in the dugout.

Well, the leadoff hitter made out, and I had to weave my way through these photographers to get to home plate. I was like a zombie. I stepped into the batter's box. Doc Medich was on the mound.

Strike one, swinging.

Strike two, called.

I felt a little lost, so I stepped out of the box, shook my head, and stepped back in.

To this day, I don't really know what happened because I wasn't in the moment. It was like I was in a fog. I just kind of flicked the bat out of the next pitch and fouled it off. I stepped out of the batter's box again and thought to myself, He didn't even try to waste a pitch. He's trying to embarrass me. That snapped me out of it.

This is my day, I'm thinking. This is my home park. Fifty-six thousand people have turned out. Rachel Robinson has made the trip to be here. And this guy is trying to strike me out on three pitches.

Now I'm in the moment. I get back in and run the count to 2-2. Then Doc throws me a slider away, and I reach out for it and make good contact and hit a line drive. I start out of the batter's box, and I'm looking at the ball to see if it's high enough to carry the fence. I step and stumble. I right myself, look up for the ball again, and stumble again.

Have you ever seen the clip? Not once, but twice I nearly fell flat. That would've been a real sight, wouldn't it? Ball's going over the fence, and I'm down on my face. Oh my goodness, as if wearing those red uniforms the Indians had back then wasn't bad enough.

But I caught myself, and when I reached first, I saw the ball had cleared. I don't know how I got around the bases.

The next thing I knew, all my teammates were running to home plate. That kind of snapped me out of it again. I waved to my wife and kids. I turned and saw Rachel sitting in her box. I went to the dugout, took off the hard helmet, and put on the soft hat. That's the moment I became a manager.

We won the game 5-3. The last out was a bouncer to Gaylord Perry. He threw out the runner, and I ran out to shake his hand. Without either of us even thinking about it, we put our arms around each other.

Gaylord gave me the game ball.

◆ ◆ ◆

GETTING MORE BLACKS into management has to be handled correctly, because this country has heard the same thing for years: I've been discriminated against in the voting booth because of the color of my skin, or I didn't get the big job because I'm black, or . . . see what I'm saying?

People get to the point where they don't want to hear it. It's like, We've heard this tune before. And it *is* an old tune. But hey, rewrite the damn lyrics. These are different times with different problems that need to be addressed.

Today, you've got Omar Minaya with the Mets and Kenny Williams with the White Sox as general managers—that's it for minority representation. Where are the presidents of ball clubs? Where are the minority owners? Do you mean to tell me that blacks in this country don't have enough money for groups to get together and buy one or two franchises? Oprah Winfrey, if she wanted, could buy a ball club all by herself.

There are enough black CEOs and black presidents of companies and wealthy black people that they could pool their resources together to buy ball clubs. But do you see anybody trying to pull minority groups together? No. It's going to take somebody like a Jackie Robinson to do it, somebody who can break new ground, and sad to say, there aren't many Jackie Robinsons around.

So what's the next step here? The commissioner has to almost demand of teams trying to buy teams that they have to have some minority interest or they won't be allowed to do the deal. It shouldn't be that way. But how else are we going to fix this?

Baseball's a very small circle. A lot of hiring is based on friendship and trust. A lot of guys who become managers go on to become managers somewhere else. Same with general managers. But in a small circle like that, how do you become a manager or a general manager in the first place?

LEN COLEMAN
◆◆◆

WHEN IT COMES to hiring managers, you've got the two R's: the Runners-up and the Recycles. The Runners-up are the minority guys who always seem to be among the finalists for a job but never get it. They always seem to come out of the process as the runner-up. The Recycles get four or five chances, while the black guy or the Hispanic guy usually doesn't get a first chance. You have to hammer at the two R's. You've got to keep pushing. You've got to keep the pressure on. If you just sit back and wait for it to come, it ain't gonna happen.

FELIPE ALOU
◆◆◆

FRANK ROBINSON GAVE us the hope that one day we could maybe be managers ourselves. We knew there were fears about hiring a black. But we finally reached a day when there was not such a thing as questioning the intellect or knowledge of a black manager. There were many qualified blacks, but I believe there were also fears about marketing your teams.

How was a black manager going to be received in his community? How was the market in a particular city going to respond to a team with a black manager? These were fears that turned out to have no foundation. But you have to understand that the fears existed.

When Frank Robinson was hired, progress was made. For the black, yes. But there was still the Latino waiting.

How would a city—I don't want to mention a particular city and get in a controversy—deal with the differences? I believe even today there are teams that might be hesitant. Here's a guy with an accent. He was born in Cuba or

Venezuela. Or he lives in Puerto Rico. Can we have this guy speak for the team at a banquet?

Is there some merit to that point of view? Let's just say there are people who might be hesitant to accept a Latino as the voice of a team. I'll give you an example of how they can look at it.

I went to a restaurant in Tampa back in the 1960s. Very nice people own the restaurant. I've been there many times since this happened.

I was with the Atlanta Braves at the time, and a bunch of us took cabs over. It was me, Ozzie Virgil, and Rico Carty, plus a couple of other guys. We got on line, and then it was our turn.

The host must have heard us talking, because he said, "You're baseball players, right?" And he said it in Spanish, because it was a Spanish restaurant.

"Yes," somebody said, "we're baseball players."

He said, "I'll be right back."

As soon as he said that, a couple of us turned to each other. We knew: We're going to have a problem here.

After a while, the guy came back and said, "We have a place for you guys to eat." And he began to take us to a room that was separate from the main dining room.

Then Ozzie Virgil, who was the oldest person in the group—and whose English was good because his family had moved to New York City when he was a teenager—said, "What's going on here? Why can't we eat with the rest of the people?"

This guy was honest enough to give us a straight answer: "We love baseball players. But we're not totally integrated in this restaurant. We have customers who may never come back to eat here if we let you eat with them. We have a nice place here. The food is great. We'll treat you great. And other ballplayers have accepted eating alone."

At that point, I took over and said, "No. We're going to eat with the rest of the people or we're going home."

A few minutes later, we were piling back into cabs. Our cab driver happened to be black, and he took us to a place booming with blacks and Latinos, and we ate pork chops with black-eyed peas, and we had a good time.

In the end, it's about the money. The restaurant was scared that our presence would cause it to lose business. That's what may be going on in the minds of major league executives when they're trying to choose a manager. Whether we like it or not.

FRANK ROBINSON

◆◆◆

ONCE YOU'VE BEEN a manager, the job comes looking for you.

Back in 1981, I was doing one of those Miller Lite commercials when I got a call from the Giants. I was in Denver, and they wanted me to come to San Francisco the next day to talk about the managing job. "I only have the clothes I'm wearing," I told them. "I don't even have a tie on." No problem, they said, we'll meet you at the airport.

The only jacket I'd brought with me had a Miller Lite patch on it. I met the Giants people at the airport, and they offered me the job. I took it on the spot. They wanted me to stay so they could announce it, and at the press conference I was still wearing that Miller Lite jacket.

The next time came in 1988. I was an assistant to the president of the Orioles. Cal Ripken Sr. was managing the club. He'd been in the Baltimore organization for 35 years. He'd wanted the job real bad, and he finally got it in 1987. We didn't have a good year, and the owner, Edward Bennett Williams, wanted to fire Ripken at the end of the season but was talked out of it. There was more talk about firing him in spring training the following year but nothing came of it. But, after we lost our first two games of the season at home and our first four games on the road, the phone in my hotel room rang.

It was Roland Hemond. There'd been a major shake-up in the front office over the winter, and Roland was in his first season as general manager. He asked me if I wanted to manage the ball club.

"Manage the ball club?" I said. "I appreciate that, but you have a good manager. Cal's only had one year, and he deserves another."

Hemond said, "No, I want you to manage."

"If I don't take it," I asked him, "what's going to happen?"

"I'll get somebody else."

It was kind of selfish on my part, but I didn't want anyone else to have the job. I thought I could do more to help turn around the team as manager than I could as assistant to the president. So I said, "How much are you going to pay me?" (It was a little more than $28,000 a year, thank goodness.)

After he gave me the number, I said to him, "Okay, I've got to go back and talk to my family first."

So I called my wife, and she said, "Are you crazy? Stay where you are. Stay in your suit and tie. You don't want to go though all that stuff in uniform again, all the sleepless nights and losing your hair and being on the road and . . ."

"But it's an opportunity . . ." I started to tell her.

"You don't need an opportunity," she said. "We're in a good position now. We enjoy having you at home."

So I called Roland back and said to him, "Okay, I'll take the job."

Later on, my wife said to me, "Why'd you call and ask me my opinion? You don't listen anyway."

"Well," I told her, "I always listen. But I have to make up my own mind."

Point is, that's how it happens once you're in the circle. The trick is to get inside the first time.

◆ ◆ ◆

WHY DID IT take Willie Randolph so long to get a manager's job? That's a little complicated. He was the third base coach for the New York Yankees. He was in a winning organization, he was being paid very well, he was collecting a bunch of extra money all the time from being in the playoffs and the World Series, and there were a lot of speaking engagements coming his way.

Milwaukee interviewed him but didn't offer him the job. Cincinnati offered him the job, but the money was ridiculously low, and he turned them down. A lot of people said, "Can you believe he turned down that job?"

And I said, "Yeah, I can believe it, and I'm kind of proud of him for doing it, because very few of us of color are secure enough to say no." White guys have turned down managerial positions that they didn't feel were right for them, and nothing was said about it. So why was everybody getting on Willie?

I called Willie and told him, "In my heart, I was hoping you'd take the Reds job because that would mean another minority manager. But I'm proud that you were strong enough and secure enough financially to turn that job down. There's probably something around the corner that's going to be better suited for you."

I had no idea that the Mets would drop in his lap. But it couldn't have worked out any better. Look what happened. During his first year, there was some grumbling from fans and writers, but the team finished 12 games better than the season before. His second season, Willie took them to the playoffs. Now he's a genius, and everybody's singing his praises.

LEN COLEMAN

◆◆◆

YOU CAN ONLY share what you've got. You can't share what you don't have.

I was hired by Fay Vincent in 1992 as director of marketing development in the commissioner's office. Then, in 1994, I was elected president of the National League. In his tenure, Fay broke down a number of racial barriers in the front offices of major league baseball.

One of the things I feel best about is when I was charged with planning the festivities to commemorate the 50th anniversary of Jackie Robinson breaking the color barrier.

Jackie was a great player. Were there better players? Sure there were. Yet nobody had done what he'd done within the game, so how do you salute him properly? Think about all the great moments in baseball, the pennant races and the home run races and the All-Star Games and the World Series. Yet the greatest moment of them all was when a black man ran out of a dugout in Brooklyn in 1947 and took the field.

But what do you do to celebrate the 50th anniversary of that moment in a befitting manner? I'll never forget when the answer came to me. I was driving on the Garden State Parkway in New Jersey, and it hit me like a flash: Retire Jackie Robinson's number from baseball.

Teams have always retired the numbers of their greatest players. Go out to the ballpark in Cincinnati and you'll see Frank Robinson's number hanging there, Joe Morgan's number, Johnny Bench's number. But at that time, there wasn't a single player in any sport whose number had been retired from the whole game, and I thought I could pull it off. Hey, I was president of the National League.

It took a little discussion. I won Gene Budig over. He was president of the American League. And then I had to get the team owners on board. Bud Selig, the acting commissioner, was all in favor. Truthfully, the hardest part was convincing Rachel Robinson. Rachel's position was that if Jackie inspired someone to want to wear 42, they should be able to wear 42. In the end, I think she went along just because she liked me.

On the night of the celebration, there was Rachel, out on the field at Shea Stadium with President Clinton, as Bud Selig made the announcement: No. 42 was being retired from baseball. We grandfathered all the major leaguers who were wearing 42 at the time. Mariano Rivera of the Yankees is the last one to wear that number. I love going into all the ballparks and seeing that number hanging in a place of honor.

We look for symbols in life. You know, I have a friend named Bill Madden who's a longtime writer for the New York *Daily News*. Bill went into the archives and found this old *Daily News* that I now have hanging at home. The front page headline says: "Dodgers Acquire Robbie."

There Jackie is in a Montreal uniform, and he's walking into the clubhouse. A sign on the door says "Clubhouse—Keep Out." He's got a smile on his face and his hand on the knob—and the door is open slightly.

◆ ◆ ◆

CHAPTER FOURTEEN

THE HOME RUN KING

FOR SOMEONE LIKE me, who grew up sharing a pillow with a baseball mitt in the 1960s, meeting the ballplayers of my youth was a fantasy come to life.

Yet only once during a year spent talking to men who followed Jackie Robinson was I nervous. That was when I met with the Home Run King, Henry Louis Aaron.

Not that Hank Aaron was my hero as a kid. No, my hero was Willie Mays. I used to spread my glove and other hand out at navel height to make basket catches in the outfield just like him, and for one whole summer, I even insisted that people call me Willie.

There were no black kids in the Long Island neighborhood where I grew up or in my elementary school. And looking back, it was through Willie that I would come to understand the power of Jackie Robinson. Jackie's integration of baseball had opened the door for Willie—and ended up integrating me.

Of course, Willie could have had no idea how close we were when, decades later, he turned down my request for an interview for this book. Now that his godson, Barry Bonds, was on the verge of passing Aaron's home run record, Willie might have been wary about where my questions might lead because of the controversy swirling around Bonds and steroids.

Aaron wasn't granting many interviews these days either. But maybe because he'd stood with an open mouth as a boy outside a drugstore looking up at Jackie Robinson, he agreed to meet with me. I knew that Henry could be wary of the media, but I also knew that his voice was critical to this book.

After all, no black player since Jackie had become the racial lightning rod that Aaron had.

It was more than the letters he received during his pursuit of Babe Ruth's home run record, one of which began as follows:

Dear Nigger,

You can hit all dem home runs over dem short fences, but you can't take dat black off yo face.

Death threats touched his parents and children. His mother and father received telephone calls at home telling them they'd never see their son again. And when a picture of Aaron and the youngest of his daughters ran in a newspaper after a Father-Daughter Day game in Atlanta, somebody mailed it to him with these words crudely scribbled on the photo: "Daddy, please think about us! Please!"

On one occasion during his home run chase, FBI agents came to Aaron's home after reports that his daughter, off at college, had been kidnapped. The reports were unfounded, but undercover agents were dispatched to the campus disguised as maintenance men to keep her under surveillance.

As the 1973 season wound down and Aaron closed in on the record, a policeman was assigned to escort him to and from the ballpark. Aaron's standard practice on road trips was to register in two rooms at hotels, one in his own name, where the hateful phone calls could be directed, and another under a fictitious name, where he could sleep. The sports editor of the *Atlanta Journal* had Aaron's obituary written—just in case.

Nine hundred and thirty thousand letters were sent to Aaron as he approached the mark of America's most beloved white sports hero. Most of them were supportive, but many were vile. Once, a parcel arrived containing a roll of toilet paper with a picture of a gorilla affixed to it and a note that said, "This is your mother." And when his secretary, who was white, was photographed with sacks of letters, she received hate mail of her own from people incensed that a white woman would work for a black man.

And then, on April 8, 1974, at Atlanta-Fulton County Stadium, Henry Aaron lofted a pitch off Al Downing of the Los Angeles Dodgers over the left-centerfield fence. The record was his at 715.

That night, Aaron returned home for a small party with family and friends. Before anyone arrived, he stepped downstairs, locked the door, dropped to his knees, and thanked God for getting him through the ordeal as tears rolled down his cheeks.

When I sat down with Aaron and began to nudge him gently back toward those moments he'd referred to in his autobiography, *I Had a Hammer*, his eyes glazed and his body shifted back slightly in his chair. He nodded affirmation but wouldn't elaborate.

For half an hour or so, Aaron didn't say much. I floundered, wondering how to reach through an invisible wall and gain his trust. "What I'm trying to do, Hank," I finally explained, "is follow the path of Jackie Robinson and look at race in America through the lens of baseball."

He edged his chair closer, his eyes no longer distant. They pierced straight into mine as if searching for something. There was a long silence. All right then, his eyes seemed to say, if that's where you want to go . . .

Then he said six words: "Cut the head off the snake."

❖   ❖   ❖

HENRY AARON

◆◆◆

CUT THE HEAD off the snake. That's how they look at it: *Cut the head off the snake.* Kill the spirit of the black man, and it'll kill the whole family.

Many years ago, I was honored in Mobile by an organization of white men. My daddy came. But they didn't want to let him in. See, I could go in and be honored, but they wouldn't accept *him*. This is what I'm talking about. Cut the head off the black man. Demoralize him. Tell him, "Even though the home run hitter's your son, we don't want you." That kills the family.

My oldest grandson—I remember once going to his school to speak to his teacher. My daughter was very young when she had him, so I kind of watched out for him. It was right around the time of integration, when they were taking the best black teachers and putting them into the white schools and taking the worst white teachers and putting them into the black schools. And now this white teacher was there in this black school.

This woman, she was already angry that she'd been sent there. She was like, "Hey, don't tell me I gotta go in and teach these kids." Anyway, my grandson was 8 years old and one day he came home crying. This teacher had told him that he would never be no good, never do this, never do that, never do nothing in life.

I went down to the school to find out about it, and she said she didn't say it exactly like that, but he needed to bring his pencil to class.

"Wait a minute," I said. "He comes home crying, and the only reason that you were talking to him like that is because he didn't have a pencil?"

Now see, the difference is that if it had been a little black girl, the teacher wouldn't have said that. But a little black boy? Somebody who would grow up to be a black *man*? Oh yeah, cut the head off the snake. Demoralize him. Tear him up. Tell him you can't do this, you can't do that. Tell him what he *can't* be.

And you'd be surprised how successful that has been. That's why you have to keep looking back on the things that Jackie Robinson went through, because it all comes back to the same thing.

They just kept beating on him, beating on him, beating on him. They were thinking they could cut the head off the snake. And Jackie couldn't fight back. That's the first thing Branch Rickey told him: *You can't fight back.* If Jackie hadn't been strong enough in his mind, he'd never have made it. The whole thing would have been set back years.

If he'd made one mistake, if he'd crossed the line Rickey laid out for him, everybody would have said, "Told you so. He can't do it."

And if he hadn't done it, you'd never have seen a Henry Aaron. You'd never have seen a Willie Mays. You'd never have seen an Ernie Banks.

What I went through was basically the same thing that Jackie went through. They hounded him because they knew he could play baseball, and they didn't want him to. They hounded me because they knew I was going to break the record, and they didn't want me to.

If I'd been white, it would have been another story. But if a black person is breaking a white man's record, well, let's just say people weren't prepared to succumb to that easily.

I tried not to let it bother me as much as they wanted it to. I tried to stay as calm as I could. I tried to do my job. But some of those letters were filled with vicious hate, crazy hate. Sometimes they made you wonder if maybe somebody might be crazy enough to do something. If those people are still living, do they stop and wonder, How silly could I have been? To sit down and write those letters . . . Man, it's just plain crazy.

What was I doing? Playing baseball. What was I doing? Hitting home runs. What was I doing? Entertaining people and trying to win a pennant with my teammates. Was I doing something wrong?

If you look back in history, and if you read the books about slavery, you'll see. It's always the same thing: *Cut the head off the snake.*

This is the way it works: If they can demoralize me, then I'll go home and demoralize my family. I'm going to be hard on my wife, my kids, and everybody around me. If they can make me feel small while I'm at work, then I'll take it home. And when you take all this crap back to your home, your wife and children have to eat it and suffer with you. Destroy the spirit of a black man, and you destroy the whole black family.

Cut the head off the snake.

That home run chase was supposed to be a really great thing in my life, and yet it was probably one of the saddest. I try not to dwell on it. I don't try to avoid looking at that videotape or anything, but I sure don't go out of my way to look at it.

It's just that there were so many unhappy moments going through the last part of the chase that I want to forget it. It's better for my mental health to look forward. Because when I talk about these kinds of things, it brings up sad moments, and I don't like to dwell on sad moments.

I'm sure right now people are writing Barry and telling him, "You ain't never gonna get Hank's record whether you break it or not."

I think the circumstances are different with Barry because he's going through all this steroids stuff. Most of it is simply because of the press. They've accused Barry of taking these prohibited substances.

Go back to O.J. Simpson. The reason most blacks were behind him was simply because of the way the press came out and ate him up alive. Ate him up, ate him up, ate him up. Whether O.J. did it or not, the press wouldn't look at how *we* were seeing what they were doing. We were looking at it and thinking, If they can do that to O.J., they can do it to any of us.

Most black people in this country have been victimized at one time or another by circumstantial evidence. We've been judged a lot of times before we ever went to court. We've been judged for a long, long time, and we've been suffering for a long, long time.

As much evidence as everybody said there was, that's why 99% of black people were in O.J.'s corner. So I'm not going to sit here and say that Barry is guilty. I can't do that. Because black people have been found guilty before we were *proven* guilty for many, many years.

Hell, we walked across the *track*s and we were found guilty.

Barry going after my record doesn't put me in a conflicted position. None whatsoever. Records are made to be broken. It doesn't really make a difference to me whether he breaks it or Ken Griffey Jr. breaks it or if years ago Harmon Killebrew had broken it. I've held the title long enough, and now it's time for somebody else to have it.

For me, breaking the record is something that happened in the past. What's important for me now is what I'm doing now.

What am I doing for my brothers? As long as one of us is in the hole, hollering for help, then all of us need to be down there.

Jackie used baseball as a platform to help others do other things. But collectively, we haven't stuck together and helped each other out. Those of us who've been successful have to learn how to pull the others up. Is it ever going to happen? Collectively, we haven't been able to do that.

The other day, I was talking with one of the boys who's been in my Chasing the Dream Foundation since he was 9 years old. He's now in a performing arts school. This boy plays the harp. He's getting ready to go to college. And there were 11 colleges after him. *Eleven!* Trying to give him scholarships. He sat talking with me and my wife, and it made me feel so good, I wrote him a check over and above what he would be getting from the scholarship. I don't want him to have to worry about money as he's getting ready to make a giant leap into another world. He's going to be able to study without having to worry.

Now, I'm not a big fan of the harp. I don't know what the heck's going on with the harp, really. About the only thing I know about harps is that you don't see too many black people playing 'em. But whatever the top of the line for the harp is, I told him, "You've got to go for it."

I don't think this young man understands what's in front of him. But he'll learn. He *will* learn.

It's like I try to tell my sons and my grandsons. No matter what you do in this country, remember one thing: You may have a pocketful of money, and you may have reached halfway to the stars, but you're going to be looked at as a second-class citizen.

I hate to say that, but that's the way it is, because this society has figured out one thing: If they cut the head off the snake, they can kill the entire family.

I have small grandkids now. And I preach to my son-in-law: You see these two children right here? Let me tell you, this little girl will go anywhere she wants. She will get anybody she wants. Black, white—people'll just slobber all over her like nobody's business.

But this little boy here? Let me tell you, you've got to teach him everything, and especially you've got to teach him to be strong.

The one thing you've got to make sure of is that the young black male grows up strong. Because if he's not strong, he'll get torn up, and if he gets torn up, he'll tear the family up, and another black family will be destroyed.

That's it in a nutshell. Kill the spirit of a black boy, and it'll end up killing a family.

Our job is to stop letting that happen. And this keeps coming back to Jackie, because Jackie showed us the way.

◆ ◆ ◆

CHAPTER FIFTEEN

FAST BACKWARD

HOW COULD I have imagined, the first time I laid eyes on Jamie Mallard, that I might be staring at the next Jackie Robinson?

After all, the kid was 10 years old, a child of prodigious size and strength for his age, and he was driving pitch after pitch over a chain-link fence on a Tampa Little League ball field. Sure, he was African-American, but his heft and his skills suggested nothing at all of the swift Brooklyn Dodger legend in his early days.

It was 2000 when I began hearing whispers about Jamie, a prepubescent phenom who, oddly enough, might never have existed if not for George Steinbrenner.

You see, Jamie's dad was a sprinter in Tampa who couldn't get to the Junior National Track and Field Championships in Indiana back in 1978 because he had no affiliation, no sponsor, and no money. Word reached the Yankees owner, who lives in Tampa and who has always been a cross between George Patton and Mother Teresa. Steinbrenner never spoke to James Mallard, but he made sure the sprinter got to Indiana.

Because George bankrolled that trip, an Alabama track coach saw Mallard, who would run the fastest 200-meter time in the country the following year. He received a scholarship to Alabama, played wide receiver for Bear Bryant, and—most important—met Kim Taylor, who became his wife and the mother of their son.

No George, no Jamie.

From the time Jamie could swing a bat, his dad threw pitches to him every day after work. Jamie became a local legend at age 9 when he hit 26 balls over a 150-foot fence in a home run derby. By age 12, Jamie had hit more than 250 home runs in organized kids' baseball, some that traveled more than 350 feet. He blossomed to six feet and 260 pounds by age 16, joined a select team run by former major leaguer Chet Lemon, and was a high school junior when baseball celebrated the 60th anniversary of Jackie Robinson's rookie season.

Given the intensity of the competition, I used to wonder about Jamie's chances of ever making it to the major leagues. Now I wonder something else. Let's say he makes it. Now I wonder whether in 20 years or so, when he retires, Jamie Mallard might be the *only* African-American in Major League Baseball . . . just like Jackie was on Opening Day in 1947.

In 2006, three teams in the majors had no African-Americans on their Opening Day rosters. The major league-wide percentage has dwindled from a high of 27% in the 1970s to just barely over 9% on Opening Day in 2006.

Competition from other sports, like basketball and football, has skimmed away athletic talent. The burgeoning number of Latinos, who get to play year-round in the Caribbean, has also had an impact. Much deeper than that lies the changing nature of youth baseball, from local leagues to extensive travel teams, and that the fatherless home so sadly prevalent in urban black communities makes it difficult to compete in a sport that has always been about fathers and sons playing catch.

It's a complicated issue. But baseball has always been one of America's most faithful mirrors, a way for a large, complicated, and multicultured nation to get a look where it is and where it's heading. In a funny way, it often answers that age-old mirror question: Who's the fairest—and the unfairest—of them all?

We'd be fools to avert our eyes from what's in the looking glass today.

◆ ◆ ◆

TORII HUNTER

◆◆◆

MY FIRST FULL year with the Twins was 1999, and that's when I really noticed it. All the teams would come to town and I'd say to myself, Man, there's only one over there, none over there. Awhile back Cincinnati had eight. I was, like, Whoa, only two now . . .

We talk about it as players. I remember one time, Derek Jeter came over to me and said, "Hey, we're getting scarce."

Sometimes you look out in the crowd at a ballpark and you don't see *any* black faces. If you pay attention, you'll see that's the way it is. After glancing over 5,000 people, maybe you find a few black faces.

I look for them, black faces. I don't think that means I'm a racist or anything. It's natural. If you were playing in Japan and you looked up in the stands and saw some American faces, you might say, Hey, there's Americans out there tonight.

It makes you think of the guys who were fighting a long time ago. Satchel Paige. Josh Gibson. Cool Papa Bell. Finally, Jackie broke into the major leagues, and we get up to where we were nearly 30%. Now, we're down to less than 10%.

There are so many reasons why African-Americans have turned away from baseball, and I've heard 'em all. The money. The father-son thing. The marketing.

Look back to Michael Jordan and those shoes. Every kid wanted Air Jordans. Everybody knew Jordan played basketball, and now you see every kid with a basketball.

It translates. I went back home to Arkansas, and I was talking to a group of kids, and I mentioned Ken Griffey Jr. They said, "Who's that?" I said, "Are you kidding me?" But they didn't even know who he was.

Barry Bonds is supposed to be the Michael Jordan of our game, but he's getting scrutinized with all these steroids accusations, and the game of baseball is running away from him.

Meanwhile, the NBA is showcasing Shaquille O'Neal, Dwyane Wade, Kobe Bryant, LeBron James, and Carmelo Anthony. You see 'em on commercials. They're always happy. You see it so much it kind of brainwashes you. It makes you want to play basketball. A kid sees himself as a little Dwyane Wade, not a little Torii Hunter. We all know you have to be 6'5" to be Dwyane Wade. But a dream doesn't care about reality.

The reality is that baseball has become a country club sport, like tennis or golf. You have to pay for equipment—and that's expensive. A glove sets you back a hundred bucks, minimum. How much does a basketball cost? Twenty bucks? One's enough for 10 kids to have a game. And if you live near a hoop, you don't need another kid to practice with. You just go to the park and shoot. A baseball glove won't do you much good if you're by yourself.

And that glove is just for starters. A bat's gonna get you for another $50. Then, if you want to play organized ball, like Little League, there's uniforms. And if you want to compete against the best kids, you're gonna need to get on a traveling team and go to tournaments. That's where the scouts will see you. There's not too many scouts going into the 'hood. They're waiting until a select team is playing at a tournament in a nice area. Everybody who's good will be there, and that's where you'll get seen.

Everybody knows you need some money to get into the country club.

That's how kid baseball's being played these days.

DARRELL MILLER

The older brother of basketball stars REGGIE MILLER and CHERYL MILLER, DARRELL MILLER played five seasons with the California Angels. He is now director of the Urban Youth Academy, whose mission is to reintroduce baseball to inner-city kids in Compton, California.

◆◆

IT WAS ALMOST like an ambush. But there was no way anyone could have orchestrated what happened. All these different forces came to work against baseball at roughly the same time, one on top of another. It was silent, and it was deadly.

You can't identify the exact moment it started. You won't find the answer when you ask why I went into baseball, and why my younger brother went into basketball.

That was an individual situation. Reggie was a really good baseball player. At the time, the coaches at Riverside Poly wanted to make him a pitcher. But he had grown from 6′1″ to 6′5″ all of a sudden, and pitching was putting a strain on his arm.

Reggie was an incredible hitter with really good vision and kind of a Darryl Strawberry-like swing. I don't know if he had that kind of power, but he had a really smooth swing. For some reason, though, the baseball coach said, If he's gonna play for me, he's gonna have to pitch.

Well, that coach did Reggie a favor. Reggie went full-time into hoops and became a potential Hall of Famer. But that was a onetime kind of thing.

What we're talking about gets to huge social issues. We're talking about the breakdown in the fabric of the family that has devastated the inner-city Little Leagues.

It's also about the competition for talent that's come about with the emergence of the NFL and the NBA. If you look back at the origins of the Super Bowl, you'll see in the beginning that they were practically giving seats away. Try buying a ticket now. I can remember when the NBA playoffs were on tape delay.

Colleges cut back on baseball in part because of Title IX. Then look at the history of the junior colleges. Baseball has evaporated at junior colleges. There are four junior colleges in LA alone that no longer have baseball teams. All that would also coincide with the dearth of African-Americans playing now.

DON B. MOTLEY

The executive director of the Negro Leagues Baseball Museum in Kansas City, MOTLEY serves on the board of the Major League Baseball program known as RBI (Reviving Baseball in Inner Cities).

◆◆

LAST YEAR, ALABAMA A&M called me looking for some ballplayers. I've been managing for nearly 40 years in the Ban Johnson League in Kansas City. For the first time in all those years, I didn't have a black player to send.

I'm telling you, I've seen the black baseball player disappear right in front of my eyes. Now, people are coming around and asking what's going on. A guy I coached a while back said to me recently, "I remember you telling us this 20 years ago."

That's when it really started. Basketball became the sport for those on a fixed income.

I once heard Torii Hunter speak. He said in his hometown when he was a kid it cost $90 to join his local youth baseball league. Ninety dollars would pay the light bill. A light bill or a league fee? That's the bottom line.

KIM MALLARD

JAMIE MALLARD's mother offers an insider's perspective on youth baseball.

◆◆

INNER-CITY KIDS get priced right out of baseball.

We traveled to 20 or 30 games in the summer of 2006. Hotel rooms that the tournaments had reserved ran up to $100 a night. Sometimes it'll take eight or nine games to get to a championship. If it rains, that's an extra night of hotel and food.

When you travel to these tournaments and see how it all works, you realize that the kids your kid is competing against have private hitting or pitching instructors. You realize raw talent isn't going to do it anymore. You need an edge. Hitting coaches can run anywhere from $40 to $50 for 30 minutes. Some kids go a couple of times a week.

There are times my husband and I just have to say no. Sometimes it gets out of hand. We think about the money. But we just want to make sure we give our son every opportunity to fulfill his dreams even if we have to stretch ourselves financially. We don't want to have any regrets.

A single-parent family can't pull this off, at least not a working-class single-parent family. Sometimes, if the kid is truly elite, a coach or a sponsor will pay his way. Maybe the kid will room with the coach on the road. But the kid has got to be a stud.

JAMES MALLARD

◆◆

WHAT PEOPLE NEED to understand is that you have to keep black kids from getting discouraged at a very young age. Many are discouraged right at the start. You've got to look at what I call Daddy Ball. When you go into the parks and to the Little League fields, everything's run by dads. The dads are coaching the teams. The dads are white. And the dads are naturally going to make sure their kids get the best chances.

When a kid is young and his parents aren't there to support him, it's easy for him to get discouraged. Maybe the black kid is at the bottom of the lineup or not on the field. Maybe the parent has car problems and the kid can't get to practice on time. Maybe the coach decides the kid isn't dependable. Maybe he's pretty good and thinks he should be on the All-Star team, but when the dads vote they vote for each other's sons. They're gonna pick the very best kids first, but if it's neck and neck . . . well, let's just say it's much easier to vote for the kid of another dad who's there all the time. Then, when the black kid starts to become discouraged, he might say, Guess I'll just go play basketball.

How many black dads are Daddy Ball coaches? Go to your local park and you can probably count them on one finger. Now, if it were just the opposite, if every park you went into had black coaches, you'd see major league baseball a whole lot differently.

Some of it's understandable. You have dads giving the park money, fixing the fields, buying equipment, putting in the time. A lot of the black kids are coming from single-parent households. The mom in that situation can't be in two or three places at once. So she'll drop the kid off and run some errands and come back and pick him up. But somebody's got to be there watching.

If you're not willing to spend money *and* time, your kid's baseball career is going to be done between 13 and 15.

Right here in Tampa, there are a lot of Doc Goodens and Gary Sheffields walking the streets because of this.

SHARON ROBINSON

KIDS START DROPPING out in all sports after the age of 12. Baseball does all right in the 9-12 group and then loses them, partly because of natural attrition and partly because they're choosing soccer, basketball and football.

It's a complicated problem. We're a much-faster-moving society, and basketball is a faster-moving sport. So is football. So is soccer, and the cost of playing is miniscule in comparison. There aren't a lot of African-American players in baseball anymore, so it's harder for the kids to know them and be excited about seeing them.

KIM MALLARD

WE MET CARL Everett when he played for the White Sox. He was talking about how there were only three black guys on the team. I looked around the field and said, "No, there's seven or eight of y'all."

"No, only three," he said. "The rest are Latino."

If you're looking from the outside, you'd never notice.

DARRELL MILLER

◆◆

WHEN THE FAMILY started to break down in the inner cities, that attacked the No. 1 place where kids start playing baseball: Little League.

You can see what I mean by looking at healthy suburban Little Leagues. The mothers and fathers are on the board of directors. They do the fund-raisers. The fathers coach the kids. They get together and take care of the fields. They water the grass and put down the baselines.

The Little League model is predicated on the parents being heavily involved. Well, if you're working two or three jobs, you don't have the time to serve on the board of directors or coach or take care of the fields. And you don't have the resources to support the fund-raisers.

If you're a single mother working two jobs, you're looking for a turn-key sports program that the parks offer in football and basketball. You drop your kid off, then come back and pick him up.

There are quite a few Little Leagues that were very healthy in Los Angeles during the 1960s and 1970s that do not exist anymore. They're gone. There's only two or three left in inner-city LA.

So you go from 20 to two. That means fewer kids are starting to play at 6, 7, 8 years old. And that means that they're way behind if they do start playing later on.

We have RBI—Reviving Baseball in Inner Cities. Well, RBI starts at 13. Now, the suburban Little League kids may have a five-year head start. Think about a beginner having to face a kid who's been in travel ball since he was 9, and who's getting private instruction for $50 an hour from someone who may have played some in the big leagues.

The kid just starting may have played 20 games. The kid he's competing against has played hundreds. You've got to be some kind of athlete to overcome a head start like that.

There's something very specific to baseball that you have to understand, too. Baseball is the most failure-oriented game you'll ever see. It's a game predicated on failure and the ability to handle failure.

In the other sports, you can kind of hide when you do something wrong. You make a bad pass in basketball and you can say, Ahhh, he should have gotten to it. You get tackled at the line of scrimmage in football and you can always say, Well, there wasn't a hole to run through.

Baseball is different. A ground ball goes through your legs and everybody sees whose legs the ball went through. You swing and miss, and there's no one else to blame. This cultivates personal responsibility. You need a lot of confidence to play baseball.

After you strike out 10 times in a row, what do you want to do? You want to quit. You want to go somewhere where you can dominate because you can run fast or jump high. And right now baseball's got all this competition from these other sports.

The more you look at it, the deeper the problem gets. Back when I played, the coaches at school were all on the faculty. They knew each other, and they ran their programs with each other in mind. Now, the coaches are all hired guns.

The high school football coach makes 10 grand to coach the team. He comes in from the outside and brings in his own assistants. He *has* to win. He doesn't want to let his players play baseball. There's spring football. In the summertime, that football coach wants that kid to be part of the team's weight program. Basketball, you've got summer camps. There's soccer, too.

It's a whole new ballgame out there. And this is just the competition in our backyard. We haven't even talked about what's going on in Latin America.

When I was playing in the big leagues, there were Latin Americans who came over to play. You saw some athleticism. But most didn't know English. Their stomachs were bothering them because they weren't used to the food. They didn't understand how to hit the relay man or open a bank account.

Nowadays, many major league teams have an academy in Latin America. They can control the player at 16 years old. They can actually sign 30 or 40 guys in the Dominican and have them in the system. Then they can see who can play and who can't, who's gonna get stronger and who's not. By the time these kids are 18 or 19, the team has a little feeder system, another farm club.

People wonder why so many guys playing baseball here are from the Dominican or Venezuela. Well, it's cost effective. You can get 20 guys in your minor league system with a budget of a million a year in the Dominican. Here, it might cost you a million dollars to sign one guy. The odds are pretty obvious. You're going to have a better chance of success with 20 guys than one.

The academy in the Dominican is feeding the kids, organizing them, teaching them a little bit of English, and drilling them in the fundamentals so that they'll have a better chance to be successful.

That's exactly what we're doing at the Urban Youth Academy here in Compton. We opened up last February. The difference between us and the Dominican academies is that no single team has control of the kids. We have about 1,000 kids, starting at 7 years old. We're all about teaching. How to hit. How to turn two. That's why we call ourselves an academy.

We probably need a baseball academy wherever there's a city. Philly. Detroit. DC. Houston. Atlanta. *Everywhere* there's a city. Once we get a bunch of these up and running, you're gonna see some players.

I really think we can solve this because we're seeing Major League Baseball starting to get involved. We're seeing major league players getting involved.

But right now, we're the only one in America.

FRANK ROBINSON

◆◆◆

WHEN I CAME into professional baseball, we used to leave our gloves in the outfield after the third out. That was 1953. You left your glove right there on the field. If you ask people who played back then when gloves stopped being left on the field, they can't tell you. They just know the practice stopped.

And that's what's so disturbing about this business of the dwindling number of African-Americans in the major leagues. It's happening right in front of us. We see it. If we don't address it, pretty soon, there's not going to be any of us here to remember when there stopped being blacks in baseball.

Just like the gloves in the outfield.

◆ ◆ ◆

CHAPTER SIXTEEN

RESPECT

I T'S CUSTOMARY IN baseball to celebrate the start of every season by having an honored guest throw out the ceremonial first pitch.

Try, then, to imagine Jackie Robinson walking to the mound to make that first pitch at the home opener at Dodger Stadium on April 9, 2007, a few days shy of 60 years after he'd trotted onto Ebbets Field and changed this country and your life in ways that we're still trying to understand.

Jackie would be 88 years old.

His hair would be snow-white, of course—it already was by the time he retired from baseball, at the age of 37.

"Jackie was as fiery as any man who ever lived," said Buck O'Neil. "But for a few years, he had to live in a role that wasn't in his character whatsoever. The stress got all holed up inside of him."

Added Billy Williams: "I had the chance to talk to him around the batting cage after he'd retired. Everything that Jackie had endured was on his face. You could see the scars. He didn't have any physical scars, but you could see the mental scars. You know what I mean?"

And Spike Lee: "When you're not able to vent, it just eats you up inside. Those years before the handcuffs were off, all that stuff was just killing him. Usually, African-Americans don't look old. They say black don't crack. Jackie looked *way* old."

The sad truth is, it would have been impossible for Jackie to walk unaided to the mound to throw out that first pitch. He was nearly blind when he collapsed in Rachel's arms and died from a heart attack and complications from diabetes at age 53—nine days after throwing out the first ball in the second game of the 1972 World Series.

We don't like to see our heroes like that. We don't like to *think* of them like that. So maybe it's best to look at him one last time through the eyes of his daughter, Sharon, from her days growing up in Connecticut.

There was a large pond on the property that generally froze in winter before the nearby lake did, and many families in the area came down to skate on that pond. But not before an annual ritual was performed: Jackie Robinson would have to check the ice to make sure it was frozen and therefore safe for everybody to skate on.

The Robinson home sat on a hill. Jackie ambled down the hill to the pond each year carrying a broomstick and a shovel. Year after year, Sharon, her brothers, and all their friends would sit on the bank and cheer him on.

Jackie would step out on the pond, shovel off the recent snow, then tap with the broomstick to make sure, with each step, that the frosted white pond could bear his presence.

Jackie was a large man, much heavier then than in his playing days, and none of the kids quite knew what to do if the ice broke and he fell through. But it was Jackie Robinson's job. Nobody else could do it.

The kids knew every inch of the pond because they swam it in the summer. They knew exactly where its depth reached 10 feet. If Jackie reached that mark and the ice hadn't cracked, he'd give an official okay, and there'd be a great cheer. Everybody in the neighborhood could skate.

"To me," his little girl remembers, "that made my father this super-giant of a man. Because the amazing part was my father couldn't swim."

JACKIE ROBINSON

◆◆

"A LIFE IS not important except in the impact it has on other lives."

◆ ◆ ◆

VOICES

HENRY AARON

Hit record 755 homers in 23-year career for Milwaukee/Atlanta Braves and Milwaukee Brewers . . . Broke Babe Ruth's mark of 714 with blast off Al Downing in 1974 . . . Played for Indianapolis Clowns in 1952. Last Negro Leaguer to play in major leagues . . . Three-time Gold Glove outfielder . . . 21-time All-Star . . . Elected to Hall of Fame 1982.

DICK ALLEN

Belted 351 homers and drove in 1,119 runs in 15-year career for Philadelphia Phillies, St. Louis Cardinals, Los Angeles Dodgers, Chicago White Sox and Oakland Athletics . . . Began as third baseman; also played outfield and first base . . . 1964 NL Rookie of the Year . . . 1972 AL MVP . . . Seven-time All-Star.

FELIPE ALOU

Major league outfielder/first baseman for 17 seasons, primarily with San Francisco Giants, Milwaukee/Atlanta Braves . . . Hit over .300 three times . . . Three-time All-Star . . . Oldest of three Alou brothers in majors . . . Managed 14 seasons, with Montreal Expos and Giants, before retiring at age 71 . . . Native of Dominican Republic who has spent half a century in baseball.

YOGI BERRA

Superior catcher and dominant hitter in 18-year career with New York Yankees . . . AL MVP 1951, 1954, 1955 . . . All-Star every year from 1948–1962 . . . Played on more pennant winners (14) and World Series winners (10) than anyone else in history . . . Manager of Yankees and New York Mets . . . Elected to Hall of Fame 1972.

BOBBY BRAGAN

Infielder who played seven seasons with the Philadelphia Phillies and Brooklyn Dodgers . . . Manager of the Pittsburgh Pirates (1956–57), Cleveland Indians (1958) and Milwaukee/Atlanta Braves (1963–66) . . . Founder in 1991 of the Bobby Bragan Youth Foundation, which recognizes students for achievements and citizenship.

LOU BROCK

Outfielder played 19 seasons with Chicago Cubs and St. Louis Cardinals . . . Revolutionized art of base stealing. Left game as all-time leader with 938 steals and had NL record 118 in 1974 . . . Trade to Cardinals in 1964 among the most lopsided in baseball history . . . Member of 3,000-hit club . . . Batted .391 in 21 World Series games. . . . Six-time All-Star . . . Elected to Hall of Fame 1985.

JIM BROWN

One of the most dominant running backs in football history . . . Played nine seasons for the Cleveland Browns and led NFL in rushing eight times . . . Walked away from game in 1966 at age 30 to devote more time to acting career . . . All-around athlete also was one of greatest lacrosse players in history . . . First-team All-American in both sports at Syracuse . . . Hall of Famer in pro football, college football, and lacrosse.

WILLARD BROWN
(1915–1996)

Powerful slugger in the Negro Leagues and the Puerto Rican League . . . Led Kansas City Monarchs to six Negro League pennants . . . Signed by the St. Louis Browns for brief stint in 1947 . . . His only home run in the major leagues—an inside-the-park job off Hal Newhouser on August 13, 1947—was the first home run hit by a black man in the AL . . . Elected to Hall of Fame 2006.

KEN BURNS

Emmy Award-winning filmmaker best known for documentary series . . . Unveiled *Baseball*, an 18-hour series in 1994 that chronicled the sport and its influence on society . . . Became nationally known with 1990 series *The Civil War.*

ROY CAMPANELLA
(1921–1993)

Eight-time All-Star catcher in 10-year-career with Brooklyn Dodgers (1948–57) . . . Set records for catcher with 41 homers and 142 RBI in 1953 . . . Had best fielding percentage for catchers four times . . . NL MVP in 1951, 1953, 1955 . . . Before joining Dodgers, played for Baltimore Elite Giants of the Negro Leagues . . . Paralyzed in January 1958 auto accident. . . . Elected to Hall of Fame 1969.

ROY CAMPANELLA II

Son of Roy Campanella . . . Award-winning documentary film director, producer.

JOSÉ CANÓ

Father of New York Yankees second baseman Robinson Canó.

ORLANDO CEPEDA

Powerful first baseman nicknamed "Baby Bull" and "Cha-Cha" . . . Played 17 major league seasons for six teams . . . 1958 NL Rookie of the Year for San Francisco Giants . . . Hit NL-high 46 homers in 1961 . . . 1967 NL MVP for world champion St. Louis Cardinals, first unanimous choice in NL since 1936 . . . Led NL in RBI in 1961, 1967 . . . Batted .300 nine times and hit 379 homers . . . Seven-time All-Star . . . Elected to Hall of Fame 1999.

ROBERTO CLEMENTE JR.

Son of Roberto Clemente . . . Broadcaster . . . Played minor league baseball in the Phillies (1984–85), Padres (1985–86) and Orioles (1990s) organizations.

LEN COLEMAN

President of the National League (1994–1999) . . . Highest-ranking African-American in commissioner's office . . . Baseball's director of marketing development 1992–1994 . . . Former Princeton outfielder.

BILL COSBY

Renowned comedian, actor . . . Undergraduate degree from Temple University, doctorate in education from University of Massachusetts . . . Creator of *The Cosby Show* (1984–92), one of the most popular shows in television history, which chronicled the life of a middle-class black family.

WALTER CRONKITE
Anchor of *The CBS Evening News* from 1962 to 1981 . . . Called "the most trusted man in America" . . . Native of St. Joseph, Missouri . . . Attended University of Texas.

RAY DANDRIDGE
(1913–1994)
Known as one of the best defensive third basemen in Negro Leagues history . . . 16-year career in Negro Leagues (primarily with Newark Eagles), and Mexican League . . . Played 11 winters in the Cuban Winter League . . . Signed by New York Giants in 1949 and played four seasons for Triple-A Minneapolis Millers of American Association . . . Elected to Hall of Fame 1987.

TOMMY DAVIS
Outfielder for 18 seasons with 10 different teams . . . NL batting champion 1962, 1963 with Los Angeles Dodgers . . . Drove in 153 runs in 1962 . . . Hit .400 in 1963 World Series for Los Angeles . . . High school basketball teammate of Lenny Wilkens.

PHIL DIXON
Negro Leagues historian . . . Author of various books on black baseball, including *The Negro Baseball Leagues: A Photographic History* . . . Has written extensively about the Kansas City Monarchs.

LARRY DOBY
(1924–2003)
First black player in AL for Cleveland Indians in 1947 . . . Power-hitting center fielder starred for Negro League's Newark Eagles . . . Hit .318 in 1948 World Series . . . Two-time AL home run champion . . . Seven-time All-Star . . . Managed Chicago White Sox for part of 1978 season . . . Elected to Hall of Fame 1998.

LARRY DOBY JR.
Son of Larry Doby . . . First African-American to play baseball at Duke . . . Played briefly in minor leagues in Chicago White Sox system . . . Concert tour stagehand for numerous performers.

AL DOWNING
Lefthander pitched 17 seasons with New York Yankees, Oakland Athletics, Milwaukee Brewers and Los Angeles Dodgers . . . Gave up Henry Aaron's 715th home run in 1974 . . . Called the "Black Sandy Koufax" early in career . . . Led AL with 217 strikeouts in 1964 . . . 1967 All-Star . . . Won 20 games with an NL-high five shutouts in 1971.

LEE ELDER
PGA Golfer from 1966 to 1990 . . . First African-American to play at the Masters (1975). Went on to play in five more Masters . . . Winner of four events on PGA Tour and eight more on Senior Tour . . . First African-American to play on the United States Ryder Cup Team, in 1979.

CARL ERSKINE
Pitched 12 seasons for Brooklyn/Los Angeles Dodgers (1948 to 1959), anchoring staff with Don Newcombe . . . Won career-high 20 games in 1953 . . . All-Star in 1954 . . . Pitched no-hitters against Chicago Cubs in 1952 and New York Giants in 1956 . . . Struck out 14 in Game 3 of 1953 World Series.

BOB FELLER
Nicknamed "Rapid Robert," his blazing fastball set the standard by which others of his era were judged . . . Spent all 18 of his major league seasons with the Cleveland Indians, amassing 266 wins with 2,581 strikeouts . . . Led AL in strikeouts seven times . . . Fanned record 348 batters in 1946 . . . Six-time 20-game winner . . . Threw three no-hitters and 12 one-hitters . . . Eight-time All-Star . . . Decorated Navy veteran who missed nearly four seasons while serving his country in World War II . . . Elected to Hall of Fame 1962.

CURT FLOOD
(1938–1997)
St. Louis Cardinals outfielder for 12 seasons . . . Challenged baseball's reserve clause after being traded to the Philadelphia Phillies in 1969 . . . Following long legal battle, finished career with Washington Senators in 1971 . . . Three-time All-Star . . . Seven-time Gold Glove winner.

BOB GIBSON
Won 20 games five times in 17 seasons for the St. Louis Cardinals . . . His minuscule ERA of 1.12 in 1968 was the lowest in the majors since 1914 . . . Known as a big-game pitcher, earned MVP awards in the 1964 and 1967 World Series . . . Posted World Series records with seven consecutive wins and 17 strikeouts in a game . . . Played basketball for Harlem Globetrotters . . . Elected to Hall of Fame 1981.

JOSH GIBSON
(1911–1947)
Power hitting catcher for Pittsburgh Crawfords, Homestead Grays in Negro Leagues . . . Called "Black Babe Ruth" . . . Credited with almost 800 homers in 17-year career . . . Once nearly hit homer out of Yankee Stadium . . . Negro Leagues home run champ 10 straight years . . . Elected to Hall of Fame 1972.

SEAN GIBSON
Great-grandson of Josh Gibson . . . Executive director of Josh Gibson Foundation, established in Pennsylvania in 1999 to aid the communities where Josh Gibson left his mark.

GREGG GONSALVES
Jackie Robinson Foundation Scholar . . . Partner at Goldman Sachs, a New York-based investment firm.

JIM "MUDCAT" GRANT
Pitched 14 seasons in major leagues, the first six-plus with Cleveland Indians . . . Led AL with 21 wins and six shutouts in 1965, helping the Minnesota Twins reach the World Series . . . Two-time All-Star . . . Started first game in Montreal Expos history in 1969.

BILL GREASON
Negro League pitcher for Birmingham Black Barons, 1948 to 1951 . . . Teammate of Willie Mays in Birmingham . . . Pitched in three games for St. Louis Cardinals in 1954 at age 29 . . . Finished career with minor league stops at Houston and Rochester . . . Became a minister after retiring from baseball in 1959.

OZZIE GUILLEN
Native of Venezuela became first Latino manager to win a World Series, leading the Chicago White Sox to their first title in 88 years in 2005 . . . AL Manager of the Year in 2005 . . .

Three-time All-Star shortstop who played 16 seasons with the White Sox, Baltimore Orioles, Atlanta Braves, and Tampa Bay Devil Rays . . . 1985 AL Rookie of the Year . . . 1990 Gold Glove winner.

BRYANT GUMBEL

Emmy Award-winning broadcaster . . . Host of HBO's *Real Sports With Bryant Gumbel* and play-by-play voice for NFL Network broadcasts . . . Spent over 20 seasons at NBC, hosting NFL and Olympic broadcasts . . . Former host of *Today* show . . . Former host of CBS's *The Early Show* . . . Has anchored and reported from all over the globe.

TORII HUNTER

Minnesota Twins outfielder . . . 2002 All-Star . . . Six-time Gold Glove winner . . . 2002 Twins representative for Roberto Clement Award for community service.

MONTE IRVIN

Star outfielder in Negro Leagues with Newark Eagles . . . Won 1946 Negro Leagues batting title . . . Joined New York Giants in 1949 and helped them to 1951 NL pennant . . . Became first ex-Negro Leaguer to win major league RBI title with 121 in 1951 . . . Hit .458 in 1951 World Series . . . Elected to Hall of Fame 1973.

JERRY IZENBERG

Longtime columnist for *Newark Star-Ledger* . . . Third in seniority among members of Baseball Writers' Association of America . . . Gave a eulogy at funeral of longtime friend and Newark neighbor, Larry Doby.

LOU JOHNSON

Played parts of eight seasons in major leagues from 1960 to 1969 . . . Nicknamed "Sweet Lou" . . . Had game's only hit and run in Sandy Koufax's perfect game over Chicago Cubs in September 1965 . . . Homered in Game Seven of 1965 World Series, helping Koufax to 2-0 win over the Minnesota Twins.

JAMES EARL JONES

Actor known who won a 1969 Tony Award for role in *Great White Hope* . . . Native of Mississippi whose family moved to Michigan when he was 5 . . . Overcame stuttering problem as a child . . . Voice of Darth Vader in *Star Wars* movie series.

BOB KENDRICK

Director of Marketing for the Negro Leagues Baseball Museum in Kansas City.

SAM LACY

(1903–2003)
Pioneer journalist who pushed for integration of baseball in career that spanned almost seven decades . . . One of the first black members of the Baseball Writers' Association of America . . . 1997 recipient of the J.G. Taylor Spink Award . . . Long-time columnist, editor for *Baltimore Afro-American*.

SPIKE LEE

Filmmaker, actor . . . Director of numerous films with racial themes, including *Do The Right Thing, Jungle Fever,* and *Malcolm X* . . . Home away from home: courtside at New York Knicks games.

DR. LASALLE D. LEFFALL

Renowned surgeon, oncologist whose professional life has been devoted to the study of cancer, especially in African-Americans . . . Named chairman of the President's Cancer Panel, 2002 . . . First African-American president of the American Cancer Society and of the American College of Surgeons . . . Professor of Surgery, Howard University.

LARRY LESTER

Negro Leagues historian . . . Member of special committee to select Negro Leagues and pre-Negro Leagues candidates to the Hall of Fame.

JAMES MALLARD

Father of Jamie Mallard, baseball prospect from Tampa . . . Former world-class sprinter . . . Split end for University of Alabama under Bear Bryant.

KIM MALLARD

Mother of Jamie Mallard . . . Husband of James Mallard.

JUAN MARICHAL

High-kicking right-hander won 20 games six times over 16 major league seasons, primarily with the San Francisco Giants . . . Nicknamed "Dominican Dandy," he won 243 games with a career 2.89 ERA . . . Threw a no-hitter against the Houston Colt .45s in 1963 . . . After playing career, became a minister of sports in Dominican Republic . . . Elected to Hall of Fame 1983.

TIM McCARVER

Catcher for 21 seasons with St. Louis Cardinals, Philadelphia Phillies, Montreal Expos, and Boston Red Sox . . . Two-time All-Star . . . Hit .478 in 1964 World Series . . . Three-time Emmy Award winning broadcaster . . . Lead baseball analyst for several networks, most recently Fox Sports . . . Called 17th World Series in October 2006.

DARRELL MILLER

Director of the Urban Youth Academy in Compton, California, a program formed by Major League Baseball to reintroduce baseball to inner-city kids . . . Utility man who played five seasons for the California Angels (1984-88) . . . Older brother of basketball stars Reggie Miller and Cheryl Miller.

MARVIN MILLER

Hired as executive director of the Major League Baseball Players Association in 1966. Turned it into one of the most powerful unions in America, shifting baseball's balance of power . . . Led strikes by the players in 1972 and 1981 . . . During his tenure, the reserve clause was overturned and free agency flourished . . . Former assistant to the president of the United Steelworkers union.

MANNY MOTA

Considered one of the best pinch hitters in baseball history, collecting 150 in a 20-year career. It was said Mota could wake up on Christmas morning and hit a line drive . . . Native of the Dominican Republic hit .304 with the San Francisco Giants, Pittsburgh Pirates, Montreal Expos, and Los Angeles Dodgers.

DON B. MOTLEY

Executive Director of the Negro Leagues Baseball Museum in Kansas City . . . Board member of Major League Baseball's RBI program (Reviving Baseball in Inner Cities).

DON NEWCOMBE

Three-time 20-game winner for Brooklyn Dodgers from 1949 to 1957. . . First African-American to win 20 games in majors . . . Had a .271 career batting average with 15 homers. . . . Only player in major league history to earn Rookie of the Year, MVP, and Cy Young Award . . . Four-time All-Star . . . Director of Community Relations for the Los Angeles Dodgers since 1970.

TONY OLIVA

Native of Cuba is only player to win batting titles in his first two full seasons . . . Outfielder who played entire 15-year career with Minnesota Twins (1962 to 1976). Knee problems forced him to be a designated hitter late in his career . . . 1964 AL Rookie of the Year . . . 1966 Gold Glove winner . . . Career .304 hitter . . . Eight-time All-Star.

JOHN "BUCK" O'NEIL

(1911–2006)
Negro Leagues first baseman . . . Won batting titles in 1940 and 1946 while with Kansas City Monarchs . . . Manager of Monarchs, 1948 to 1955 . . . Named scout for Chicago Cubs in 1956 . . . Became first black coach in major leagues, with Cubs in 1962, and worked with future Hall of Famers Lou Brock and Ernie Banks . . . Baseball ambassador who gained national attention in Ken Burns' 1994 *Baseball* documentary . . . Helped lead effort for Negro Leagues Baseball Museum.

JUDY PACE

Actress . . . Wife of Curt Flood.

LEROY "SATCHEL" PAIGE

(1906–1982)
Legendary pitcher for at least eight Negro League teams in career that spanned three decades . . . Huge gate attraction who starred in many barnstorming tours . . . Made major league debut for Cleveland Indians in 1948 at age 42 . . . All-Star 1952, 1953 . . . Pitched three scoreless innings for Kansas City Royals in 1965 at age 59 . . . Elected to Hall of Fame 1971.

ROBERT PAIGE

Son of Satchel Paige . . . Volunteer for Negro Leagues Baseball Museum Traveling Exhibit . . . Truck driver for Roadway Express.

VIOLET PALMER

Palmer and Dee Kantner became the first female referees of a major U.S. professional sport when they began to call NBA games in 1997 . . . First woman to referee an NBA playoff game, in 2006 . . . Officiated in WNBA and CBA . . . Worked five NCAA Women's Final Fours.

TONY PÉREZ

First baseman was a fixture of the Cincinnati Reds' "Big Red Machine" of the 1970s . . . Had seven 100-RBI seasons and drove in 1,652 runs over 23-year career . . . Seven-time All-Star and MVP of 1967 Mid-Summer Classic . . . Hit three homers in 1975 World Series . . . Manager of the Reds (1993) and Florida Marlins (2001) . . . Longtime Marlins executive . . . Elected to Hall of Fame 2000.

VIC POWER

(1927–2005)
Native of Puerto Rico played 12 major league seasons for five different teams . . . Seven-time Gold Glove-winning first baseman . . . Stole home twice in the same game for the 1958 Cleveland Indians . . . Known for flamboyant style on and off the field . . . Hit 126 homers and batted .284.

CHARLEY PRIDE

Acclaimed country western singer who was the first African-American inducted into the Country Music Hall of Fame, in 2000 . . . Gained membership in the Grand Ole Opry in 1993, 26 years after he first played as a guest . . . Negro Leagues pitcher, outfielder in mid-1950s . . . Sang national anthem at 2006 Baseball Hall of Fame induction ceremony.

CHARLES RANGEL

New York Congressman currently serving his 18th term . . . Harlem native . . . Ranking member of the Committee on Ways and Means . . . Served in U.S. Army in Korean War, winning Purple Heart and Bronze Star.

BILL RHODEN

Sports reporter for *The New York Times* since 1983 . . . Consultant on ESPN *SportsCentury* series and regular guest on ESPN's *The Sports Reporters* . . . Former columnist for *The Baltimore Sun* . . . Former associate editor of *Ebony* magazine.

BRANCH RICKEY

(1881–1965)
Visionary executive who spent half a century in baseball front offices with the St. Louis Browns and Pittsburgh Pirates . . . Signed Jackie Robinson for the Dodgers in 1945 and promoted him to the majors in 1947 . . . Founder of the modern farm system, copied throughout the game . . . Brief major league playing career from 1905 to 1907 and 1914 . . . Managed Browns and Cardinals between 1913 and 1925 . . . Elected to Hall of Fame 1967.

BRANCH RICKEY III

Grandson of Hall of Fame baseball executive Branch Rickey . . . President of the Pacific Coast League since 1997 . . . Spent 20 years in major league baseball with Pittsburgh Pirates and Cincinnati Reds as a scout, assistant scouting director, and director of player development . . . Served in the Peace Corps.

DAVID ROBINSON

Son of Jackie Robinson . . . Co-founder of Sweet Unity Farms, a cooperative of coffee farmers in Tanzania.

FRANK ROBINSON

Star outfielder for 21 years, primarily with Cincinnati Reds, Baltimore Orioles . . . 1956 NL Rookie of the Year . . . First player to be named MVP in both leagues (NL in 1961, AL in 1966) . . . 12-time All-Star . . . AL Triple Crown winner in 1966 . . . Hit 586 homers in 32 different parks . . . Became baseball's first black manager, with Cleveland Indians in 1975 . . . Managed 16 seasons in majors with Indians, San Francisco Giants, Baltimore Orioles, and Montreal Expos/Washington Nationals . . . Elected to Hall of Fame 1982.

RACHEL ROBINSON

Widow of Jackie Robinson . . . Founded The Jackie Robinson Foundation in 1973.

SHARON ROBINSON

Daughter of Jackie Robinson . . . Vice chair of The Jackie Robinson Foundation . . . Author of several books for young readers, including *Promises to Keep: How Jackie Robinson Changed America*.

ROB RUCK

Senior lecturer, historian, University of Pittsburgh . . . Author of *Sandlot Seasons: Sport in Black Pittsburgh* and *The Tropic of Baseball: Baseball in the Dominican Republic* . . . Member of special committee to select Negro Leagues and pre-Negro Leagues candidates to the Hall of Fame.

QUINCY TROUPE

Acclaimed poet and biographer of Miles Davis . . . Son of Quincy Trouppe.

QUINCY TROUPPE

(1912–1993)

Strong-armed catcher in Negro Leagues, Mexican League . . . Lifetime .300 hitter, career-best .352 in 1948 . . . Played six games for 1952 Cleveland Indians . . . Scout, St. Louis Cardinals, 1953-57.

BOB VEALE

Lefthander pitched 13 seasons in majors with Pittsburgh Pirates and Boston Red Sox . . . All-Star 1965, 1966 . . . Led NL with 250 strikeouts in 1964 and had a career-high 276 in 1965.

BILL VEECK

(1914–1986)

Innovative, flamboyant entrepreneur-owner of Cleveland Indians, St. Louis Browns, Chicago White Sox . . . Signed AL's first black player (Larry Doby, 1947) and brought Satchel Paige to the majors at age 42 . . . Set major league attendance record of 2.6 million with 1948 Indians . . . Introduced exploding scoreboards and player names on uniforms . . . Known for cutting-edge promotions such as "Grandstand Managers Day" . . . Elected to Hall of Fame 1991. HOF plaque refers to him as "a champion of the little guy."

MIKE VEECK

Son of Hall of Fame owner Bill Veeck . . . Worked for father in 1970s and promoted the ill-fated "Disco Demolition Night" . . . Worked for four major league teams . . . Owner of six minor league teams . . . Developed unique promotions of his own, including Bob Dylan concert tour in minor league parks, Dawn Baseball, and Mime-O-Vision . . . Co-author of *Fun is Good*.

MAURY WILLS

Elite base runner in 14-year major league career, primarily with Los Angeles Dodgers . . . Stole record 104 bases in 1962 and led NL in steals six times . . . Five-time All-Star . . . Two-time Gold Glove shortstop . . . 1962 NL MVP . . . Hit .367 in 1965 World Series . . . Manager of Seattle Mariners for parts of 1980 and 1981 seasons.

BILLY WILLIAMS

Soft-spoken outfielder known for his sweet yet powerful swing . . . Hit .290 with 426 home runs over 18 major league seasons for the Chicago Cubs and Oakland Athletics . . . Hit 20 or more homers for 13 straight seasons . . . 1961 NL Rookie of the Year . . . 1972 NL batting champion . . . Six-time All-Star . . . Played in 1,117 straight games . . . Elected to Hall of Fame 1987.

ERNEST WITHERS

Acclaimed photojournalist . . . Best known for evocative photos of civil rights movement, Negro Leagues baseball, and blues musicians . . . Spurred push for equal rights with photo book on the Emmett Till murder.

—DOUG MITTLER
JANUARY 2007.

THE FACTS ABOUT MEMORY

◆◆

IT'S A FUNNY thing how a batting average can shoot up more than a hundred points when a hitter recalls it 50 years later.

Pain can hide facts that we don't want to remember. Anger can distort them when we want to prove a point. And age can cloud even the best-intentioned memory. Tommy Davis likes to joke, "I don't have Alzheimer's. I have Some-timer's."

So how is it possible to set in print stories that are straight from the tellers' mouths *and* simultaneously insure their accuracy?

You try your best, and you make adjustments.

Accurate batting averages are the only ones you'll find on these pages. Whenever possible, corrections were made in the text so that accuracy would prevail over faulty memory.

A few players pointed me to their autobiographies to confirm events and retrieve information so they could best relate their experiences. I used this license grudgingly. My intent was to render their stories as they came directly to my ears.

Other compromises were made for clarity. Often players spoke of team-mates without introduction. So "Hilton Smith" now comes to you as "a pitcher on our team, Hilton Smith." Details like the full names of teams, the scores of games and the years they were played were also inserted into the voices. Though people don't generally speak in such precise detail, it was sometimes necessary to establish time and place.

The only area where I deliberately didn't set down voices from mouth-to-ear was recounting conversations with Latino ballplayers. I once read that Roberto Clemente resented being quoted exactly the way he spoke in his second language. Out of respect for Roberto, I smoothed out the accents and cadences of the Latino players to give the appearance that the words were as fluent as they would have been in their native tongue.

Other than that, I let the spoken word flow. That's why you'll find play-ers jumping back and forth from past to present tense in the same paragraph. While this may seem unusual on the printed page, it's often the way people tell a story.

Everything I did was rooted in a single hope—that you'd feel like you were sitting next to me along the journey.

—CAL FUSSMAN
JANUARY 2007

ACKNOWLEDGEMENTS

MANY, MANY PEOPLE richly deserve my heartfelt thanks for their contributions, conscious and otherwise, to this project. They know who they are, and now so will you.

To Rachel, Sharon and David Robinson, and The Jackie Robinson Foundation, for guidance, assistance and support.

To all the players and witnesses whose voices you have just heard, for sharing their time and opening up their lives.

To my wife, Glória, and my children, Dylan, Keilah, and Bridgette, for all their sacrifices.

To my parents, for waiting so long.

To Gary Hoenig, for his friendship, the idea to do this, and the strength to get it done, and Betsy Carter, for continually sparking Gary's mind.

To editor Glen Waggoner, the Chateau Cheval Blanc of partners, for making sure every word was as clear as crystal; to writer-reporter Doug Mittler, for digging up so much good stuff and turning so many errors into clean base hits; managing editor John Glenn, for keeping all the balls in the air; and copy chief Steve Horne and his crack crew—Ethan Lipton, Roseann Marulli, Margaret McNicol Robbins—for making me love copy editors.

To all the rest of the gang at ESPN Books: Chris Raymond, for the relentless encouragement; Michael Solomon, for the lightning bolt flashes; Henry Lee, for his keen eye; Sandy DeShong, for always pointing in the right direction; Nigel Goodman, for showing me the future; Carmen Camacho & Co., for pulling off the impossible on demand; Jessica Welke and Ellie Seifert, for spreading the word; Craig Winston, for the fine-tooth comb; Doris Alvarez-Ramirez and Tricia Reed, for always being there; and Keith Clinkscales, for coming through at crunch time.

To Gary Smith, for taking every journey with me and making them all better; John A. Walsh, for teaching me for 27 years—and counting;

Peter Bonventre, for being between every line for just as long; and David Granger, for lifting me to new heights with silence.

To Bob Costas, for a letter I'll never forget; Jay Lovinger, for always looking at the situation from a different angle; Geoff Reiss, for picking me up when I was down; John Skipper, for believing in second chances; Roxanne Jones and Carmen Renee Thompson, for listening while I figured it out; Grace Gallo, whose first name perfectly suits her; and Robyn Crawford, for keeping her cool (and me cool) until the good times arrived.

To Connor William Schell, for the kindness and scholarship; Santa Brito, for welcoming me to the Caribbean; Ray Stallone, for the ever-present helping hand; Jerry Lewis, for the cup of coffee; and David Black, for decades of free advice.

To Lindsay Berra, Dave Kaplan and the folks at the Yogi Berra Museum, for treating me like family; Tonya Tota, Bob Kendrick, Don B. Motley, and everyone at the Negro Leagues Baseball Museum in Kansas City for treating me like family; and The Bethel Baptist Church in Birmingham for treating me like family.

To Andy Ward, for showing me that deadline miracles are nothing but reality; Roger Jackson and Dan Galvin, for starting before I did; and Larry Lester, Jerry Malloy, and Ike Brooks for transporting me back in time.

To Don Newcombe Jr., for his patience and good spirit; Bill White, for declining with *respect*; Leah Keith, for explaining skin color; Tim Buckman, for hooking things up; Paul Melvin, for persistence that insures a great marriage; and Mark Durand, for sharing.

To John Hassan, for making the right connections; John Papanek, for linking this up with The Big Train; Jon Pessah, for guiding me to Claire Smith who guided me to so many others; Jon Scher, for tapping into his connections; Nate Guerin, Brian Ma, Savi Smith, and Noah Smith for enjoying the transcription; Howard Bingham, for showing me the ropes; and Gary Schueller, for his indefatigable assistance and for caring so much.

To Della Britton-Baeza, America's best hope, for her spirit; Tom Breitling, for opening the door; Tim Scanlon, for doing all he could; Larry Lundy, for always answering on the first ring; Sandra Richards, for making me at home from the start; Michelle Rowland, for knowing the way; Bernadette Weeks, for chipping in; and Barbara Gothard, for always making it a party.

To Brooklyn, because that's where I'm from.

To Gary Belsky and Neil Fine, for the comic relief; Steve Wulf and Dan Okrent, for technical support; Mike Tollin & son and Marshall Goldberg & daughter, for the great pizza in Pittsburgh; and Jerry Remolt, for an overview of the past.

To Ernie Harwell, Ted Tolls and Bud Collins, for the background; and Gerry Groh, for making the difficult seem easy.

To photo researcher William Nabers, for finding that great pic of Maury Wills; designer Richard Berenson, for making the look capture the feel; and Arthur Hochstein, for showing me how much it matters.

To Buck O'Neil, for letting me tap his amazing memory bank, and for endorsing my nickname as if it were Gates Barbecue.

To all those I didn't mention, for your forgiveness.

And still, even with all the positive energy and good spirit supplied by everyone listed above, this book would never have been bound if not for two people. And so a special tip of the cap goes to David Cummings and Ricky Clemons, for making it happen.

—C.F.

◆ ◆ ◆

PHOTOGRAPHY AND ILLUSTRATION CREDITS

Front Jacket: Jersey worn by Jackie Robinson during 1955 season (courtesy the National Baseball Hall of Fame Library) ◆ **Spine:** Jackie Robinson, c. 1948–50 (courtesy the National Baseball Hall of Fame Library) ◆ **Back Jacket:** Jackie Robinson, 1948 (Bettmann/Corbis) ◆ **Pages ii–iii:** Jackie Robinson stealing home against the Cubs, May 1952 (Bettmann/Corbis) ◆ **Page viii:** *Time* magazine cover, September 22, 1947 (Time Life Pictures/Getty Images) ◆ **Chapter 1 (page 1):** Jackie Robinson, 1948 (Bettmann/Corbis) ◆ **Chapter 2 (page 7, top):** Zulu Cannibal Giants player Robert Bissant, 1936 (Phil Dixon/American Baseball Chronicles) ◆ **Chapter 2 (page 7, bottom):** Zulu Cannibal Giants broadside, c. 1938 (Bert Orlitzky/NLBPA.com) ◆ **Chapter 3 (page 19):** Steve Gromek (left) and Larry Doby (right) after Cleveland wins Game 4 in 1948 World Series (Ed Nano/Bettmann/Corbis) ◆ **Chapter 4 (page 38):** Satchel Paige, 1948 (George Silk/Time Life Pictures/Getty Images) ◆ **Chapter 5 (page 58):** Don Newcombe on the mound, 1955 (Francis Miller/Time Life Pictures/Getty Images) ◆ **Chapter 6 (page 77):** Maury Wills stealing third, c. 1962 (Francis Miller/Time Life Pictures/Getty Images) ◆ **Chapter 7 (page 99):** Ernie Banks, c. 1955 (Carl Kidwiler/Diamond Images) ◆ **Chapter 8 (page 115):** Buck O'Neil, date unknown (courtesy the National Baseball Hall of Fame Library) ◆ **Chapter 9 (page 131):** Jackie stealing home in Game 1 of 1955 World Series against Yankees (Ralph Morse/Time Life Pictures/Getty Images) ◆ **Chapter 10 (page 153):** Jesus, Matty, and Felipe Alou, 1963 (AP Photo) ◆ **Chapter 11 (page 167):** Dick Allen, 1969 (Charles Bonnay/Time Life Pictures/Getty Images) ◆ **Chapter 12 (page 184):** Curt Flood (right foreground) and Marvin Miller on steps of New York Federal Courthouse, 1970 (Bettmann/Corbis) ◆ **Chapter 13 (page 200):** New Indians manager Frank Robinson at Cleveland's 1975 home opener against Yankees (Ron Kuntz/Diamond Images) ◆ **Chapter 14 (page 214):** Hank Aaron at press conference after breaking Babe Ruth's career HR mark, April 8, 1974 (AP Photo) ◆ **Chapter 15 (page 222):** Jackie Robinson on UCLA basketball team, 1941 (UCLA/Collegiate Images/Getty Images) ◆ **Chapter 16 (page 233):** Jackie Robinson throw outs first ball in Game 2 game of 1972 World Series, his last public appearance (AP Photo)